To Alyssa and Alana
With confidence and hope that your generation will do
better than mine

BENIGN BIGOTRY

While overt prejudice is now much less prevalent than in decades past, subtle prejudice – prejudice that is inconspicuous, indirect, and often unconscious – continues to pervade our society. Laws do not protect against subtle prejudice and, because of its covert nature, it is difficult to observe, and frequently goes undetected by both perpetrator and victim. *Benign Bigotry* uses a fresh, original format to examine subtle prejudice by addressing six commonly held cultural myths based on assumptions that appear harmless but actually foster discrimination: "those people all look alike"; "they must be guilty of something"; "feminists are man-haters"; "gays flaunt their sexuality"; "I'm not a racist, I'm colorblind" and "affirmative action is reverse racism." Kristin J. Anderson skillfully relates each of these myths to real-world events, emphasizes how errors in individual thinking can affect society at large, and suggests strategies for reducing prejudice in daily life.

KRISTIN J. ANDERSON is Associate Professor of Psychology in the Social Sciences Department at the University of Houston-Downtown. She teaches college courses on prejudice, discrimination, and stereotyping, and her work has been published in many academic journals including *Developmental Psychology, Journal of Language and Social Psychology, Sex Roles,* and *Journal of Latinos and Education.*

Benign Bigotry

THE PSYCHOLOGY OF SUBTLE PREJUDICE

Kristin J. Anderson

CAMBRIDGE UNIVERSITY PRESS
Cambridge, New York, Melbourne, Madrid, Cape Town, Singapore, São Paulo, Delhi

Cambridge University Press
The Edinburgh Building, Cambridge CB2 8RU, UK

Published in the United States of America by Cambridge University Press, New York

www.cambridge.org
Information on this title: www.cambridge.org/9780521702591

First published 2010

Printed in the United Kingdom at the University Press, Cambridge

A catalogue record for this publication is available from the British Library

Library of Congress Cataloging-in-Publication Data
Anderson, Kristin J., 1967–
Benign bigotry : the psychology of subtle prejudice / Kristin J. Anderson.
p.   cm.
ISBN 978-0-521-87835-7 (Hardback)
1. Prejudices. 2. Toleration. I. Title.
HM1091.A53 2009
303.3'85–dc22
                                                          2009030204

ISBN 978-0-521-87835-7 Hardback
ISBN 978-0-521-70259-1 Paperback

Contents

Acknowledgments

I owe a major debt of gratitude to several individuals whose generous and useful contributions have made this work possible. Christina Accomando provided hours of stimulating conversation and ideas in the early stages of development of this book. Throughout this process many students in their capacity as research assistants have made valuable contributions. Tenille Duncan, Adela Garza Sopheap Im, Patricia Jefferson, Cynthia Pope, Marisa Ramirez, Monica Romo, and Fransheneka Watson each provided support in the many mechanical tasks that require patience and precision. To them, I offer heartfelt thanks. Dianne Wells deserves special recognition for her clarity, thoroughness, and painstaking attention to detail, combined with an impressive grasp of the larger issues in this project. Victor Vasquez deserves special mention in this regard as well. Over the course of this research and writing many colleagues have provided thoughtful and constructive comments on drafts of chapters. These people include Christina Accomando, Gail Burns, Judith Coker, Shauna Curtis, Thierry Devos, Roger Dunn, Bonnie Field, Dave Georgetti, and Douglas teDuits, and the students enrolled in my spring 2008 Psychology and the Law and spring 2008 Psychology of Women courses.

These individuals have my profound thanks and I hope that their efforts are clear in the following pages. I thank Rebecca Counnels for her help with the book cover design. Without institutional support this project would not have been possible, and I thank my colleagues at the University of Houston-Downtown, Adolfo Santos, Patrick Williams, and Provost Molly Woods, for their direct support. Additionally, I offer thanks to the 2007–2008 Faculty Development Leave Committee that provided support that allowed me to work on this project without distraction. Many years ago Roger Dunn introduced me to the concept of schemas and my life changed forever. The significance of that contribution is revealed in every page. From the training and patience he provided in his role as graduate advisor, to his current generous efforts as a colleague, Campbell Leaper deserves thanks for his consistent support of my work and his extremely useful contributions to the effort of making it as effective as possible. Finally, I express my thanks and appreciation to Melinda Kanner for her extraordinary intellectual, emotional, political, and moral support. Several key concepts and arguments in this book come from her, or conversations with her. It is difficult to imagine how this book could have come to life without her.

The changing place of prejudice: a migration underground

The secret life of subtle prejudice

You used to be able to spot them a mile away. Bigots. If they weren't wearing white hoods, you could count on their willingness to identify themselves in conversation by their unabashed use of racial epithets and sexist stereotypes. They were the co-workers telling homophobic jokes in the break room. They were the people who insisted that a woman could never be president because her pre-menstrual syndrome might one day lead to nuclear war. Bigots – loud and proud and easy to recognize from their behavior and conversation. The bigot was able to find justification and comfort in a deeply rooted set of ideas supported by prejudice at cultural and institutional levels.

Regardless of the precise stereotypes, people of color, women, poor people, and sexual minorities have historically been represented as genetically inferior. Since the 1950s, academics, activists, and policy-makers have made serious efforts to focus on social and political conditions, and to challenge the very concept of a biological basis of "race."[1] The sixties and seventies saw massive social movements advocating civil rights, feminism, and gay liberation. There have been distinctive shifts that indicate a greater willingness to understand the shaping role of environmental factors, to explore differences without always assuming deficits, and at least to *pretend* to value egalitarianism and equal opportunity. As biological and social sciences have challenged claims regarding the biological basis of human differentiation, legislative (e.g. *Brown vs. Board of Education*) and cultural transformations have made overt racism, sexism, and homophobia less socially acceptable. Many individuals now acknowledge that prejudice has had devastating consequences, but they also believe that prejudice is largely a thing of the past.

That overt and conspicuous bigotry has decreased is supported by research. In the United Kingdom, in 1987, 75% of people polled expressed the view that homosexuality was always or mostly wrong. By 2008, only 32% expressed this view.[2] In 1989, a third of British men agreed with the statement, "*A man's job is to earn money; a woman's job is to look after the home and family.*" By 2008, agreement with that statement had dropped to 17%.[3] In the early 1960s, only one third of white Americans believed that blacks and whites should be allowed by law to marry one other. By 1995, four of every five whites believed they should be.[4] Are such changes in reported attitudes reflecting heartfelt beliefs or is this surface reporting? Susan Fiske[5] observes that the more public the arena, and the more abstract the principle, the more marked the change in attitudes toward tolerance. For instance, in the United States, 68% of respondents endorsed racial segregation in schools in the 1940s and only 4% endorsed it by 1995. This sounds like tremendous progress. But while most white Americans now report being willing to live next door to a black family, 70% report that they would move away if blacks came into their neighborhood in "great numbers." Whites appear, then, to be more supportive of equal rights in principle than of equal rights in practice. When commitment is required to perform specific actions involving their own lives and the status of their own group, they are much less receptive to the idea of equality. For example, only about 15% of whites believe that the government should help African Americans improve their living standards because of past discrimination. Among Britons, a substantial number of people think that equal opportunity measures for blacks and Asians have "gone too far."[6]

On the one hand, overt bigotry appears to have decreased, but on the other hand, people are not necessarily willing to give up their own privileged status. Dominant groups appear increasingly tolerant, but when it comes to sacrificing some of their own comfort or endorsing government assistance for subordinate groups, they are disinclined to favor these remedies. In terms of racial and ethnic attitudes, it appears, then, that whites' attitudes toward ethnic minorities in the early part of the twenty-first century are ambivalent and consist of both positive and negative elements. There is a consensus among social scientists that prejudice has changed in the last several decades. The number of individuals *reporting* prejudiced attitudes has decreased. At the same time, the *location* of prejudice has changed; it now resides underground, in a subtler form. This change of location in social space can manifest in a discrepancy between what people report and how they behave. Angela Davis[7] talks about the *migration* of racism. "It moves, it travels, it migrates, and it transmutes itself."[8] Her analysis of the ability of racism to change its form and location can apply to other forms of prejudice as well. It is this changing place of prejudice that is examined in this book.

Benign bigotry: an introduction to the harm of subtle prejudice

Given the changing nature of prejudice and its often covert and unconscious forms, how do we go about studying it? How do we make subtle prejudice visible, and how do we reveal its effects? This book examines various manifestations of subtle prejudice. This analysis harnesses the power of social psychological theory and research to explain common, everyday manifestations of subtle prejudice and deconstructs the myths created to maintain these attitudes. I will use *benign bigotry* as an umbrella term to describe subtle prejudice – prejudices that are automatic, covert, often unconscious, unintentional, and sometimes undetectable by the target. The term is not intended to suggest that the subtle forms of bigotry described in this book are less harmful than other forms. They are not. In fact, benign bigotry is extremely harmful because it is insidious. With an understanding of benign bigotry comes the recognition that behaviors and attitudes may appear harmless and even positive, when they represent only a shift in the salience, not the strength, of prejudice. In the remaining pages of this introduction, I discuss some of the technical and analytical ways by which social psychologists examine subtle forms of prejudice. Some of this research focuses on one particular kind of bigotry and some applies to various myths and faulty assumptions. The introduction ends with a discussion about the scope of this book.

Because of the changing place of prejudice, social psychologists now distinguish between explicit and implicit prejudice.[9] Explicit prejudice is a set of feelings about others that are consciously accessible, seemingly controllable, and self-reported. Racism based on explicit prejudice is referred to as *old-fashioned* or *overt* racism. Implicit prejudice may or may not be consciously accessible, and may be difficult or impossible to control. Implicit prejudice is believed to be a consequence of years of exposure to associations in the environment, it tends to be impervious to conscious control, and it is relatively stable. Racism based on implicit prejudice has various names: *subtle, covert, modern, ambivalent,* or *aversive.* Because prejudice has changed, we can no longer detect its presence simply by interviewing people and asking whether or not they dislike certain groups. Most people would not admit to being prejudiced nowadays and many of them truly believe they are not prejudiced. This subtle form of prejudice is often studied by capturing the difference between overt self-reports of attitudes and results obtained using more covert measures in which research participants are unaware that their prejudice is being studied.

Scholars in any of the social sciences may study prejudice and bigotry but it is my contention that social psychologists are well positioned to study subtle forms of prejudice because they, more than those in other disciplines, rely on the experimental method. The experimental method allows the researcher to recreate real-life settings through controlled situations in which measures of prejudice can be taken without the research participant realizing that prejudice is being examined. For instance, a personnel manager might be asked to evaluate resumes of job candidates. The manager is asked to carefully review the applications and to decide whether or not each candidate should be hired. Unbeknownst to the manager, the resumes have been manipulated so that some of the resumes have women's names at the top, while others have men's. The candidates' qualifications are equivalent in the two sets. How qualified is each applicant? Research finds that the answer to that question depends on whether the evaluator believes the applicant to be a woman or a man. Do evaluators have any idea sexism is being measured? Probably not. Do they believe they are discriminatory? Probably not.

Another way to study subtle prejudice using the experimental method is to set up a situation in which respondents can be given the option of responding without appearing that they are actually biased. John Dovidio and Samuel Gaertner's[10] research compares people's tendency to express old-fashioned (overt) racism and what they describe as *aversive* (subtle, ambivalent) racism. They surveyed two sets of white students from the US: one group in 1989 and the second in 1999. In the first phase of the study, they asked students about their racial attitudes (the overt measure). Students responded to statements such as: "*Blacks shouldn't push themselves where they are not wanted,*" and "*I would probably feel somewhat self-conscious dancing with a black person in a public place.*" Later, in the second phase of the experiment, students were asked to select applicants for a peer counseling program, using interview excerpts as the basis for their choices. The information was manipulated such that the job candidate was either African American or white, and had one of three types of qualifications: clearly strong, ambiguous, or clearly weak. Students were asked whether or not they would recommend each job candidate, and how strongly. Note that, from the student raters' point of view, there was nothing about this procedure that would suggest the students' prejudice was being measured, except at the earlier and seemingly disconnected phase of the experiment. Dovidio and Gaertner hypothesized that, due to the continued emphasis in the US on egalitarian values, the general trend toward the expression of less prejudiced attitudes would be reflected from the earlier sample to the later one. They predicted that over the ten-year testing period, students' overt attitudes about African Americans would become more tolerant. They also speculated that bias in favor of whites and against African Americans would still appear in the subtler measure of assessing job candidate qualifications. Their hypotheses were borne out in their results. Students surveyed in 1999 had lower overt prejudice scores than did those surveyed in 1989. In terms of the students' ratings of job candidates, an interesting pattern emerged that is consistent with the notion of subtle prejudice. There were no differences in the recommendations for black and white candidates who had strong and weak qualifications – clearly qualified black and white students were recommended for hire, while clearly unqualified black and white candidates were not. However, black candidates with ambiguous qualifications were recommended less often than were whites with ambiguous qualifications. When a white job candidate's qualifications were ambiguous, students rated the candidates as if their qualifications were strong, whereas when a black candidate's qualifications were ambiguous, they rated the candidates as if they were weak. Thus whites seem to have been given the benefit of the doubt by other whites, a benefit not extended to African Americans. Dovidio and Gaertner write:

> Because [subtle] racists consciously recognize and endorse egalitarian values, they will not discriminate in situations in which they recognize that discrimination would be obvious to others and themselves . . . However, because aversive racists do possess negative feelings, often unconsciously, discrimination occurs when bias is not obvious or can be rationalized on the basis of some factor other than race. (p. 315)

So, although the students in the 1999 study reported less overt prejudice, they manifested subtle prejudice through the differential treatment of black and white candidates who had ambiguous qualifications. The fact that the discrimination against black candidates and favoritism of white candidates only took place when the applicants had ambiguous qualifications is significant because, in real life, many people's qualifications are not clearly outstanding or clearly deficient. Most individuals fall in the middle. Comedian Chris Rock agrees that most Americans are average, and points out that "average" has different consequences depending on one's race:

> Now when you go to a class there are 30 kids in the class: 5 smart, 5 dumb and the rest they're in the middle. And that's just all America is: a nation in the middle, a nation of B and C students . . . [A] black C student can't even be the manager at Burger King. Meanwhile the white C student just happens to be the President of the United States of America![11]

Chris Rock is referring to the widely known fact that the President of the United States at the time, George W. Bush, was a marginally good student. This observation is borne out in Dovidio and Gaertner's findings – subtle prejudice often operates in ambiguous conditions in which there is a lot of room for idiosyncratic interpretation. When a white person's qualifications are ambiguous, people tend to elevate that person, whereas when a black person's qualifications are ambiguous, people tend to devalue that person. Many of the examples in this book deal with applications for employment because the consequences of benign bigotry affect people's livelihood and their ability to work and earn income.

Subtle prejudice can also be measured using physiological measures – comparing what participants *say* (an explicit measure) with physiological measures (e.g. changes in heart rate, sweating) indicative of how they *feel* (implicit measures). The implicit measure that has received the most attention since the mid 1990s is the Implicit Association Test (IAT). The IAT measures the strength of association between mental constructs.[12] This computer-based task is essentially a sorting task during which the participant combines people, objects, or symbols with evaluative statements. For instance, a typical IAT on race would have the participant sort white faces and black faces and sort "Good" (e.g. paradise) and "Bad" (e.g. abuse) words at a fast pace. The ease (speed) with which one can sort black faces using the same response (a key press) as for "Good" or for "Bad" words is compared to the ease with which one can sort white faces sharing the same response as "Good" or "Bad" words. This speed reflects the strength of associative links between blacks and goodness/badness and between whites and goodness/badness. Whites tend to sort faces more quickly if white faces are aligned with "good" words and black faces aligned with "bad."[13] This means that whites react more quickly when the prompt matches the dominant stereotype and react more slowly if the association challenges the stereotype. Studies tend to find a discrepancy between results on the IAT, an implicit measure of attitudes, and responses from self-report surveys, which capture explicit measures of attitudes. This discrepancy suggests that the implicit responses from the IAT reveal one's unguarded, actual attitudes whereas responses from explicit measures reflect one's attitudes filtered through impression management.

Sources of subtle prejudice

Where does subtle prejudice come from? It comes from an internal conflict in people who want to comply with their non-prejudiced ideals, but who are still affected by the stereotypes about groups in the culture that surrounds them. Prejudiced values and ideas originate from many sources and influences. Prejudiced attitudes can come from the media, from growing up in a prejudiced familial environment, and from not having much contact with people different from oneself. Because of norms against prejudice and anti-discrimination legislation (in many cases it is illegal to discriminate), many people's prejudices take on hidden and sometimes unconscious forms. Subtle racism, for instance, is different in significant ways from *old-fashioned racism*. Old-fashioned racism might produce beliefs articulated as: *"Blacks are lazy,"* or *"Blacks are stupid."* Differently phrased, but no less pernicious, subtle racism produces statements that disguise prejudice, sometimes even from the speaker. *"I don't have anything against blacks,"* one might say, *"but this particular applicant is not a good fit for our company."*

Features of subtle prejudice

What are the features of subtle prejudice? First, subtle prejudice tends to be automatic, covert, unconscious, ambiguous, ambivalent and often unintentional. As will be demonstrated throughout this book, prejudice isn't merely antipathy toward a given group. The content of many prejudices consists of both negative and positive attributes. Unfortunately, "positive" attributes often function to perpetuate a target group's subordination in that the target is perceived as incompetent or in need of protection. It is the ambivalent feelings and subtle behaviors that explain, for instance, how it happens that one member of a minority group is discriminated against in a workplace while another is not. Subtle prejudice also tends to manifest in ambiguous conditions, as was demonstrated in the evaluation of applicants with mixed qualifications in the Dovidio and Gaertner study described above.

Second, unlike the extreme and overt prejudice of hate group members, subtle prejudice is not assumed to be the result of individual psychopathology but rather of the collision of two processes: normal cognitive processes, such as shortcuts in thinking and hasty generalizations, and the influence of sociocultural and historical processes, such as laws and policies that relegate certain groups to low status (e.g. laws prohibiting same-sex marriage). This is not to imply that prejudice is normal or that those who are prejudiced cannot help themselves and are therefore excused from self-examination. It does mean that categorizing and generalizing are part of our cognitive make-up – we all make generalizations that simplify our social worlds. However, *what* we generalize, *who* we categorize, and the content of our stereotypes can be modified and changed, and certainly should be modified and changed in the case of prejudice and discrimination.

Third, most people go out of their way to appear non-prejudiced – to themselves and to others; in many cases they truly believe they are not prejudiced. These three features make subtle prejudice insidious because they cause it to be widespread, normalized, resistant to change, and difficult for both the perpetrators and the targets to detect. The work on subtle bias suggests that, while we still find evidence of overt prejudice in people, these more contemporary forms of prejudice may account for the persistence of disparities in society.

Schemas and prejudice

It is clear that all of us categorize people, objects, and events. All of us, regardless of where we live or how much money we earn, create *schemas*, mental frameworks of beliefs, feelings, and assumptions about people, groups, and objects. Schemas help us make sense of the world. We incorporate new information into already existing schemas so that we do not have to treat all new information as though it is totally unfamiliar, requiring slow, deliberate, and thorough examination. Schemas, the foundation for assumptions, help us interpret our world and organize new information. When applied to categorization of people, schemas often manifest as stereotypes. Schemas work as filters that help us determine what aspects of a person or object are important to observe carefully and what can be disregarded, thus minimizing the drain on cognitive resources. They affect what we pay attention to and what we will remember later.

Power and prejudice

All of us create and utilize these cognitive structures to help us make sense of the world. Prejudice, however, including seemingly benign bigotry, necessarily involves power. Power, in addition to privilege, interacts with schemas to produce benign bigotry. Although both powerful and powerless people can be prejudiced, the prejudice of the powerful is more consequential. In terms of an organization, the prejudice of CEOs and middle managers can affect who gets hired, promoted, and fired. If receptionists in that same organization have prejudices, their prejudices will affect fewer people and have less of an impact.[14] On a national scale, the prejudices of presidents, Supreme Court justices, and law-makers reverberate through a society in a way that the prejudice of a factory worker does not. In addition, individual prejudices that tap into common stereotypes are reinforced in the media and have more staying power. Another hallmark of power and prejudice is the tendency for the powerful to harbor prejudiced attitudes toward the powerless and to see their lack of power as having been caused by some deficiencies in their characters.[15] So one thing to keep in mind about prejudice, stereotyping, and discrimination is, *Who is doing it?*

Throughout this book, in addition to referring to *majority* and *minority* groups, I will also use the terms *high status* and *low status* groups, and *dominant* and *subordinate* groups, to refer to groups with more or with less access to resources, power, and privilege in a society, regardless of actual group size. For instance, women are the numerical gender majority; however, they are a subordinate group because they lack power, resources, and status, relative to men. Those in power have more influence over their own lives and the lives of those immediately around them, but they also have more influence over cultural messages about who is valued and who is not, and who is considered normal and who is considered deviant. Racism, as an example, is based on a *system* involving cultural messages and institutional policies and practices, as well as the beliefs and actions of individuals. Racist ideas are also supported by decades, even centuries, of historical trends, laws, and policies that support them.

Beverly Daniel Tatum defines *cultural racism* as the images and messages in a culture that affirm the assumed superiority of white people and the assumed inferiority of people of color. Tatum uses a metaphor that equates cultural racism to smog in the air. "Sometimes it is so thick it is visible, other times it is less apparent, but always, day in and day out, we are breathing it in. None of us would introduce ourselves as 'smog-breathers' (and most of us don't want to be described as prejudiced), but if we live in a smoggy place, how can we avoid breathing the air?"[16] Tatum's point is that while many individuals may not feel prejudiced, or believe they do not discriminate, everyone is involved in prejudice. We all see the same cultural messages about high status and low status groups, whether by viewing television, using the Internet, or being subjected to discriminatory laws and Supreme Court decisions. None of us can disengage from racism, sexism, heterosexism, and classism. All of us are part of a system that values certain groups and devalues others. Tatum illustrates the ongoing cycle of racism by using a metaphor describing a moving walkway that you might see at an airport. The overt or *active* racist, to use Tatum's term, walks fast on the conveyor belt, which is moved along with racist ideology. Subtle racists, what Tatum terms *passive* racists, stand still on the moving walkway, exerting no visible effort, but, nonetheless, the conveyor belt moves them along in the same direction it moves active racists. Some people will feel the movement of the conveyor belt under their feet and choose to walk in the opposite direction, actively working against racism. But unless they turn around and walk in the opposite direction they are carried along with the others in racist traditions and practices.

Benign Bigotry: The Psychology of Subtle Prejudice addresses six commonly held cultural myths and faulty beliefs that are based on assumptions that *seem* relatively benign but actually foster and justify prejudice and discrimination. Each chapter provides a detailed discussion and dismantling of one of the six myths. Each chapter includes references to real-world events that illustrate the myth; examples in popular culture and politics; a discussion of the myth and corresponding stereotypes associated with it; a presentation of the "facts" about the phenomenon via systematic research studies (i.e. how and why the myth is believed); a discussion highlighting real-life consequences; and, finally, recommendations for the reduction of the beliefs that perpetuate the myth.

The first chapter, "Those people all look alike": the myth of the other, examines the tendency to erase individual differences in people who are different from oneself. Social psychologists refer to "they all look alike" thinking as the *outgroup homogeneity effect*, and the chapter moves this concept from the laboratory to the interpersonal, business, social, and political settings in which it is experienced on a daily basis. The chapter begins with a description of how, shortly after September 11, 2001, there was a dramatic increase in hate crimes in the US against Muslims, and against those who were thought to be Muslims or Arabs. Anyone who appeared "different" or from "over there" was a target, including Sikhs and Persians. One result of treating all members of a category as if they are the same is that they become interchangeable in people's minds. This phenomenon helps support, for example, Americans conflating Osama bin Laden and Saddam Hussein in the lead-up to the 2003 US invasion of Iraq. Americans saw little difference between the two men, and because of this, the invasion may have become more palatable. I also discuss how the *they all look alike* phenomenon may have contributed to why many of the Guantánamo Bay detainees were apparently captured by mistake.[17] Also discussed in this chapter, both in terms of actual events and systematic experimental research, is human *categorization*, and concepts related to the outgroup homogeneity effect including *ingroup favoritism* and *outgroup derogation*, the *ultimate attribution error*, the *linguistic intergroup bias*, *dehumanization*, and *scapegoating*. Finally, the chapter ends with strategies for change that are relevant to the outgroup homogeneity effect. These include *intergroup contact*, *stereotype suppression*, *values confrontation*, and the role of *empathy* in prejudice reduction.

Chapter 2, "They must be guilty of something": myths of criminalization, takes aim at how individual thought processes such as mental shortcuts, the formation of stereotypes, and internalized cultural schemas interact to construct an assumption that those who are accused of a criminal act are, in fact, guilty of something. This thinking impacts criminal investigations, police interrogations, suspect confessions, jury decision-making, views about the death penalty, and ideas about individuals who have been falsely convicted and later exonerated. Because of stereotypes about African Americans and Latinos, this chapter necessarily discusses real-life events and experimental evidence on racial and ethnic bias in the criminal justice system as well as media coverage of crime. The chapter ends with strategies to reduce bias during police investigations, defense strategies to minimize bias against defendants, and suggestions for changes in policy.

Chapter 3, "Feminists are man-haters": backlash mythmaking, examines the popular belief that feminists dislike men. Relatively few women describe themselves as feminists even when they support feminist ideology. This reluctance is due in large part to women's concern that, in doing so, they will be viewed as male-bashers.[18] Feminists are believed by some to be responsible for a variety of social ills such as young men entering college at a lower rate than young women[19] and the supposed decline in "manliness" in American culture.[20] Chapter 3 examines people's beliefs and stereotypes about feminists as well as feminists' actual beliefs and attitudes. What does feminism actually critique and advocate? Do feminists really dislike men more than do non-feminists? These questions are examined through a review of the few empirical studies that have looked at this issue. Rather than finding that feminists dislike men, evidence suggests that non-feminists actually feel more hostility toward men than do feminists. Why does the myth of the feminist man-hater endure? This question is addressed in the chapter, as are the questions of why feminism is vilified and why there is cultural hostility toward strong, assertive, and non-traditional women. Attempts to trivialize the feminist movement are documented as well. Finally, strategies for change address the possibility of modifying masculine gender roles, the positive impact of gender and women's studies courses, and changes in workplace policies.

"Gays flaunt their sexuality": the myth of hypersexuality, is the popular belief explored in Chapter 4. The concepts of *illusory correlation* and *vividness* are used to help elucidate why people tend to "see" hypersexuality only in lesbians and gay men and not in heterosexuals. Heterosexual privilege is discussed as it helps explain why some groups are seen as normal, with behavior deemed as natural, while other groups are seen as foreign and deviant. In fact, the same behavior that is criticized in homosexuals is celebrated and expected in heterosexuals. Nonetheless, the belief that homosexuals flaunt their sexuality impacts how lesbians, gay men, and bisexuals are treated in their professional lives, whether or not they are viewed as adequate parents, and whether or not anti-gay violence is pros- ecuted. Strategies for change in Chapter 4 include the importance of institutional support for lesbian and gay rights, the role of increased contact and cooperation between gay and straight people as a strategy to reduce prejudice, and the role that *cognitive dissonance* can play in reducing homophobia and heterosexism.

Chapter 5, "I'm not a racist, I'm colorblind": the myth of neutrality, addresses the appeal of being racially colorblind in a time of decreased overt prejudice and increasingly prevalent norms of non-prejudice. In a multiracial society, is it possible, or even desirable, to be colorblind? There have been many legal and policy attempts at, for instance, "colorblind" admissions policies. Many people believe that colorblindness is the key to ending discrimina- tion, while others use colorblindness in a cynical attempt to maintain white privilege and to pressure people of color into assimilation. I examine the research on people's ability not to notice others' race and ethnicity. What sort of political attitudes are held by those who espouse colorblindness? Do they tend to be racially tolerant, for instance? I also compare multicultural and colorblind approaches to prejudice reduction. Chapter 5 includes *decategorization* and *recategorization* as strategies to reduce prejudice.

Chapter 6, "Affirmative action is reverse-racism": the myth of merit, deals with the ever-controversial topic of affirmative action in the United States. If you only consider media coverage of affirmative action, you would probably believe that the typical affirmative action program involves quotas and that unquali- fied women and ethnic minorities are hired over better-qualified white men. This chapter explains the difference between "equal opportunity" and affirmative action, and addresses the reasons benign bigotry makes actual equal opportunity impossible and affirmative action necessary. I then look at the stages of employment and college admissions procedures during which subtle prejudice can be manifest. I examine the social psychological literature on gender and ethnic patterns in *entitlement* as well as explanations of success and failure. Affirmative action must be considered in the context of privilege. Finally, strategies for change include suggestions for affirmative action plans including the differentiation between *process-oriented* and *goal-oriented* approaches. Additionally, a discussion of the importance of affirmative action from the leadership in organizations is crucial. Other strategies for reducing bias during interviews, the importance of standardized performance criteria, and the challenges of mentoring and "diversity" training are discussed.

Some caveats

Having outlined what this book covers, I should note some of its limitations. First, researchers make a distinction between different levels of influence on a person's behavior. The macrosystem consists of social–structural factors such as laws and religious institutions. The microsystem refers to individuals interacting in particular environments such as work, family, or school. This book focuses mainly on prejudice from a social psychological perspective and will thus tend to focus on *individual* attitudes, beliefs, and behaviors. Unlike other social sciences, such as sociology and anthropology, which use society and culture as the unit of analysis, psychology is primarily focused on the individual. Analysis of social structures is also key to addressing issues of prejudice. Therefore, a key feature of this presentation is that I make explicit connections between social psychological research and theory, and macro issues such as institutions, laws, and policies, as well as the mass media.

Second, prejudice involves both a *perpetrator* – the prejudiced or discriminatory individual, and a *target* – the recipient or victim of prejudice. In this book, I devote the majority of space to the psychology of the prejudiced individual (the perpetrator) and to the impact of prejudice on the target, and less to the psychology of the target of prejudice. Third, this book is less about what people *are actually like* – which stereotypes are true and which are false – and more about *perceptions* and *beliefs* about others that are based on social categories. Explanations about social groups are rarely based on people's direct *experiences* with those groups, and instead are more likely to be reflective of beliefs (and mythologies) shared by members of a culture.

Fourth, most of the research I describe in this book is from studies conducted in the US with American participants. There are also several studies from the UK and a few from other parts of the world. When I describe a study, I identify the demographic characteristics of the participants whenever they are available. Also, many studies on ethnic prejudice have focused on white participants, with African Americans as the targets of prejudice. The field of social psychology knows less about white stereotypes regarding other ethnic groups or the stereotypes of non-whites directed towards whites and other people of color. Finally, I include some anecdotes in this book. However, this book much more heavily emphasizes coverage of systematic research studies using experimental methods. To the extent that I rely on anecdotes, I do so only to illustrate patterns found in studies. In other words, any anecdotes I report are supported by empirical research studies.

The name of this book is *Benign Bigotry*, and this title is ironic. Bigotry is never benign, even when it exists in the form of subtle prejudice. *Benign Bigotry* is meant to capture the hidden nature of subtle prejudice; the *apparently* innocent assumptions people make based on prejudice. Of course, technically, the content of prejudices and stereotypes can be positive or negative. I can have a prejudice in favor of a certain type of music, for instance. But stereotypes are always harmful to the people who are targets of them. Even when stereotypes appear to be flattering (e.g. African Americans are good athletes, Asians are the model minority), they demand that the target either conforms or risks disappointing the holder of the stereotypes. People we stereotype are not seen as having their own individual opinions, preferences, and desires, but rather are judged as members of a group. Stereotypes erase a person's individuality. Stereotypes control and constrain people. Those who hold the stereotypes are also harmed. In his discussion of how racism negatively affects whites, Derald Sue[21] describes racism as a clamp on one's mind, distorting one's perception of reality. He explains that in maintaining one's schemas, one's perceptual accuracy is diminished. Individuals become members of categories rather than unique people. The harm to people of color diminishes white people's humanity because whites lose sensitivity to hurting others. And stereotyping nearly always involves the loss of the ability to empathize. Racism is also bad for whites because they misperceive themselves as superior, thereby engaging in elaborate self-deception. Prejudice in members of dominant groups can result in the guilt of recognizing their own privilege at the expense of others. This recognition can manifest in shame, defensiveness, and even outbursts of anger.

Understanding the nature of subtle prejudice – that prejudice comes in subtle, ostensibly "benign" forms – should not let us off the hook. We can no longer allow ourselves to think that only the Ku Klux Klan or skinheads are prejudiced. We cannot distance ourselves from bigotry once we understand that bigotry, even in a "benign" form, is part of the air we breathe, and has devastating consequences.

NOTES

1. American Anthropological Association. (1998, May 17). *American Anthropological Association statement on "race" (May 17, 1998)*. Retrieved September 13, 2004, from www.aaanet.org/stmts/racepp.htm

2. National Centre for Social Research. (2008, January 23). *New British social attitudes report published today* [Press Release]. Retrieved August 28, 2008, from www.natcen.ac.uk/natcen/pages/news_and_media_docs/ BSA_24_report.pdf
3. *Ibid.*
4. Cited in: Fiske, S.T. (2004). *Social beings: A core motives approach to social psychology.* Hoboken, NJ: John Wiley & Sons.
5. *Ibid.*
6. National Centre for Social Research, *New British social attitudes report.*
7. Democracy Now! (2006, December 28). Angela Davis speaks out on prisons and human rights abuses in the aftermath of Hurricane Katrina. Transcript retrieved November 5, 2007, from www.democracynow.org/ 2006/12/28/angela_davis_ speaks_out_on_prisons
8. *Ibid.*
9. Henry, P.J., & Hardin, C.D. (2006). The contact hypothesis revisited: Status bias in the reduction of implicit prejudice in the United States and Lebanon. *Psychological science, 17,* 862–868.
10. Dovidio, J.F., & Gaertner, S.L. (2000). Aversive racism and selection decisions: 1989 and 1999. *Psychological science, 11,* 315–319.
11. Rock, C. (Writer), & Gallen, J. (Director). (2004). *Never scared (Black ambition tour)* [DVD]. Washington, DC: Home Box Office, Inc.
12. Carney, D.R., Nosek, B.A., Greenwald, A.G., & Banaji, M.R. (2007). Implicit Association Test (IAT). In R.F. Baumeister & K.D. Vohs (Eds.) *Encyclopedia of social psychology, Vol.1* (pp. 463–464). Thousand Oaks, CA: Sage.
13. See the Harvard Project Implicit website for a review of research trends: Project Implicit (n.d.). FAQs. Retrieved August 25, 2008, from https:// implicit.harvard.edu/implicit/demo/background/faqs.html
14. Sampson, E.E. (1999). *Dealing with differences: An introduction to the social psychology of prejudice.* New York: Harcourt Brace College Publishers.
15. *Ibid.*
16. See page 6 in: Tatum, B.D. (1997). *"Why are all the Black kids sitting together in the cafeteria?" and other conversations about race.* New York: Basic Books.
17. Cited in: Walsh, J. (2006, March 14). The Abu Ghraib files. Retrieved October 20, 2007, from www.salon.com/news/abu_ghraib/2006/03/14/ introduction/
18. For instance see: Alexander, S., & Ryan, M. (1997). Social constructs of feminism: A study of undergraduates at a women's college. *College student journal, 31,* 555–567; and see: Aronson, P. (2003). Feminists or "post-feminists"? Young women's attitudes toward feminism and gender relations. *Gender and society, 17,* 903–922.

19. Sommers, C.H. (2000). *The war against boys: How misguided feminism is harming our young men.* New York: Simon & Schuster.
20. Mansfield, H.C. (2006). *Manliness.* New Haven, CT: Yale University Press.
21. Sue, D.W. (2003). *Overcoming our racism: The journey to liberation.* San Francisco: Jossey-Bass.

ONE

"Those people all look alike": The myth of the other

I watch CNN but I'm not sure I can tell you the difference in Iraq and Iran.
Alan Jackson's *"Where Were You?"*[1]

Immediately after the September 11, 2001, attacks in the United States, Sikh Americans became targets of hate crimes. Sikhism, a religion that originated in India, is not related to Islam, the religion of the hijackers who committed the attacks. Sikh men wear their hair long and in a turban or tied back. For some Americans, turbans worn by Sikh men resembled the head covering of Osama bin Laden, the Saudi who took responsibility for the attacks. Suddenly, Sikhs were the victims of crimes ranging from a woman trying to pull a man's turban off to beatings, bombings, and killings.[2] To the perpetrators of these attacks against Sikh Americans, Sikhs may as well have been Osama bin Laden himself – even though they did not share his religion, ethnicity, or nation of origin. To many Americans, *people over there* (i.e. the Middle East and Asia) are, indeed, all alike. To many Americans Sikhs look more like

Middle Easterners, Arabs, or Muslims than they do Americans, and therefore *they must be the enemy*.[3]

"They all look alike" is a fairly ordinary expression, and a phenomenon most people have encountered in one situation or another. In essence, it reflects our general inability to distinguish individuating features of members of groups to which we do not belong. This idea is applied to nearly any sort of group or category, from race to nationality to religious affiliation. This chapter examines this phenomenon, the idea that "they all look alike" as a widespread and common event, as a psychological process, and as a place where individual psychological processes and social interactions intersect. Beyond the constructive function of sorting and categorizing, the belief that "they all look alike" also leads to mistaken beliefs about people and things beyond our immediate experience. We are all familiar with the expression "they all look alike," and we are familiar with the ways in which that frame of mind can also reflect an underlying system of social status and power. After all, "they all look alike" is at the heart of racial profiling and erroneous eyewitness testimony.

Before we explore ways to identify and overcome the tendency to think "they all look alike" (whoever "they" might be), it will be useful to think about the various ways in which this phenomenon occurs, and then to introduce some of the insights offered by social psychology that help us move toward understanding the way categorization and prejudgment work, and the ways in which these ordinary cognitive processes can have unwanted and damaging results in specific social contexts. We hear this expression, perhaps even use this expression, but it is important to debunk the common-sense feeling that it conveys something meaningful and legitimate. This chapter explores the ways that social psychology can help us understand how such an expression comes to gain currency and how such a cognitive phenomenon actually works. Perhaps more importantly, social psychology provides theories, tools, and an enormous bank of experimental research to help us understand some of the real-life consequences of the erroneous belief that "they all look alike."

First, I will describe the "they all look alike" phenomenon through some real-life, contemporary examples drawn from politics, news, and popular culture. Then I will introduce some of the formal ways in which social psychology describes this phenomenon. In this section, a number of experimental studies in social psychology will allow us to see how scientific research can explain day-to-day belief and behavior. Finally, I will outline some strategies for change, emphasizing both the value of applying an analytical perspective to ordinary life and the importance of developing deliberate techniques we can all employ to help overcome benign bigotry and its often devastating consequences.

Osama, Obama – The Difference One Consonant Can Make

Governor Pataki in New York says he knows what to do. He said we should take the toppled statues of Saddam Hussein, melt them down and put them in a new World Trade Center – to serve as a permanent reminder that America is a country that cannot tell Arabs apart.

Bill Maher[4]

The war in Iraq presents some of the most vivid illustrations of how a "them" gets created in the first place and how the social construction of categories comes to substitute for actual reality. In the quote above, talk show host, Bill Maher, points out that the governor of New York (falsely) believed that Saddam Hussein, then president of Iraq, was responsible for the September 11, 2001, attacks on the World Trade Center in New York. In the examples that follow, it becomes clear that the confusion of names, faces, nationalities, and other details of "them" carries enormous implications and consequences. Let's first look at some of the public discussion around the time when US military strategy moved from the invasion of Afghanistan (in the hunt for Osama bin Laden, the leader behind the attacks of September 11, 2001) to the military action against Iraq. In the process of explaining and justifying this transition, US President George W. Bush blurred the distinction between Osama bin Laden and Iraqi president Saddam Hussein. No evidence actually linked the attacks of September 11 to Saddam Hussein, but making such links was a necessary component of President Bush's rationale for the invasion of Iraq.

Let's look at an example of how this belief works by examining a set of events with global consequences. One of the most dramatic recent examples of this phenomenon occurred when politicians and members of the George W. Bush administration began conflating Osama bin Laden, who gave orders to al-Qaeda for the September 11 attacks, and Saddam Hussein, the leader of Iraq.[5] In the fall of 2002, as President Bush was making his argument for the invasion of Iraq, he made the statement, "The war on terror, you can't distinguish between al-Qaeda and Saddam when you talk about the war on terror."[6] In order to justify the 2003 invasion of Iraq, it was important for the Bush administration to create a link between Saddam Hussein and the attacks of September 11, 2001. In the months after September 11, 2001, as the Bush administration's focus on attacking Iraq became clear,[7] George Bush's public references to Osama bin Laden began to decrease, while his references to Saddam Hussein increased. Making this false linkage between bin Laden and Hussein was relatively easy because Americans had already been led to believe that Saddam Hussein was responsible for the September 11 attacks, even though he was not.[8] For many Americans these two men were interchangeable: both were Arab and Muslim, they had dark skin and facial hair, were non-English speakers, and were enemies of the United States. The Bush administration took advantage of the public's susceptibility to blurring the distinctions between people of a large and diverse region, successfully linked the two men, and was able to gain public support for the invasion and occupation of Iraq – a country that had nothing to do with the September 11 attacks. In fact, perhaps the reason George Bush was re-elected as President in 2004 was that he successfully harnessed the American public's ignorance in order to link Saddam Hussein with the terror attacks of 9/11, thereby justifying the invasion of Iraq in 2003.[9]

The contemporary mixing up of Arabs and those from the Middle East by Westerners pre-dates September 11, 2001. Back in 1980, during the Iranian hostage crisis, when Iranian students kidnapped and held 52 American diplomats for 444 days, 70% of Americans wrongly identified Iran as an Arab country. Today, most Americans think of Iranians as Arabs,[10] but they are Persians. The view that all Middle Easterners are Arabs and that all Arabs are alike is reflected in the history of cinematic representations of Arabs. In American films from as early as the 1937 film *The Sheik Steps Out* to 1998's *Siege*, themes reflect and perpetuate the belief that all Arabs are alike, with lines from Westerners in the films such as: "They all look alike to me" and "I can't tell one from another. Wrapped in those bed sheets they all look the same to me."[11] In feature films with Arab characters, Arabs and Muslims are interchangeable, leaving the viewer with the impression that all Arabs are Muslim and all Muslims are Arab, when, in fact, only 12% of the world's Muslims are Arab.[12]

The unwillingness or inability of "us" to distinguish nationalities, physical characteristics, religions, or even names, has become an often convenient and dangerous joke in the 2008 US presidential campaign. The name of the African American democratic presidential candidate, *Barack Obama*, closely resembles the name *Osama bin Laden* in some voters' minds. One voter explained her reasoning for not supporting Obama: "Obama sounds too much like Osama."[13] More than a handful of very public instances of interchanging the names of Osama bin Laden and Barack Obama have been identified. This confusion has occurred in news broadcasts, in television talk shows, in official comments from the US senate, and in the public remarks of other presidential candidates seeking their party's nomination. Here is a sample: in a CNN report from December 12, 2006, correspondent Jeanne Moos[14] reports on what she describes as the "Obama – Osama similarity." "Only one little consonant differentiates the two names," we are told. In actuality, of course, distinctions between words based on only one consonant are not, in general, problems for American speakers of English to understand. The words, for example, "bad" and "dad" are likewise distinguished by only one consonant, but that similarity seems not to interfere with understanding meaning. The underlying issue that results in this "Obama–Osama confusion" concerns the tendency for non-Arab Americans to blend all people of color into one undifferentiated generic sound and look. Moos accounts for this "confusion" in part as a result of Senator Obama's relatively low recognition factor at the time. Her report goes on to ask viewers, "If that similarity weren't enough, how about sharing the name of a former dictator?" The report continues with a discussion of Senator Obama's middle name, *Hussein*, and its resonance with Saddam Hussein. Here is the resulting situation: an African American US senator, Barack Hussein Obama, is being linked to both Saddam Hussein and to Osama bin Laden because their names are alike or sound alike, resulting in the mistaken belief that some sort of kinship exists.

This confusion continued to receive air time throughout the campaign season, with various versions being repeated by Senator Edward Kennedy on the morning television program, *The View*, and, perhaps most notoriously, by the former governor and presidential candidate Mitt Romney. During a campaign speech in October, 2007, Romney reports: "Look at what Osama – Obama, Barack Obama said just yesterday, calling on radicals, all different types of jihadists to come together in Iraq, join us under one banner." In this instance, of course, Romney actually corrects himself, replacing the correct identification of Osama with the incorrect identification of Barack Obama. In February, 2008, as the Democratic primary contests were well under way, the MSNBC newscaster Chris Matthews reported on a story about Barack Obama while a photograph of Osama bin Laden was displayed throughout the newscast.[15] Whether or not such mistakes are made willfully and knowingly, or innocently and accidentally, they all contribute to the idea that "they all look alike."

Whether it's judgments about what a terrorist looks like, police line-ups, playground politics, or country singers like Alan Jackson not being able to distinguish between Iraq and Iran, the belief that those who are different from *us* are all alike can have devastating consequences. This chapter deals with the tendency for people to think that those who are different from them think alike, act alike, and *are* alike. This belief is the product of categorization and is referred to by social psychologists as the *outgroup homogeneity effect*. Members of one's own group appear to be highly diverse with different personalities, preferences, and tendencies, whereas members of other groups appear to be highly similar – they look alike, think alike, and act alike. Categorization leads to the outgroup homogeneity effect as well as other phenomena. This chapter explains the outgroup homogeneity effect as well as *ingroup favoritism/ outgroup derogation*, the *ultimate attribution error*, *linguistic intergroup bias*, and the implications of categorization such as the dehumanization that can lead to abuse.

Arrested on the battlefield? Guantánamo detainees

Shortly after the terrorist attacks against the US on September 11, 2001, US Defense Secretary Donald Rumsfeld ordered the building of a prison at the Guantánamo Bay Naval Base in Cuba to detain those accused of participating in or assisting in terrorist activities against the US. By the end of 2008, there had been only one trial in the seven years that suspects were detained. Who are the detainees at Guantánamo and why have they not been tried and convicted? Only 8% of Guantánamo detainees were captured on the battlefield by American troops. Instead, the detainees were captured in markets, taken from their homes, or arrested in other non-combat situations. Sixty percent of the detainees are not members of al Qaeda, or of the Taliban, the rulers of Afghanistan at the time of the September 11, 2001 attacks, but rather are accused of being "associated" with some group.[16] For instance, one detainee had been conscripted by the Taliban to work as a cook's assistant, and this fact was the sole evidence of his association with the Taliban. Many of the detainees were captured by locals who were enticed by advertised bounties.[17] The US Military had distributed leaflets throughout Afghanistan and nearby areas that read "Get wealth and power beyond your dreams. Help the Anti-Taliban Forces rid Afghanistan of murderers and terrorists" and "You can receive millions of dollars . . . to take care of your family . . . for the rest of your life."[18]

Many arrested in Iraq during the US and British invasion and occupation of the country were similarly captured under ambiguous conditions. An International Committee of the Red Cross report from February, 2004, cited military intelligence officers estimating that "between 70 to 90 percent of persons deprived of their liberty in Iraq had been arrested by mistake."[19]

There are myriad explanations as to why the evidence against many of the detainees is non-existent or thin. The false belief that Muslims are all alike could be one component of the explanation. When people were rounded up in sweeps or picked up by bounty hunters, many might have been innocent, but shared the same or a similar name with someone else who might really be a terrorist.[20] From an English-speaking Westerner's perspective, Osama and Obama and Iraq and Iran sound the same. And if you believe that all Arabs are the same, that they all hate America, that they don't value human life the way Westerners do,[21] then really what's the difference? Guantánamo detainees become interchangeable. As an example, here are two lists of names. One includes names of some of the detainees imprisoned at Guantánamo Bay as of March 2006.[22] The second contains common English names of American men.

Wazir Mohammed	Daniel Jackson
Mirza Muhammad	David Jefferson
Muhammad Ansar	John Johnston
Muhammad Anwar	Douglas Jackson
Muhammad Ashraf	Jeffrey Douglas
Ali Muhammad	John Daniels
Mohamed Al Adahi	John Jefferson
Mohamed Ahmed Al Asadi	Daniel Johnson
Abdullah Mohammed Al-Hamiri	Douglas Jefferson
Mohammed Ahmed Salam	Daniel Douglas
Mohamid bin Salman	Jeffrey Johnston
Hajii Faiz Mohammed	Jonathan Douglas
Haji Mohammed Khan	David Jackson

Social psychologists would predict that English-speaking Westerners would find it easier to distinguish the names on the second list, that there would be more motivation to remember the names on the second list, and that the names on the second list would represent distinct people. If there is a warrant for the arrest of someone named Daniel Jefferson, you will be hesitant to pick up someone named Jeffrey Daniels. But if you are an English-speaking Westerner in Afghanistan capturing terrorists and someone gives you the name Mohamed Ahmed Al Asadi, even though on the man's papers his name is Mohamed Al Adahi, that name might be "close enough" to Mohamed Ahmed Al Asadi, and so the wrong person is arrested and is detained for several years, much of the time having no access to an attorney, no contact with family members,[23] no contact with members of the Red Cross,[24] no formal charges against him, no opportunity to answer to charges, and no hope of ever leaving.[25] What this chapter will show is that employing broad generalizations and apparently innocent shortcuts in thinking can have, literally and figuratively, global implications and life-and-death consequences.

Categorization

Let's go over how this belief that "they all look alike" works. It turns out the dangerous and mistaken belief that "they all look alike" emerges from a very basic, very ordinary and mostly benign process that human beings employ to make sense of the world: the use of categories. Categorization, making a group out of items that share some characteristics, is a fundamental human cognitive process. Observing children provides many examples of this categorization process. For instance, when a child sees a camel for the first time, she might call it a "bumpy horse" until she learns that camels are a category of animals distinct from horses. She might believe that a coconut is a "furry rock" until she learns that coconuts share some of the properties of fruits and thus belong in the fruit category and not the rock category.

Categorization helps us make sense of the world and is therefore both a natural tendency and a necessary ability for human thought. Unfortunately, categorization is also the basis for stereotyping and prejudice.[26] But this is not to say that racism, homophobia, sexism, and other stereotype-based forms of bigotry and discrimination are natural and therefore not preventable. We are hardwired with the ability to think categorically; however, the *content* of our categories and the *meaning* and *significance* of those categories is socially constructed. We give categories meaning and power through social and cultural interaction, and changing contexts result in somewhat flexible categories. Historically, for instance, *Homo sapiens* was divided into three races using the following terms: Negroids (i.e. "blacks") were those whose ancestors resided in Africa; Mongoloids ("Asians") were those from Asia; and Caucasoids ("whites") came from Europe. Dividing human beings into "racial" categories is erroneous because it involves the importation of biological categories for social purposes. Even these "biological" categories have been exposed to be bankrupt in terms of explaining evolutionary relatedness or social realities. Instead social scientists encourage understanding more meaningful groups of association.

The whole concept of having distinct human races has been discredited as an ideological framework and part of a worldview rather than a set of scientific facts.[27] The concept of race, itself, has recently been explored and revised in biology and social sciences. Overwhelmingly the conclusion has been that as members of a complex society where considerable variation and diversity exist, we have been conditioned to view human races as natural and as separate divisions of the human species. Indeed, these apparent divisions do not reflect discrete, bounded categories but instead human physical variation that is understood as a continuous, unbroken gradient of a number of features, including, but not limited to, skin pigmentation.[28] Race has been discredited as a meaningful biological category, but continues to hold powerful significance as a social category. The point here is that all sorts of categories are actually highly plastic and dynamic and not the stable or objective things we think they are. Categories themselves are not intrinsically meaningful – we make categories meaningful. Nonetheless, the categorization of people forms the basis of prejudice and discrimination.

One of the most common and basic ways of categorizing people is to divide them into two groups: those in my group (members of my *ingroup*) and those not in my group (members of the *outgroup*). After all, there is no simpler way to divide people than according to a binary, either–or division. Social psychologists use the terms "ingroup" and "outgroup" to distinguish those like us from those not like us. However, there is not an inherent judgment in the terms ingroup and outgroup the way, for instance, the popular kids at school are in the "in" group while the losers are the "out" group.

Also, whites are not the ingroup and, say, Asians are not the outgroup, unless the comparison is in reference to a white person. From the perspective of an Asian person, Asians would be the ingroup and people of other ethnicities would be the outgroups. In social psychology, ingroup merely means people who have some similar characteristics to the self. If they do not, they are members of the outgroup – the other group. Now that this point has been made, we will soon see that individuals *do* tend to believe that their group is better than other groups, and various groups, such as some ethnicities and religious groups, have higher status and more power in a given culture.

One important result of classification into ingroups and outgroups is the *outgroup homogeneity effect*. Outgroup homogeneity is the technical term for our social experience that "they all look [or act] alike." This occurs when people are judged in terms of their social identities and their membership in a specific group, rather than on the basis of their individual attributes and characteristics.

They all look (and act) alike: the outgroup homogeneity effect

Social psychologist Jennifer Boldry and her colleagues[29] conducted a meta-analysis on the outgroup homogeneity effect. A meta-analysis is a statistical procedure whereby the calculations from previously conducted studies on a particular topic are combined into one giant or "meta" analysis. A meta-analysis is therefore a kind of statistical summary that gives a thorough summary of a particular topic. Boldry and her colleagues compiled the statistical information from 173 studies, carried out over several decades, which examined some aspect of the outgroup homogeneity effect. They found that, indeed, across the studies they examined, people tended to perceive people who are similar to themselves as diverse and individual, and to view those different from themselves as similar to each other. Additionally, group size affects the action of the outgroup homogeneity effect. The larger the ingroup relative to the outgroup, the more members of the outgroup will be perceived as similar to each other.[30] Homogenizing the outgroup happens in terms of a variety of social categories including gender and race. For instance, whites tend to see blacks with less complexity than they do other whites.[31]

Another factor to consider in understanding how the outgroup homogeneity effect works is *status*. Research shows that status affects our ability to make fine distinctions and to recall details about people. Groups that are considered high status and having more social, economic, and political power are thought to be more valuable, and are particularly likely to engage in outgroup homogeneity with reference to lower status group members in terms of memory tasks.[32] This finding suggests that high status people are not required to remember details about low status people and have the luxury of not having to pay attention to those "lower" than them. So the fact that high status people think low status people are alike is more consequential than low status people believing high status people are all alike.

The meta-analysis performed by Boldry and her colleagues showed that outgroup homogeneity was particularly strong when stereotyping (judging the percent of group members who possess stereotypical traits) was the task being studied, as well as when one's memory for face recognition was being tested. This point is important because these two factors are likely to lead to problems with eyewitness identification and discrimination. Stereotyping tasks prompt people to think abstractly about the group as a whole. One consistent pattern in social psychological research is that people are more accurate at recalling own-race faces than other-race faces.[33] This pattern seems to be consistent across racial and cultural groups.

Some studies have found that whites, in settings where they are the dominant group, tended to be worse at remembering other-race faces than were non-whites at remembering other-race faces.[34] While most groups tend to remember their own-ethnicity faces better than other-ethnicity faces, whites, in nations where they are the dominant group, have more same-race recall than other-race recall. One study,[35] conducted in South Africa and England, found that whites and blacks engage in this own-race bias almost equally. A few studies have found that those in the minority in a given setting do not indicate an own-race bias. For example, one study[36] tested white Australian students' and Chinese students' recall accuracy for faces. Participants viewed several photographs of white and Chinese women's and men's faces. They later had to pick out those photos they saw before that appeared in a new group of photos. White participants recognized white faces more accurately than Chinese faces. However, Chinese participants recognized both races equally well. White people are particularly likely to make false alarms – believing they had previously seen a photo when they had not. This effect is exacerbated when participants judging faces had little time to view them and when the interval between viewing and testing was increased.[37]

This is exactly the problem with eyewitnesses to crimes. People of color in the US have been falsely convicted based solely on the inaccurate recall of an eyewitness. Next to a defendant's confession – a topic described at length in the next chapter – eyewitness identification is one of the most persuasive pieces of evidence for jurors. Even when DNA tests have excluded suspects, they have been convicted on the basis of a victim's eyewitness testimony.[38] Additionally, many people think that racial stereotyping in the US has decreased over time and that "race relations" are getting better. While the ability to differentiate own- and other-race faces has improved over the thirty-year period during which most of these studies took place, it is also true that the false alarm rates *increased* over those thirty years.[39] To summarize, the meta-analytic work on the outgroup homogeneity effect finds that, although any person can view members of the outgroup as similar, dominant group members are more likely to do it than subordinate members, especially when the dominant group is also the numeric majority in a society. Furthermore, the outgroup homogeneity effect is most likely to occur when people are asked about stereotypical traits and in studies on face recognition.

The potentially horrific implications of the outgroup homogeneity effect was epitomized in the 1982 beating to death of Chinese American Vincent Chin. In 1982, the American auto market was in recession. In comparison, the Japanese auto market was going gangbusters. Chin was beaten to death with a baseball bat by angry unemployed auto workers who blamed Japan and the Japanese for having lost their jobs.[40] The men who killed Chin either mistook Chin for someone Japanese, or did not care to distinguish between Chinese and Japanese because they assumed that all Asians are alike.

The outgroup homogeneity effect finds that outgroup members are viewed as "all alike" while ingroup members are thought to be more variable. What does it mean for members of a group to be perceived as more variable? It means that those people are thought about in terms of who they are as individuals, with more complexity, rather than in terms of group stereotypes. All ingroup members are perceived to have their own individual thoughts, feelings, and characteristics. Those people are judged one by one based on their individual merits, not based on the expectations we have of them according to their group membership. In contrast, those who are thought to be homogeneous are judged in terms of their social category, not what they are like as individuals. Outgroup members' behavior is perceived through a stereotyped lens. It is always better to be judged as an individual and not in terms of stereotypes. Even positive stereotypes are bad because they reduce or remove a person's individuality. They constrain judgments of people to others' expectations. Also, when people behave in ways inconsistent with positive stereotypes about their group, there can be strong negative reactions. When we defy stereotypes about us, we are vulnerable to harsh penalties from those whose expectations were violated.[41]

Why do we think they all look alike?

In terms of the ability to recognize and recall faces, it seems that when people process own-race faces, they are able to attend to the idiosyncratic features of the face more efficiently than when they process an other-race face. When we are asked to recall a face, we can compare an own-race face to more detailed ideas of own-race faces and can remember more subtle differences.

The outgroup homogeneity effect impacts more than people's recognition of faces. It extends to judgments of personalities, preferences, and behavioral tendencies – *they all look alike, think alike, and act alike*. Why does this happen? Construing outgroup members as all alike provides a sense of welcome predictability. First, that people tend to think that outgroups "all look alike" has to do with familiarity. People in the dominant group can be more selective in their social contacts and might not have a lot of contact with outgroups due to residential and occupational segregation. For instance, poor people and rich people work in different jobs, shop at different stores, attend different schools, and live in different neighborhoods. Therefore we know more people in our ingroup and know more about them as individuals with distinct preferences and attributes, than people in the outgroup. We have more information about ingroup members and their unique qualities.

Second, we like to think of *ourselves* and those we think are similar to us as relatively individual and complicated individuals. People believe outgroup members have similar traits and occupy similar social roles. Also, people tend to ignore schema-discrepant information. In other words, when we are confronted with information about a person or group that doesn't fit our stereotype of the group, we tend to ignore the information, rather than incorporate it into a new more complex schema.[42] One consequence of this differential perception is that evaluations of outgroup members tend to be more polarized and extreme than evaluations of ingroup members.[43] For instance, outgroup members' beliefs and viewpoints are seen as more extreme.[44] Would spending more time with out-group members lessen the tendency to see them all as the same? Possibly, because the outgroup homogeneity effect is less consistent with gender – there is less gender segregation than there is racial segregation because heterosexual women and men live together and those who grow up with sisters and brothers have same- and other-gender siblings. Third, the nature of interactions with in-group members is more familiar and is less affected by social norms. We see ingroup members in multiple roles, whereas we tend to see outgroup members in more limited social roles.[45] For instance, if white people's only interactions with people of color are when they are being served by them in a restaurant, or having their house cleaned, a white person's ideas about ethnic minorities will be drawn from very narrow roles that people of color play in white people's lives. At the same time, the media provide biased images as sources of information about ethnic groups, and people can easily develop unconscious associations and feelings that reinforce bias.[46]

Fourth, people are motivated to see themselves as unique and therefore look for ways to distinguish themselves from their group in order to maintain their individuality, thus emphasizing the heterogeneity of their group. We tend to pay attention to the ways in which we are different from members of our own group. This detailed level of scrutiny is not necessary for outgroups – people already believe that outgroup members differ from them on important dimensions.[47] Finally, ingroup–outgroup compari-sons tend to happen at the group level. We tend to minimize within-group differences – especially if we are referring to an outgroup.[48]

Is there always an outgroup homogeneity effect?

Not necessarily. Indeed, an *ingroup* homogeneity effect can occur in a variety of circumstances. Sometimes you'll find an ingroup homogeneity effect in which people think of members of their own group as similar to each other. There are at least two instances in which outgroup homogeneity does not occur and ingroup homogeneity does. People in well-defined minority groups – meaning that there is specific information about them as members of a certain group, and that they are the numerical minority – will tend to engage in ingroup homogeneity. On the other hand, when people attach little importance to their group identity and define themselves in terms of their personal identities, they will engage in outgroup homogeneity.[49] So if you think about race relations in the US, you can imagine that the group membership of an Asian American is quite salient to her. People treat her differently – they might speak to her in a louder voice (thinking that she may not speak English), they may believe that she is good at math, or that she is a bad driver, etc. As an Asian American, then, she is constantly reminded of her minority group membership status. She may seek refuge in her identity as an Asian American, and her sense of Asian American identity might be a source of comfort. Therefore, she may be motivated to see her ethnic group as a cohesive category. Minorities might accentuate ingroup resemblances, particularly positive characteristics, as a way to utilize self-esteem to fight the threat of the majority group and to achieve an ingroup solidarity. Think about a white American. Racial identity for whites in the US may not be a salient part of one's identity. Beverly Daniel Tatum says that whites tend to think of racial identity as something that *other* people have.[50] Many whites believe, "*I don't have an ethnicity, I'm just normal.*" Many whites who attach relatively little importance to their membership status are therefore likely to homogenize other groups: *Asians are like this, blacks are like that.* Because whites as a category tend to not attach significance to that identity, they are more likely to engage in outgroup homogeneity. In other words, ingroup homogeneity tends to matter when the ingroup is in a subordinate position.

A second circumstance in which *ingroup* homogeneity might occur involves conditions in which ingroup members feel threatened. In one study,[51] white students were asked to respond to low and high threat statements about racism. A low threat statement would be, "*there is some racism against ethnic minority students on campus,*" and a high threat statement would be, "*whites are inherently racist.*" The white students rated the degree to which whites or African Americans would agree with the statements. High threat items elicited ingroup homogeneity and low threat items produced outgroup homogeneity. In other words, when the white students felt threatened, they perceived other whites as being similar to each other. When they did not feel threatened, the white students perceived African Americans to be very similar to each other. The threat to one's group embodied in a particular statement was a strong determinant of whether majority group members saw ingroup or outgroup homogeneity. There are two needs that the perception of variance in one's own group might serve. The perception of ingroup difference and outgroup similarity allows people to feel individualized and unique from others. Under ordinary conditions, this might be the preferred perception of majority group members. However, when issues threaten or target the ingroup, ingroup homogeneity may be evoked to enable presenting a united front and to satisfy the need to feel supported.

Another kind of threat study[52] found an interesting switch in the usual outgroup homogeneity pattern. White US college students looked at photographs of black and white men, some faces had angry facial expressions, and some had neutral expressions. Participants' memories of faces were tested later, when students were shown several photos, some of which had been seen in the previous session. The students were asked to respond using a scale ranging from *definitely did not see* to *definitely did see*. The typical outgroup homogeneity effect occurred, as expected, with the neutral black and white faces. That is, the white students were better at recognizing the previously seen white men's faces than black men's faces when those faces had neutral expressions. However, the results were flipped when it came to angry faces. Recognition accuracy was better for angry black than for angry white faces, meaning that the white participants had little difficulty differentiating between previously seen angry black faces and angry black faces they hadn't seen. White participants were also better at differentiating among angry black faces than among neutral black faces. So in the case of angry faces, an outgroup *heterogeneity* effect occurred – whites were better at differentiating angry black faces than angry white faces. Why did this flip in the typical pattern occur? The authors of this study suggest there is a different psychological mechanism at work for interpreting groups and individual group members. Effective self-protection may be facilitated by the stereotypical presumption that outgroup members (especially African American men) are potentially dangerous and so more cognitive energy goes into interpreting those faces. If society teaches white people to fear black men then these results are not surprising. A similar study to be done on other outgroups would be interesting in order to see if this instance of ingroup heterogeneity is solely reserved for the perception of African American men – a segment of the US population that is viewed as dangerous. One study found that white US undergraduates misread anger in the faces of African American men whose faces were actually neutral. This did not happen when white men's or African American *women's* faces were viewed.[53] Part of the belief systems of many whites about African American men is that they are hostile and aggressive, and this study shows that this belief system skews whites' judgments to reflect perceived hostility even when no hostility exists. Chapter 2 in this book

"They must be guilty of something" deals with a similar presumed link, in that case, the presumption of a link between blackness and criminality.

Ingroup favoritism and outgroup derogation

Categorization goes beyond overgeneralization to affect positive and negative judgments and treatment. Social psychologists use the term *valence* to describe positive or negative directional valuing. Ideas about ingroups and outgroups are *valenced*, meaning there is a tendency for people to treat members of their ingroup favorably, and members of the outgroup unfavorably. *Ingroup favoritism* and *outgroup derogation* can be illustrated by Henri Tajfel's[54] classic study using what has become known as the *minimal groups* design. Tajfel and his colleagues placed people into groups using the most trivial characteristics as the basis for division, resulting in a very minimal differentiation of the two groups. In Tajfel's study, participants were divided into groups supposedly based on the number of dots they counted on a projected screen. For instance, some participants were told that they had overestimated the number of dots, and other participants were told that they had underestimated the number of dots. The group division is truly minimal in that it was based on trivial characteristics; group members had never met each other, there was no contact between group members or between the two groups, no history of competition existed between the groups, and there was insufficient time to develop loyalty to one's group. Nonetheless, when the researchers provided money to the participants that was intended to be dispersed to other participants based on whatever criterion they wanted, the results were dramatic: participants gave more money to members of their own group than members of other groups. People did this even when giving money to others outside their group had no effect on how much they gave to own-group members.

In other words, when participants could give freely to outgroup members without penalizing ingroup members, they still gave more to ingroup members. Again, they penalized outgroup members even when doing so clearly did not benefit the ingroup. Clearly this bias goes beyond the allocation of reward. For example, partisan observers have shown bias in favor of their own group members when judging group members' ability to reason and display flexibility in negotiation tactics.[55] Despite the arbitrariness of group divisions in this case, the mere categorization of people into ingroups and outgroups was adequate to activate intergroup discrimination in the form of ingroup favoritism and outgroup derogation.

How can this be explained? Tajfel reasons that this occurs because a significant part of people's social identity is located in groups; thus, they make their own group appear in a positive light so that they can have a positive identity for themselves – *I can feel good about myself as long as I belong to an important group.* Imagine this pattern in real life, when the stakes are high and there is real competition between groups, when one group is historically more valued and powerful than another group; when there is a history of rivalry for resources, of slavery, and of genocide among groups. Another reason for outgroup derogation is that it can be a convenient, after-the-fact excuse to justify why an outgroup is mistreated.

Power, people's value, and maintaining the status quo

Thus far, I have been talking about ingroups and outgroups without much reference to the power and status of groups. But, for most groups – such as those of class, gender, and race – in the real world (not groups assigned arbitrarily in the laboratory), one group has more power and privilege than another. Powerful groups tend to be able to influence the legal system, the political system, and the educational system in ways that those without access to power do not.[56] Let's look at the idea of "separate but equal" in American history. Until the middle of the twentieth century, racial inequality was maintained through legal support. Although "separate but equal" appeared to simply segregate whites and blacks, in reality the "equal" provisions, concerning schools, public accommodation, housing, and medical care, were significantly different, with whites benefiting from the concentration of resources that accrued to the dominant group. The 1954 *Brown vs. Board of Education* Supreme Court decision finally acknowledged that racial segregation created and maintained structured and institutional inequality between whites and blacks. White children had access to resource-full schools, while black children went to resource-deprived schools. Whites rode in the front of the bus, blacks in the back.

So what is the role of power and status regarding perceiving others as all alike? Some studies have addressed this. Recall Tajfel's work on minimal groups that analyzed ingroup–outgroup behavior in the laboratory where groups were arbitrarily assigned. What happens in terms of perceptions of members of established ingroups and outgroups that are unequal in power and privilege? We have already seen that African American men are viewed as more hostile and angry than white men, even when there is no objective difference between the two groups of men.[57] Widespread preconceptions of black men prevent people from processing information about black men accurately. As you will see through several examples in this book, benign bigotry often manifests in giving one group the benefit of the doubt, while other groups that are stereotyped are held to tight standards.

The outgroup homogeneity effect refers to the perception, by the ingroup, that members of the outgroup tend to look and act similarly to other outgroup members and are distinct and different from members of the ingroup, whereas ingroup members are perceived to look and act more variably. The outgroup homogeneity effect is important because the tendency to perceive groups as more or less variable affects the extent to which group stereotypes are potent and are likely to be relied upon in the judgment of individuals. Stereotypes about groups that are viewed as diverse and variable are less potent than stereotypes about groups that are less diverse and variable. Also, status and power are relevant factors in perceived variability. Those in power seem to be more variable and diverse, whereas those without power and status all seem to act the same way.[58] The intersection of ingroup–outgroup status and power, therefore, is crucial to the exercise of dominance: those in the outgroup and those who have less power are viewed as similar to each other, whereas ingroup members who are also members of a privileged group are viewed as complex individuals.

The effects of outgroup homogeneity and the ways in which it combines with social power and privilege are revealed in a number of experiments in social psychology. This section explores several significant studies that each illuminate some of the effects that occur when outgroup homogeneity combines with power.

Do outgroup members really act alike and ingroup members act more different from each other? In other words, maybe dominant groups really are more heterogeneous in their behavior as a result of their ability to influence others and resist social control in the ways that subordinate groups cannot. This would mean that *actual* variability exists in dominant groups in addition to *perceived* variability. A study by Ana Guinote[59] and her colleagues tested this possibility. They wanted to identify the ways social power may affect the perception of group variability. They arbitrarily assigned US college students to either high status roles as "judges" or low status roles as "workers" and then organized group discussions. Participants were then asked to describe themselves and were asked about their interests and their best qualities. Participants judged themselves and others in terms of how similar they thought each group was overall. In the second part of their experiment, Guinote and her colleagues asked observers who were not part of the original study to assess videotaped group discussions and make observations. The results from the study speak to the role of power and status in accuracy of judgment as well as the importance of roles that people get assigned to in shaping behavior. According to the independent observers, high-power participants did behave more variably (less similar to each other) than did low-power participants. For instance, the high-power group members provided more individuating information about themselves than the low-power group members. Low-power participants accurately detected greater variability in the high-power group than in their own group, whereas high-power participants did not detect differences in variability between low- and high-power individuals. Thus, the low-power participants' assessment of variability was more accurate – high-power participants did behave more variably, as judged by the independent observers who watched the interactions on videotape. It's interesting to note that most of the previous work finding that more powerful people behave more variably has been found with groups already in existence (e.g. based on ethnicity). In contrast, Guinote and her colleagues *assigned* people to either a powerful or powerless group, so the extent that the powerful participants behaved more variably was due to their group assignment and not any characteristics of them as individuals. What can we take away from this study? First, the results suggest that to the extent that subordinate groups (e.g. women, people of color in white-dominated nations, lesbians and gay men) are apt to act similar to each other, it is not inherent to those individuals but to the effect of being subordinate. In other words, being in a one-down position actually constrains one's behavior. Second, individuals who are members of such groups are inhibited in the ways they can act, and the extent to which they can authentically present themselves as individuals. Therefore, lower status groups' freedom is constrained in a way that higher status groups' freedom is not. The research in this area suggests then that subordinated groups are perceived as "all alike" but, also, subordinated groups may, at least in some settings, behave similarly.

David Ebenbach and Dacher Keltner[60] examined the relationship between actual numerical majority or minority and stereotyping. This study examined whether or not a group's numerical majority or minority status related to increased stereotyping. Using opposing political opinions as the issue, they studied US undergraduates to determine whether people tended to stereotype those with political positions opposite their own. They gathered information on people's attitudes toward the death penalty and foreign military interventions. Once people were divided into opposing groups based on their beliefs about each issue, they were asked to describe the other side's attitudes and beliefs. Each person described their own attitudes about these two issues as well, and how they thought the other side would think. In this particular study, the numerical majority of students they asked were in favor of capital punishment and for military intervention, and the numerical minority was against capital punishment and anti-intervention. Similar to the findings in Guinote's study, Ebenbach and Keltner found a tendency for minority members to be more accurate in judging the two sides' attitudes than were majority members. This finding is consistent with other research findings that stereotypes of one's ingroup are more flexible than stereotypes of the outgroup.[61] Also, both sides of the debate assumed that minority viewpoints came from more sources, perhaps implying more knowledge of the topic. Nonetheless, both groups – those in the majority and those in the minority – stereotyped the attitudes of the minority viewpoint as extremist. In sum, this study found that minority group members were more accurate regarding the facts of their beliefs and came to their viewpoint drawing from more sources, yet were seen by the majority and themselves as more extreme in their viewpoints, even though they were not. Finally, minority group members, who tended to be more accurate judges, expressed more anger, contempt, and frustration than their less accurate counterparts. Perhaps those who held the minority position in this study felt misrepresented and misunderstood, as indeed they were.

Taken together, the Guinote and the Ebenbach and Keltner studies speak directly to the issue of power and privilege and their role in understanding the belief that *those people all look alike*. Susan Fiske[62] provides insight into the role of power and control in stereotyping. Recall that Guinote[63] and Ebenbach and Keltner[64] found that subordinates were more accurate judges of behavior and viewpoints than those who were dominant; and those agitating for change versus the status quo were viewed as less reasonable, less flexible, and more responsible for conflict. Fiske[65] argues that people in power stereotype in part because they do not need to pay attention and they may not be personally motivated to pay attention. The powerful are not so likely to be stereotyped because subordinates need to form detailed impressions of them. The power-less need to predict and possibly alter their own fates. People pay attention to those who control outcomes that affect them. Atten-tion follows power and attention is directed up the hierarchy. The powerful need not concern themselves very much with those with less power because less is at stake for the powerful with regard to their subordinates. Fewer bad things can happen to a powerful person if she ignores the wishes of less powerful people than the reverse. Both the powerful and the powerless can stereotype, but if the powerless do stereotype, their beliefs simply exert less control and have less impact. It matters less if the powerless stereotype because the powerful's behavior is not limited by others' stereotypes of them. The powerless are stereotyped because no one needs to, can, or wants to be detailed and accurate about them.

Fiske also notes that those whose fate is dependent upon others (e.g. an employee dependent upon a supervisor for salary, promo-tions, etc.) attend to the most informative clues they can find about those with power over them. They have a stake in being accurate. Subordinates end up with more detailed impressions and they are assessed as more accurate by observers. One study[66] found that power decreases attention paid to others. In a setting designed to mimic personnel decision making, undergraduate students were given the power to evaluate high school students' summer job applications. As the percentage of their power in the decision increased, their attention to the details of the applications decreased. While both low and high status groups succumb to the outgroup homogeneity effect, high status groups are likely to experience it more, with more serious consequences. To the extent that low status group members experience it, it matters less and has less of an impact.

Is there always outgroup derogation?

Although people show favoritism toward members of their ingroup, they do not necessarily always penalize members of the outgroup. Sometimes benign bigotry manifests, not when outgroups are treated unfairly, but rather when ingroups are treated overgenerously.[67] Also, again in contrast to overt mistreatment of outgroup members, outgroup members are often treated with indifference by ingroup members.[68] Clearly, outgroups are harmed. What conditions are usually necessary for outgroups to be mistreated? Activation of a social identity leads to such negative outcomes after two conditions are met. First, ingroup members must believe that a common set of norms and values apply to both themselves and to members of the outgroup. Second, the ingroup must see its values as the only acceptable values, so that their values overwhelm those of the outgroup and are the ones that should guide both themselves and the outgroup. The combination of these two factors leads the ingroup to perceive members of the outgroup as deviant, morally inferior, and a potential threat to ingroup values.[69] Take as an example stereotypes about lesbians and gay men. Typical stereotypes about lesbians and gay men are that they violate norms and values that heterosexuals do not. For instance, homosexuals are believed to be confused in terms of their gender roles – gay men act like, or want to be, women, and lesbians act like, or want to be, men. In this way, they are viewed as violating norms about gender. Second, lesbians and gay men are thought to be hypersexual – they are thought both to engage in sexual activity more than heterosexuals and to flaunt their sexuality (the chapter "Gays flaunt their sexuality" deals with this stereotype at length). In this way, they are seen as violating norms about sexual behavior. The belief that lesbians and gay men violate important norms justifies their mistreatment – *they do not deserve the same treatment as everyone else because they are deviants*. Research demonstrates that, all things being equal, people are more likely to expect negative qualities from outgroups than from ingroups.[70]

Other consequences of thinking categorically

Ultimate attribution error

In addition to the differential treatment, such as the allocation of rewards described above, we tend to *think* differently about people who are different from us. A common place for stereotypes to be located is in the *attributions* we make about people. In addition to a discussion here, attributions are discussed in Chapter 2 ("They must be guilty of something") and Chapter 6 ("Affirmative action is reverse racism"). Attributions are simply people's explanations of behavior. For example, if you get a promotion at work, to what do you attribute this success? Many people would attribute their success to working hard, or to their intelligence, or they might attribute their success to luck, or even a fluke. Attributions can be internal or external, temporary or stable, positive or negative. For instance, if I dislike a co-worker, I might attribute her promotion to luck, not to her intelligence or hard work. *Luck* in this case is temporary, external, and negative. If I make an attribution of intelligence, that is an internal, static, and positive attribution. A person's intelligence is within her, it is unlikely to change, and it is a good quality. A frequent effect of categorization is known as the *ultimate attribution error*[71] which is the tendency to attribute the desirable actions of ingroup members to something internal and undesirable actions to something external. The reverse is true for outgroup members. Their positive behavior is attributed to external circumstances (e.g. luck, accident), while their undesirable behavior is attributed to internal characteristics (e.g. flawed character, low intelligence). For example, people tend to make internal attributions about poor people (e.g. they are lazy, dumb) more often than external attributions (bad luck, unjust economic system).[72]

On a societal level, attributions serve those who wield the most social and political power. Those people tend to make attributions that serve to keep the powerless in their places. For example, Muslims, who are the majority in Bangladesh, engage in outgroup derogation of Hindus, who are the minority. Muslims explain the negative acts of Hindus with internal, stable, global attributions.[73] Another study looked at the attributions Dutch participants made of the Netherlands' occupation of Indonesia (Dutch were the ingroup and the colonizing force) compared to the German occupation of The Netherlands (Dutch were the ingroup and were the victims).[74] The Dutch participants were more likely to attribute the Dutch occupation of Indonesia to external factors ("*I think The Netherlands occupied Indonesia because of the circumstances*"), than to internal factors ("*I think The Netherlands occupied Indonesia because the Dutch consider themselves superior*"). When it came to explaining Germany's occupation of The Netherlands, Dutch participants explained the occupation with internal attributions (*Germans think they're superior*), compared to external factors (*it was the circumstances*).

Unfortunately, the behavior of a single minority group member may significantly influence how members of their entire group are viewed by members of the majority group, whereas this is not the case for majority members. For example, white Americans who witnessed a black person responding in a rude manner to a white person were later more likely to avoid sitting next to another black person.[75] Such an instance of negative behavior also can affect whites' overall feelings about blacks. When participants[76] overheard a description of an assault committed by a black person, participants later rated blacks as generally more antagonistic than did participants who heard the same conversation about a white assailant.[77] Observing a single instance of a negative behavior involving a member of an outgroup leads people to evaluate all members of that group negatively. While attributions could be seen as innocent explanations of behavior, systematic examinations reveal the underlying bigotry that can manifest in attributions about others.

The linguistic intergroup bias

The specific language we use when making attributions can reflect the biases we have about other groups. The research on the *linguistic intergroup bias* demonstrates attributional patterns through language. Anne Maass and Janet Ruscher have both done important work on the linguistic intergroup bias. In a series of studies, Anne Maass[78] and her colleagues found that the level of concreteness versus abstraction in the language we use to describe the behavior of others reflects the degree to which we believe others' actions are temporary or permanent. When spontaneously describing the positive behaviors of an ingroup member, people tend to use abstract, trait-like terms. On the other hand, when people describe the positive behaviors of an outgroup member, people tend to use concrete descriptions. So an ingroup member who serves meals at a local homeless shelter is "generous" or "altruistic." An outgroup member who serves meals at the shelter is described as "helping" or "volunteering." Conversely, negative ingroup behavior is described in concrete terms, while negative outgroup behavior is described in more abstract and global ways. For instance, an outgroup member might be described as "aggressive" or "violent" while an ingroup member's behavior is described as "hitting someone."[79] The linguistic intergroup bias describes the phenomenon in which behaviors that are consistent with stereotypes are described with abstract terms, suggesting the permanence of trait-like behavior – behavior that is stable and intrinsic to the person – whereas behaviors that are inconsistent with stereotypes are described with more concrete terms suggesting a temporariness to the behavior. The degree of linguistic abstractness, then, can reveal the structure of thought about the group in question because the dimension of concreteness – abstractness reveals the degree to which people think observed behaviors are tied to the circumstances (external) versus being the result of inherent (internal) traits of the group. When abstract descriptors are used they can reveal underlying cognitive associations leading to stereotypes; when concrete descriptors are used, underlying associations are not being tapped into.

Evidence of linguistic intergroup bias has been revealed in dozens of studies on topics such as racial bias, gender bias, competing sports teams, and even hunters versus environmentalists.[80] Bradley Gorham[81] found that the linguistic intergroup bias helps people make sense of television news stories. White staff members at a US university watched eight minutes of a TV news broadcast in which run-of-the-mill news stories were played with a crime story imbedded in the middle of the broadcast. The story, which was about a murder, contained a picture of either a white or black suspect. After the participants watched the news segment, they completed a survey, in which, for each of the news stories, they chose the appropriate description of what they saw. The descriptions ranged on a continuum from concreteness to abstractness. As predicted by the work on linguistic intergroup bias, respondents who saw a white suspect tended to choose the concrete descriptor ("The man police want to talk to probably hit the victims") while those who saw the black suspect tended to choose the abstract descriptor ("*The man police want to talk to is probably violent*"). Studies that find evidence for the linguistic intergroup bias demonstrate this pattern whether the research participants write descriptions in their own words, or choose from alternatives, such as was the case in the Gorham study.

What does the linguistic intergroup bias have to do with *benign bigotry*? The linguistic intergroup bias allows for maintenance of stereotypes. Statements made at a high level of abstraction are more resistant to change than concrete statements because abstract descriptions are difficult to confirm or disconfirm. Concrete descriptions can be more easily discounted. People gain an advantage if they describe their group's positive behaviors in abstract terms that are hard to disprove.[82] The ultimate attribution error and the linguistic intergroup bias are manifestations of subtle prejudice. They function as a window into people's schemas as they betray people's stereotypes about the outgroup.

Are there any individual characteristics associated with the tendency to make attributions about others? For whites at least, the more prejudiced the person, the more likely they will make negative dispositional (internal) attributions about minority groups.[83] *Modern* racism, a specific form of subtle prejudice, seems to be correlated with this tendency. Modern racism is the tendency to recognize that racism is wrong and socially inappropriate yet believe that prejudice is largely a thing of the past and that lack of hard work and diligence are the reasons minorities haven't achieved what whites have. Typical of benign bigotry, modern racists do not express prejudice explicitly and overtly but instead look for race-irrelevant reasons to express bias against subordinated groups. Modern racists, compared to non-prejudiced individuals, are more likely to engage in linguistic intergroup bias. Also, people who have a strong need for definitive answers and cannot tolerate confusion or uncertainty, known by social psychologists as *need-for-closure*, have a tendency to be susceptible to the linguistic intergroup bias. They exhibit greater linguistic abstraction when describing positive behaviors of ingroup members and negative behaviors of outgroup members.[84]

In addition to attributions, other uses of language reflect the importance of categorization for people. The first person plural ("us," "we") reflects a sense of belongingness and ingroup cohesion. In contrast, the third person plural ("them," "theirs") is associated with the outgroup and therefore negative evaluation. For instance, because a main function of belongingness to a group is to validate one's self esteem and identity, sports fans will often describe their winning team with "we won" and their losing team with "they lost." Also, after victories, college students at US universities are more likely to wear clothing with their school's logo than if their team loses.[85]

Former US President George W. Bush used similar us/them rhetoric after the attacks of September 11, 2001. While many writers have criticized Bush's descriptions as overly simplistic, categorical statements that reduce various nations, cultures, and political groups into "evildoers" (a good example of a "trait-like" description), his rhetoric served a psychological function. For example, consider the following statements by Bush: "Every nation, in every region, now has a decision to make. Either you are with us, or you are with the terrorists"[86] and "No threat, no threat will prevent freedom-loving people from defending freedom. And make no mistake about it: this is good versus evil. These are evildoers. They have no justification for their actions. There's no religious justification, there's no political justification. The only motivation is evil."[87] Statements such as these erase the complexities of those seen as enemies. Terrorism, Iraq, Osama bin Laden, and Saddam Hussein become one threatening category.[88] Complexities get reduced to dichotomies: good versus evil, peace versus violence, civilization versus chaos – all grandiose variations on the us-versus-them division.[89]

Dehumanization and responsibility of outgroup pain

Reducing complex individuals to simplistic dichotomies such as good versus evil can lead to dehumanization. Dehumanization is a process whereby a person or group is treated as less than human. It occurs when an individual or group is denied some of the characteristics that makes us human. Dehumanization can take the form of treating others as if they lack refinement and culture and therefore do not merit humane treatment; or when it is believed that a person or group lacks human feelings, warmth, and human agency (empowerment) resulting in a fundamental lack of empathy toward those who are subjected to dehumanization.[90] When you think people are less than human you tolerate their mistreatment. As an example, dehumanization of the enemy is one way in which soldiers prepare themselves to overcome the repugnance of killing other humans. The use of derogatory names such as *Haji* (Gulf Wars), *Gook* (Vietnam War) and *Jap* and *Kraut* (WWII) helped to trivialize, marginalize, and dehumanize the enemy. Photographs of the abuse in the Abu Ghraib prison in Iraq, made public in 2004, illustrated the effects of dehumanization with detainees being treated like animals; for example being led around on dog leashes. One military police officer who testified during the abuse hearings referred to one of the detainees as "it" instead of "him": "I saw two naked detainees, one masturbating to another kneeling with its mouth open."[91] "It" is the way you might describe an animal, not a human being with human feelings, desires, needs, and thoughts. When the US Central Intelligence Agency (CIA) debated the methods of interrogation about definitions of torture, John Fredman, Chief Counsel to the CIA's counter terrorism center explained that torture "is basically subject to perception." "If the detainee dies, you're doing it wrong."[92] Similarly, *No Humans Involved* (NHI) is a term that has been used by judges and police to refer to crimes involving victims who are "undesirables" – ethnic minorities, prostitutes, or prisoners.[93]

Historically, marginalized groups have been depicted as sub-human animals in popular culture. People of African descent were portrayed in the US and Europe as monkeys, cannibals, and savages during the twentieth century,[94] Jews in Europe and the United States were caricatured as dogs.[95] In American films, Arabs have been described as dogs and monkeys.[96] Viewing characters from marginal groups as less than human normalizes their mistreatment, encourages viewers to not empathize or understand their pain, and gives viewers a sense of solidarity as they become united by their shared distance from marginalized people. Empirical studies find support for people's tendency to dehumanize outgroups. On both implicit and explicit measures, people attribute words that are commonly associated with humans (e.g. *people, citizen*) to ingroup members while attributing words commonly associated with animals (e.g. *breed, creature*) to outgroups.[97]

One significant way of erasing a person's humanity is to assume that the person does not feel the full range of human emotions that others do. Research on dehumanization[98] and emotion examines attributions about *primary emotions*, those emotions experienced by all humans and most primates, such as joy, anger, fear, and sadness – and *secondary emotions*, those emotions that are thought to be uniquely human and not experienced by non-human animals, such as pride, guilt, shame, and embarrassment. People tend to attribute fewer secondary emotions to outgroups.[99] What does it mean that people attribute fewer secondary emotions to members of the out-group? It implies outgroup members do not share the same human-ity as ingroup members, that people different from us do not feel the same range of emotions as fully human individuals feel. It puts outgroup members closer in our minds to how we might think about and treat animals. For example, one may not be bothered by a homeless person begging for money if one thinks that homeless people wouldn't be embarrassed or ashamed to beg for money. However, for a middle-class person, the idea of begging for food could be shameful.

If recognition of another's humanity activates empathy such recognition would, we might suppose, make it difficult to mistreat that person without feeling personal distress. If denying others' humanity facilitates violence against them, do people use the same disengagement strategy when reminded that their own group has committed violence against an outgroup? Emanuele Castano[100] and his colleagues conducted three experiments to test this theory. They hypothesized that after being made aware of atrocities for which their ingroup is responsible, ingroup members may derogate the victims (outgroup members) by developing the belief that they are not fully human, particularly in terms of emotional capacity. In the first experiment, British undergraduates read one of two scenarios involving humans and aliens from another planet who are working together in a mine. In one scenario, there is a mining accident that kills 10,000 aliens, while the humans are away on Christmas vacation. In the second scenario 10,000 aliens are killed in the mine but their deaths are caused by the humans. In the first scenario, humans are not responsible for the alien deaths but in the second scenario they are. The participants were asked to identify what emotions the aliens would feel. The authors found that those who perceived ingroup responsibility – either in the accidental or killing condition – showed stronger dehumanization in the form of attributing fewer human-related emotions to the aliens than those who did not perceive responsibility. In other words, the realization that humans were responsible triggered a reaction among the participants to reduce their discomfort by believing the aliens didn't feel the emotions that humans would – but only when respondents felt that humans were responsible. So the thinking might be: *Yeah, humans were responsible but it probably didn't hurt the aliens all that much, so it doesn't really matter.* A second experiment[101] conducted by Castano and his colleagues was based on a real-life set of events. This study examined the attributions of emotions to Australian Aborigines based on whether or not the British were presented as responsible for atrocities against Aborigines after British colonization. British undergraduate participants perceived the Aborigines as less human when they read that British colonization resulted in quasi-extermination than when they read that British colonization did not produce negative effects on the Aboriginal population. In a third experiment,[102] attributions of emotions to Native Americans by white Americans were examined. White New Yorkers recruited from an Internet site were presented with a brief history of Native Americans and the effects on them with the arrival of Europeans. When Native American deaths were attributed to killing by Europeans, more dehumanization occurred than when Native deaths were attributed to disease. Making people aware of their ingroup's past wrongdoings did increase their feelings of guilt, but the guilt did not increase their willingness to support collective reparations to Native Americans.

The results from Castano's studies are paradoxical. Wouldn't you think that, if your group was responsible for the mistreatment of others, such recognition would make you feel sympathy and concern about their humanity? Instead, the more that people believed their group was responsible, the less they viewed the harmed group as human. According to the findings in Castano's studies, dehumanization is not intensified merely by perception of the suffering of another group, it requires the attribution of responsibility to the ingroup. This is a self-defensive process.

Individuals are even capable of *misremembering* mistreatment for which their group is responsible. Baljinder Sahdra and Michael Ross[103] examined how group identity affects memory of past events, including memories of violence involving ingroup members as perpetrators and victims. They hypothesized that historical memory would be biased to support a favorable view of the ingroup, and that this positivity bias would be particularly strong for those who are highly identified with their group. In their first study, they examined how respondents' memories differed as a function of their identification with their ethnic group and the role of violence perpetrated by their group. They asked Sikhs and Hindus living in Canada to reflect on several actual events of the 1980s and 1990s during which either Sikhs committed abuse against Hindus (e.g. assassination of Indira Gandhi, a Hindu) or Hindus committed abuse against Sikhs (attack on the Golden Temple, a holy Sikh shrine in India). Participants were also asked how much they identified with their group. Sahdra and Ross found that participants more readily recalled events, and thought about these events more often, when the ingroup members were victims than when they were perpetrators. This was especially the case for those who were highly identified with their group. Those not highly identified with their group remembered fewer harms to the ingroup. High-identifiers also recalled more incidents of ingroup suffering than of ingroup violence. And, finally, high-identifiers were more likely to advocate that the victim group should forget and move on when their ingroup perpetrated the harm but not when their ingroup was victim to the harm.

Sahdra and Ross subsequently replicated their results in a laboratory study.[104] Results from both studies suggest that those who identify highly with their group recall their group's history in a manner that limits any damage to their social identity. There are positive and negative functions of this: positive ingroup biases do enhance commitment to one's group, but are also likely to contribute to conflict and misunderstanding between individuals and outgroups. Sahdra and Ross's work also demonstrates how social identity influences individual-level memory processes. Acts of violence and hatred by ingroup members are stereotype-inconsistent and therefore less accessible in memory.

Scapegoating and genocide

Scapegoating is the process of blaming and punishing an innocent outgroup for the misfortunes of one's ingroup. Perhaps the most well-known scapegoating in modern history is the scapegoating of Jews in Germany under the Nazi government during World War II. Scapegoating provides a "designated villain" to explain the frustration caused by social and economic problems. The preferred target of aggression is designated as the cause of the frustration, but if it is not possible to be aggressive toward the source of the frustration, aggression will be displaced and directed toward a more readily available target. The scapegoat is not actually or factually responsible for the perpetrator's problems – it often just makes intuitive sense to blame the scapegoated group.

Outgroups make convenient scapegoats. Several factors increase the likelihood that a group will be scapegoated.[105] First, scapegoats tend to have little social, political, and economic power so they do not have the means to effectively resist the actions taken against them. Second, the group that is scapegoated is usually visible enough in society to be salient to the ingroup. Visibility can be in the form of skin color or other physical features, or can be the violation of social norms, such as lesbians and gay men who violate the norm of heterosexuality. Third, the group will tend to be disliked and to have negative stereotypes associated with it in order to set the stage for scapegoating. Finally, the group should be viewed as a threat to the ingroup. When the differences between the ingroup and outgroup are particularly large in terms of religion, manners, or customs, then the outgroup is seen as less than fully human: pagans, savages, or animals. In order to perform a genocide the perpetrator first organizes a campaign that redefines the victim group as worthless, outside the web of mutual obligations, a threat to the people, immoral sinners, and/or subhuman.[106] Edward Sampson[107] puts ingroup favoritism, which I discussed earlier in this chapter, on a continuum with genocide. At one end is *ingroup favoritism or ethnocentrism* – the favoring of one's own group over the other. Ingroup favoritism can also include *outgroup derogation*, which then can, in some cases, lead to scapegoating and genocidal actions.

Putting it all together

Sorting people into categories is a routine and inevitable aspect of cognition. Categorization becomes problematic when it is based on prejudice and when a power difference exists between those who create categories and those who are sorted into categories. Categorization produces the "they all look alike" effect but status, power, and privilege determine who is harmed by it. For while everyone is capable of seeing people outside their own group as looking and acting alike, dominant groups, such as whites in the US, are more likely to think members of subordinate groups look and act alike, rather than vice versa.[108] The stereotypes of the dominant group are more consequential than the stereotypes of the subordinate group. As I stated in the Introduction to this book, stereotypes control people[109] but the consequences to those with less power, such as people of color, can be disastrous. Believing that people with different ethnicities and religions are all alike could be one reason a reported 70–90% of those captured in Iraq by American troops were captured by mistake.[110] The outgroup homogeneity effect also affects how whites interpret the faces of black men – for example, as being angry even when their faces are, in fact, neutral.[111] As we will see in the next chapter, "They must be guilty of something," that whites read anger into the faces of African American men, while they do not into the faces of African American women and white men, surely plays a role in the belief that black men are linked with criminality. The perception of outgroup homogeneity is often, though not always, accompanied by outgroup derogation. Ingroups, as revealed in the studies in this chapter, as well as the studies in the other chapters in this book, are often given the benefit of the doubt, while outgroup members' feet are held to the fire. And those agitating for change are viewed by the status quo as extremists, even when their arguments are more accurate and are not more extreme.[112]

Cousins to the outgroup homogeneity effect are the ultimate attribution error and the linguistic intergroup bias. Individuals' explanations of their own and others' behavior involve more charitable attributions of ingroup compared to outgroup behavior. People tend to attribute the desirable behaviors of ingroup members to dispositional, stable, and inherent characteristics; they attribute the undesirable behaviors of their group to external, temporary circumstances. Positive outgroup behavior is attributed to external, temporary circumstances, while negative behavior is attributed to stable, inherent characteristics. An African American man who is a murder suspect may be described in more abstract terms, suggesting that African American men are close to criminality, while a white murder suspect may be described in more concrete ways, suggesting a more tenuous and temporary link between whiteness and criminality.[113] Linguistic intergroup bias is likely among benign bigots (modern racists,[114] specifically) because it provides a useful cover for more overt forms of prejudice.

The outgroup homogeneity effect is likely a necessary, although not a sufficient, phenomenon for dehumanization. Effective dehumanization allows for groups to be scapegoated and mistreated without compunction by mistreating groups. In order to justify or cope with the mistreatment of others, individuals may misremember their own or their government's bad deeds.[115]

Strategies for change

Confronting the unwanted and dangerous manifestations of social categorization can be quite challenging. The research findings and insights of social psychology offer both explanations of social categorization and helpful strategies for overcoming the dangers of this kind of stereotyping.

Contact complicates conceptions

One explanation for the occurrence of the perception of outgroup homogeneity and its effect on prejudice and discrimination has to do with familiarity. People in the dominant group can be more selective in their social contacts and might not have a lot of contact with outgroups in their daily lives due to residential and occupational segregation. In many cases, we know more people in our ingroup and know more about them as distinct individuals with distinct preferences, attributes, and values, than people in the outgroup. We simply have more information about ingroup members and their unique qualities.

One of the richest areas of research on prejudice reduction is the work on the *contact hypothesis*. The contact hypothesis is the notion that contact between members of different groups will improve relations between them. Because thinking that outgroup members are all alike, to some degree, probably has to do with familiarity, increased contact is a good bet as a method of reducing perceived outgroup homogeneity. Increased contact should produce increased familiarity, which should complicate our schemas of those different from us. Not just any contact will work, however.

In order for the contact hypothesis to have an effect on reducing prejudice, four conditions must be met.[116] First, *cooperation* between groups is necessary. If members of a university Muslim student organization are required to work with a Jewish student alliance toward some overarching goal that benefits both groups, a reduction in stereotypes may result. Second, the interactions have to be on *equal footing*. A white person who employs a Latina for maid service will probably not feel much inclination to get to know the maid as an individual who has a unique personality. Third, contact over an *extended period of time* is much more effective than a brief encounter between group members. For instance, if a friend or relative becomes involved with someone who has a different religion to you, your acceptance of that particular person and your acceptance of that religion in general may increase more than if you have occasional contact with an acquaintance whose religion is different from yours. Barry Goldwater, the conservative Republican senator from Arizona and 1964 Republican presidential candidate, had attitudes about gay rights that might surprise some when compared with conservative Republicans presently. Prior to his death in 1998, he actively worked on behalf of lesbian and gay rights making gay rights part of his larger, libertarian political ideology. His progressive views regarding lesbian and gay rights may have been due, in part, to his having a gay grandson as well as other relatives who are gay.[117] Finally, the reduction and eventual elimination of prejudice requires consistent *institutional support*. Intergroup contact works best as a prejudice-reduction tool when it occurs in a formal or established setting in which existing norms favor group equality. Those in authority – school officials, politicians, and others – must unambiguously endorse egalitarian norms. You can imagine the impact when, for instance, the president of the United States declares Saddam Hussein and Osama bin Laden to be similarly guilty of terror against the United States.[118] The President's merging of two very different people does not help to complicate Americans' ideas of Islam. These four factors: requiring groups to work together; interacting on equal footing; contact over an extended period of time; and institutional support, have been shown to break down divisions between groups and complicate our ideas of outgroup members.

Toward a complex identity

To the extent that it is possible, fostering complex social identities might reduce perceptions of outgroup homogeneity. A person with a simple social identity (e.g. "I am a Christian" or "I am Asian") focuses on only that one identity and sees only people who share that one identity as part of the ingroup. In contrast, a person with a complex social identity (e.g. "I am a mother *and* a Latina *and* a Catholic") sees herself as having more than one meaningful identity. A complex social identity leads people to be more tolerant of group differences because a complex identity reduces the motivation to self-categorize as a member of any one group.[119] Having multiple concurrent identities reduces feelings of distinctiveness. A person with a complex identity can see commonalities with more people than can a person with a simple identity. Also, if people have more than one social identity, a threat to one identity can be offset by focusing on a more positive identity until the threat has passed.[120] Chapter 5 ("I'm not a racist, I'm colorblind") elaborates strategies for creating more complicated categories and identities.

Contact and the jigsaw classroom

The jigsaw classroom is one method of encouraging structured positive contact between groups and fostering more complex identities of individuals within different groups. The jigsaw method, originated by Elliot Aronson,[121] was developed as a response to the difficulties of integrating classrooms when schools desegregated in Texas in the early 1970s. When Mexican American, African American and white students were put together in classrooms, soon after there was open conflict and marginalization of the students of color followed. In many cases the students of color came from resource-deprived schools and, due to decades of school segregation, were not as prepared academically as the white students. Aronson, a social psychologist, developed an intervention with the goal of creating a more harmonious environment. The result was the jigsaw classroom. Here's how it works: Let's say you have 36 students in a class. The teacher divides his lecture for the day into six components. He divides the class into six-person groups. The teacher gives each group one of the pieces of the lecture. Each member of these "expert" groups masters the piece of the lecture. Expert groups review their assigned material and ensure that all group members understand the material. High ability students can assist low ability students to ensure that they are capable of presenting the material. Next, students are put into "jigsaw" groups. The jigsaw groups then are made up of one expert of each component of the lecture who teaches the others in her group the component they need to learn the day's lesson in its entirety. Like the pieces of a jigsaw puzzle, each piece of information must be put together before anyone can understand the whole lecture. Each student learns her own section and teaches it to the other members of that group who do not have access to that material.

Unlike traditional classrooms that foster competition, the jigsaw arrangement fosters interdependence and cooperation as well as empathy and perspective-taking (the ability to view something from another's perspective). Because students are dependent on each other, if there is one student who is not very articulate, or who has a speech or presentation style that other students are not accustomed to, the listener must ask questions that will elicit the information the listener needs. In order to accomplish this goal the listener must put herself in the place of the speaker and see things from his perspective. She learns how to treat each child as an individual, not as a category. The jigsaw method requires people to participate more actively when they are required to recite and when they raise questions as active listeners. Active participation produces better learning than the passive condition of merely receiving information, resulting in children taking responsibility for their learning.

Diane Bridgeman[122] conducted an experiment with 10-year-old children to test whether or not kids who learned in jigsaw class-rooms for two months behaved differently than children from tradi-tional classrooms. Bridgeman found that children from jigsaw classrooms were better able to take the perspective of another person and had more developed empathy than the children from the traditional classroom. Overall, Bridgeman found that jigsaw classrooms: (1) required interdependence and social reciprocity by which students depend on each other to learn all of the material; (2) involve equal status cooperative interaction in which each student has a vital role in the process; (3) provide a consistent opportunity to be an expert which allows for a better developed sense of self; (4) encourage the integration of varied perspectives; and (5) involve a highly structured process which allows easy replication of the above interactions on a consistent basis.

Elliot Aronson reports that if the jigsaw method is used for as little as one hour per day, the positive effects are substantial. Aronson's jigsaw classes in Texas demonstrated that compared to students in traditional classrooms, students in jigsaw classes showed a decrease in prejudice and stereotyping and an increase in their liking for their groupmates, both within and across ethnic groups. Learning in this manner also improved student performance for the Mexican American and African American children, while the white students performed equally well in jigsaw and traditional classrooms.[123]

Controlling your cognitions and values confrontation

Our own thoughts are spontaneous, and feel both natural and inevitable to us. Stereotype reduction can also be practiced at the individual cognition level through a strategy called *stereotype sup-pression*. This mental strategy, which has been used for a range of goals from curbing food cravings to controlling depressing thoughts, entails avoiding thinking of negative thoughts and replacing them with distractor thoughts. In the case of stereotyped thinking, when you find yourself applying stereotypes to a member of a certain group, you replace them with non-stereotypical thoughts. Research on the efficacy of stereotype suppression is mixed.[124] In some cases, deliberately trying to avoid thinking about a topic makes you think about it even more, especially if you are a person with strong prejudices. Margo Monteith[125] and her colleagues tested this strategy in a study in which people were given a photo of two gay men who were a couple and were asked to write a passage about a typical day in their life. Some of the participants were instructed to avoid stereotypical preconceptions in their description, while others were not given such instructions. For participants low in prejudice, suppressing stereotypes was effective, while for those with strong prejudice toward gays, suppressing the stereotypic thoughts actually increased the accessibility of the stereotype.

Some individuals can avoid prejudicial responses if they have the motivation and ability to do so. As a result of living in a prejudiced society, stereotypes are often highly accessible and easily used. However, for those individuals who strongly endorse egalitarian values that conflict with initial stereotypical thinking (those who fit the description of someone with a subtle prejudice), this discrepancy in thinking can induce guilt which can be a motivator to suppress prejudicial thinking. According to Patricia Devine[126] and her colleagues, many people want to do and say the right thing, and the discrepancy between their spontaneous stereotypical thinking and their nonprejudiced standards leads to feelings of compunction. As a result, these individuals will be motivated to avoid subsequent stereotyping.

Several researchers have found that when low-prejudice people have been made aware that they have behaved in a way inconsistent with their egalitarian values, they feel guilty and are motivated to change their future behavior. This line of research is one of the few that have examined subtle or benign forms of bigotry and prejudice reduction. Leanne Son Hing[127] and her colleagues examined the role of *hypocrisy induction* as a successful prejudice reduction technique. White Canadian college students who were *aversive racists* (those with low levels of explicit prejudice and high levels of implicit prejudice) were compared with non-racists (those with low levels of both implicit and explicit prejudice) on a hypocrisy induction task. Both groups were asked to write an essay on the importance of treating people equally regardless of their race, gender, etc. This was an easy task for all participants because they all espoused non-prejudiced beliefs (at least explicitly). Next, half of the participants in each group experienced the hypocrisy induction condition: they were asked to write about situations in which they acted negatively toward an Asian person. Later, all participants were asked to respond to an initiative to make financial cuts in various student clubs, including the Asian Students' Association's budget. They were told that the budget cuts were inevitable but that they should give their opinion on which groups should be given reduced budgets. Son Hing and her colleagues found that the hypocrisy induction had a different effect on the participants' behavior based on whether or not the participant was truly non-prejudiced versus only explicitly non-prejudiced (i.e. an aversive racist). Aversive racists who were confronted with the discrepancy between publicly advocating for equal rights in their essays, but then having to admit to discriminating against Asians in the past, were less likely to cut funds from the Asian Students' Association compared to aversive racists who did not experience the hypocrisy induction. Being confronted with their own hypocrisy forced aversive racists to become aware of the negative aspects of their attitudes that they usually suppressed. In contrast, the truly low-prejudiced participants had a different reaction to the hypocrisy induction. They we no less likely to cut funds to the Asian Students' Association compared to those in the control condition (who did not experience hypocritical feelings). To summarize, aversive racists in the non-hypocrisy inducing control condition tended to discriminate against Asians by cutting their funding. However, in the hypocrisy condition, aversive racists treated Asians positively when their negative attitudes were made salient. The researchers suggest that aversive racists need to experience consciousness raising to avoid behaving in a discriminatory manner. When people are made aware of the discrepancy between their ideal attitudes and the actual attitudes reflected in behavior, negative feelings act as a sort of self-punishment and motivate people to behave in non-discriminatory behavior. The results of Son Hing's study found that these processes work for benign bigots (in this instance, aversive racists) but not for truly low-prejudiced people.

Inducing empathy

Getting people to feel empathy toward a stigmatized group can play a powerful role in prejudice reduction – particularly when, without empathy, there is a risk of dehumanization. The work of Daniel Batson and his colleagues demonstrated that attitudes toward people with AIDS, homeless people, drug addicts, and even murderers, in addition to whites' attitudes toward people of color, can become more positive with empathy. Much of this research happens in a laboratory setting where participants are induced to feel empathy toward members of some target group and then are asked about their attitudes toward the target group later. One of Batson's studies[128] found that, in addition to attitude change, empathy can lead to behavior change in a positive direction toward a target group. In this study, American college students (ethnicity unknown) listened to a taped interview of a drug addict in which he discusses his addiction and incarceration. In the control condition, participants were asked to remain "objective" while listening to the interview, while in the "empathy" condition, participants were asked to imagine the feelings of the person being inter-viewed. This simple difference in instruction had a significant impact on how participants viewed, not only this particular addict, but drug addicts in general. Participants in the empathy condition were later found to feel more positive toward drug addicts and were more likely to recommend increasing student funds for an agency to help drug addicts, even while it meant taking money away from other agencies and would not help the particular addict they heard in the interview. So not only did participants who were primed to think empathically feel different about drug addicts than those told to remain "objective," they also supported *taking action* to help addicts to a greater degree. The participants' responses were not simply a reflection of sympathy expressed to help relieve an *individual's* need – they made choices about helping the stigma-tized *group*, even though it did not benefit the particular person who evoked the sympathy. In other words, care evoked by empathy felt for a member of a stigmatized group can generalize to the group and create motivation for action on behalf of the entire group.

These strategies, as well as the strategies outlined in subsequent chapters, should help in reducing reliance on schemas when processing information about others, particularly those who are different in some demographic characteristic.

NOTES

1. Jackson, A. (2001). *Where were you (when the world stopped turning)*. On promotional single [CD]. Arista, Nashville.
2. Goodstein, L., & Lewin, T. (2001, September 19). A nation challenged: Violence and harassment; victims of mistaken identity, Sikhs pay a price for turbans. *The New York times*. Retrieved November 12, 2007, from http://query.nytimes.com/gst/fullpage.html?res=9C06EED9123 BF93AA2575AC0A9679 C8B63
3. Obviously hate crimes of any kind are unjustified, even when the "correct" category of person, actual Arabs in this case, is targeted.

4. Maher, B. In list of quotes compiled by Daniel Kurtzman. Retrieved December 14, 2007, from http://politicalhumor.about.com/library/blsaddamjokes.htm

5. President Bush, Colombia President Uribe Discuss Terrorism (2002, September 25). Remarks by President Bush and President Alvaro Uribe of Colombia in Photo Opportunity. The White House: Office of the Press Secretary. Retrieved October 15, 2007, from http://georgewbush-whitehouse.archives.gov/news/releases/2002/09/20020925-1.html

6. Ibid.

7. Althaus, S.L., & Largio, D.M. (2004, October). When Osama became Saddam: Origins and consequences of the change in America's public enemy #1. PS: Political science and politics, 795–799.

8. Ibid.

9. Ackerman, S. (2004, January/February). Saddam and Osama's shotgun wedding: Weekly Standard beats a long-dead horse. Extra! Retrieved November 4, 2007, from www.fair.org/index.php?page=2829&printer_friendly=1

10. Reported by: Shaheen, J.G. (2003). Reel bad Arabs: How Hollywood vilifies a people. Annals of the American academy of political and social science, 588, 171–193.

11. Ibid.

12. Ibid.

13. See page 66 in: Kirkpatrick, D. (2007, October 28). The evangelical crackup. The New York times magazine, pp. 38–66.

14. Moos, J. (2006, December 12). In transcript of CNN broadcast aired December 12, 2006. Retrieved April 22, 2008, from http://transcripts.cnn.com/TRANSCRIPTS/0612/12/cnr.04.html

15. Chris Matthews apologizes again – this time for Obama/Osama error. (2008, February 19). Retrieved April 22, 2008, from www.huffingtonpost.com/2008/02/19/chris-matthews-apologizes_n_87324.html

16. Bowker, D., & Kaye, D. (2007, November 10). Guantánamo by the numbers. New York times. Retrieved April 28, 2008, from www.nytimes.com/2007/11/10/opinion/10kayeintro.html?n=Top/News/U.S./U.S.%20States,%20Territories%20and%20Possessions/Guantanamo%20Bay%20Naval%20Base%20(Cuba)

17. Denbeaux, M.P. (2007, April 27). The 14 myths of Guantánamo. Testimony to the [United States] Senate Armed Services Committee. Retrieved November 4, 2007, from http://law.shu.edu/publications/guantanamoReports/fourteen_myths_of_gtmo_final.pdf

18. See reprints of the leaflets in: Denbeaux, M., & Denbeaux, J. (2006). Report on Guantanamo detainees: A profile of 517 detainees through analysis

of Department of Defense data. Retrieved November 4, 2007, from http://law.shu.edu/news/guantanamo_report_final_2_08_06.pdf
19. Cited in: Walsh, J. (2006, March 14). The Abu Ghraib files. *Salon.com*. Retrieved October 20, 2007, from www.salon.com/news/abu_ghraib/2006/03/14/introduction/
20. Denbeaux, The 14 myths of Guantánamo.
21. Shaheen, Reel bad Arabs.
22. Names of the Detained in Guantanamo Bay, Cuba. (2006, March 15). Retrieved November 4, 2007, from http://projects.washingtonpost.com/guantanamo/
23. Margulies, J. (2006). *Guantánamo and the abuse of presidential power*. New York: Simon & Schuster.
24. Glaberson, W. (2007, November 16). Red Cross monitors barred from Guantánamo. *New York Times*. Retrieved April 14, 2008, from www.nytimes.com/2007/11/16/washington/16gitmo.html?scp=1&sq=red+cross+monitors& st=nyt See also: Soldz, S., & Assange, J. (2007, November 17). Guantanamo document confirms psychological torture. Retrieved April 29, 2008, from www.wikileaks.org/wiki/Guantanamo_document_confirms_ psychological_torture
25. Margulies, *Guantánamo and the abuse of presidential power*.
26. Sampson, E.E. (1999). *Dealing with differences: An introduction to the social psychology of prejudice*. New York: Harcourt Brace College Publishers.
27. AAA Statement on Race (1998, May 17). Statement adopted by the Executive Board of the American Anthropological Association. Retrieved April 29, 2008, from www.aaanet.org/issues/policy-advocacy/AAA-Statement-on-Race.cfm#
28. American Psychological Association Public Policy Office. (n.d.). Can or should America be color-blind? Retrieved July 2, 2007, from www.apa.org/ppo/issues/pcolorblind.html
29. Boldry, J.G., Gaertner, L., & Quinn, J. (2007). Measuring the measures: A meta-analytic investigation of the measures of outgroup homogeneity. *Group processes and intergroup relations, 10,* 157–178.
30. Mullen, B., & Johnson, C. (1993). Cognitive representation in ethnophaulisms as a function of group size: The phenomenology of being in a group. *Personality and social psychology bulletin, 19,* 296–304.
31. Linville, P.W., & Jones, E.E. (1980). Polarized appraisals of out-group members. *Journal of personality and social psychology, 38,* 689–703.
32. Meissner, C.A., & Brigham, J.C. (2001). Thirty years of investigating the own-race bias in memory for faces: A meta-analytic review. *Psychology, public policy, and law, 7,* 3–35.
33. *Ibid.*

34. *Ibid.*
35. Wright, D.B., Boyd, C.E., & Tredoux, C.G. (2001). A field study of own-race bias in South Africa and England. *Psychology, public policy, and law, 7*, 119–133.
36. Ferguson, D.P., Rhodes, G., & Lee, K. (2001). "They all look alike to me": Prejudice and cross-race face recognition. *British journal of psychology, 92*, 567–577.
37. Meissner & Brigham, Thirty years of investigating the own-race bias in memory for faces.
38. For a discussion, see page 126 in: Greene, E., Heilbrun, K., Fortune, W.H., & Nietzel, M.T. (2007). *Wrightsman's psychology and the legal system.* (6th edition). Belmont, CA: Thomson Higher Education.
39. Meissner & Brigham, Thirty years of investigating the own-race bias.
40. Described in: Shah, S. (2007). Asian American? In P.S. Rothenberg (Ed.) *Race, class, and gender in the United States* (7th edition, pp. 221–223). New York: Worth.
41. Smith, G., & Anderson, K.J. (2005). Students' ratings of professors: The teaching style contingency for Latino/a professors. *Journal of Latinos and education, 4*, 115–136.
42. Valian, V. (1999). *Why so slow? The advancement of women.* Cambridge, MA: The MIT press.
43. Linville & Jones, Polarized appraisals of out-group members.
44. Keltner, D., & Robinson, R.J. (1996). Extremism, power, and the imagined basis of social conflict. *Current directions in psychological science, 5*, 101–105.
45. Whitley, B.E., Jr. & Kite, M.E. (2010). *The psychology of prejudice and discrimination.* Belmont, CA: Wadsworth.
46. Fiske, S.T. (2004). What's in a category? Responsibility, intent, and the avoidability of bias against outgroups. In A.G. Miller (Ed.), *The social psychology of good and evil* (pp. 127–140). New York: Guilford Press.
47. Whitley & Kite, *The psychology of prejudice and discrimination.*
48. *Ibid.*
49. Simon, B., & Pettigrew, T.F. (1990). Social identity and perceived group homogeneity: Evidence for the ingroup homogeneity effect. *European journal of social psychology, 20*, 269–286.
50. Tatum, B.D. (1997). *"Why are all the black kids sitting together in the cafeteria?" and other conversations about race.* New York: Basic Books.
51. Thompson, S.C., Kohles, J.C., Otsuki, T.A., & Kent, D.R. (1997). Perceptions of attitudinal similarity in ethnic groups in the US: Ingroup and outgroup homogeneity effects. *European journal of social psychology, 27*, 209–220.

52. Ackerman, J.M., Shapiro, J.R., Neuberg, S.L., *et al.* (2006). They all look the same to me (unless they're angry): From out-group homogeneity to out-group heterogeneity. *Psychological science, 17,* 836–840.

53. Maner, J.K., Kenrick, D.T., Becker, D.V., *et al.* (2005). Functional projection: How fundamental social motives can bias interpersonal perception. *Journal of personality and social psychology, 88,* 63–78.

54. Tajfel, H., Billig, M.G., Bundy, R.P., & Flament, C. (1971). Social categorization and intergroup behaviour. *European journal of social psychology, 1,* 149–178.

55. Kray, L.J., & Robinson, R.J. (2001). Partisanship and the status quo. *European journal of social psychology, 31,* 321–335.

56. For a thorough discussion of power and privilege, see: Johnson, A.G. (2006). *Privilege, power, and difference* (2nd edition). New York: McGraw Hill.

57. Maner *et al.* Functional projection.

58. Fiske, S.T. (1993). Controlling other people: The impact of power on stereotyping. *American psychologist, 48,* 621–628.

59. Guinote, A., Judd, C.M., & Brauer, M. (2002). Effects of power on perceived and objective group variability: Evidence that more powerful groups are more variable. *Journal of personality and social psychology, 82,* 708–721.

60. Ebenbach, D.H., & Keltner, D. (1998). Power, emotion, and judgmental accuracy in social conflict: Motivating the cognitive miser. *Basic and applied social psychology, 20,* 7–21.

61. Fiske, S.T., & Taylor, S.E. (1991). *Social cognition* (2nd edition). New York: McGraw Hill.

62. Fiske, Controlling other people.

63. Guinote *et al.* Effects of power on perceived and objective group variability.

64. Ebenbach & Keltner, Power, emotion, and judgmental accuracy in social conflict.

65. Fiske, Controlling other people.

66. Goodwin, S.A., & Fiske, S.T. (1993). Impression formation in asymmetrical power relationships: Does power corrupt absolutely? Unpublished manuscript, University of Massachusetts at Amherst. Cited in: Fiske, Controlling other people.

67. Dovidio, J.F., & Gaertner, S.L. (2000). Aversive racism and selection decisions: 1989 and 1999. *Psychological science, 11,* 315–319.

68. Whitley & Kite, *The psychology of prejudice and discrimination.*

69. Mummendey, A., & Wenzel, M. (1999). Social discrimination and tolerance in intergroup relations: Reactions to intergroup difference. *Personality and social psychology review, 3,* 158–174.

70. Howard, J.W., & Rothbart, M. (1980). Social categorization and memory for in-group and out-group behavior. *Journal of personality and social psychology*, 38, 301–310.
71. Pettigrew, T.F. (1979). The ultimate attribution error: Extending Allport's cognitive analysis of prejudice. *Personality and social psychology bulletin*, 5, 461–476.
72. Cozzarelli, C., Tagler, M.J., & Wilkinson, A.V. (2002). Do middle-class students perceive poor women and poor men differently? *Sex roles*, 47, 519–529.
73. Islam, M.R., & Hewstone, M. (1993). Intergroup attributions and affective consequences in majority and minority groups. *Journal of personality and social psychology*, 64, 936–950.
74. Doosje, B.J., & Branscombe, N.R. (2003). Attributions for the negative historical actions of a group. *European journal of social psychology*, 33, 235–248.
75. See Study 1 in: Henderson-King, E.I., & Nisbett, R.E. (1996). Anti-black prejudice as a function of exposure to the negative behavior of a single black person. *Journal of personality and social psychology*, 71, 654–664.
76. The ethnicity/race of the participants in the study was not reported by its authors.
77. See Study 3 in: Henderson-King & Nisbett, Anti-black prejudice.
78. For a review, see: Maass, A. (1999). Linguistic intergroup bias: Stereotype perpetuation through language. In M.P. Zanna (Ed.), *Advances in experimental social psychology* (Vol. 31, pp. 79–121). New York: Academic Press.
79. These examples come from chapter 6 in: Jones, M. (2002). *Social psychology of prejudice*. Upper Saddle River, NJ: Prentice Hall.
80. For a summary of work on the linguistic intergroup bias, see: Ruscher, J.B. (2001). *Prejudiced communication: A social psychological perspective*. New York: The Guilford Press.
81. Gorham, B.W. (2006). News media's relationship with stereotyping: The linguistic intergroup bias in response to crime news. *Journal of communication*, 56, 289–308.
82. Whitley & Kite, *The psychology of prejudice and discrimination*.
83. Schnake, S.B., & Ruscher, J.B. (1998). Modern racism as a predictor of the linguistic intergroup bias. *Journal of language and social psychology*, 17, 484–491.
84. Webster, D.M., Kruglanski, A.W., & Pattison, D.A. (1997). Motivated language use in intergroup contexts: Need-for-closure effects on the linguistic intergroup bias. *Journal of personality and social psychology*, 72, 1122–1131.

85. Cialdini, R.B., Borden, R.J., Thorne, A., Walker, M.R., Freeman, S., & Sloan, L.R. (1976). Basking in reflected glory: Three (football) field studies. *Journal of personality and social psychology, 34*, 366–375.
86. Address to a Joint Session of Congress and the American People (2001, September 20). The White House: Office of the Press Secretary. Retrieved October 15, 2007, from www.dhs.gov/xnews/speeches/speech_0016.shtm
87. International Campaign Against Terror Grows (2001, September 25). Remarks by President Bush and Prime Minister Koizumi of Japan in Photo Opportunity. The White House: Office of the Press Secretary. Retrieved October 15, 2007, from http://georgewbush-whitehouse. archives.gov/news/releases/2001/09/20010925-1.html#
88. Snow, N. (2003). *Information war: American propaganda, free speech and opinion control since 9–11.* New York: Seven Stories Press.
89. Frank, J.A. (2004). *Bush on the couch: Inside the mind of the president.* New York: Regan Books.
90. Haslam, N. (2006). Dehumanization: An integrative review. *Personality and social psychology review, 10*, 252–264.
91. Cited in: Hersh, S.M. (2004, May 10). Torture at Abu Ghraib. *The New Yorker.* Retrieved October 15, 2007, from www.newyorker.com/archive/2004/05/10/040510fa_fact
92. Warrick, J. (2008, June 18). CIA played larger role in advising Pentagon: Harsh interrogation methods defended. *The Washington post,* p. A1.
93. See references to NHI in: Judges behaving badly: Low pay and partisan elections are threatening judicial integrity (2007, June 28). *The Economist, 383*, 36–38. Duersten, M. (2005, February 3). Who'll stop the reign? *LA Weekly.* Retrieved October 7, 2007, from www.laweekly.com/news/features/wholl-stop-the-reign/968/; Livingston, G. (1999). Beyond watching over established ways: A review as recasting the literature, recasting the lived. *Review of educational research, 69*, 9–19.
94. Strömberg, F. (2003). *Black images in the comics: A visual history.* [No location]: Fantagraphics Books.
95. Kingston, P.J. (1983). *Anti-semitism in France during the 1930s: Organisations, personalities and propaganda.* Hull, UK: University of Hull Press.
96. Shaheen, Reel bad Arabs.
97. Viki, G.T., Winchester, L., Titshall, L., Chisango, T., Pina, A., & Russell, R. (2006). Beyond secondary emotions: The infrahumanization of outgroups using human-related and animal-related words. *Social cognition, 24*, 753–775.
98. Leyens, J.-P., Rodriguez-Perez, A., Rodriguez-Torres, R., *et al.* (2001). Psychological essentialism and the differential attribution of uniquely

human emotions to ingroups and outgroups. *European journal of social psychology, 31*, 395–411. Leyens *et al.* refer to this as *infrahumanization*. I am using the more commonly used term *dehumanization*.

99. *Ibid.*

100. Castano, E., & Giner-Sorolla, R. (2006). Not quite human: Infrahumanization in response to collective responsibility for intergroup killing. *Journal of personality and social psychology, 90*, 804–818.

101. *Ibid.*, Experiment 2.

102. *Ibid.*, Experiment 3.

103. Sahdra, B., & Ross, M. (2007). Group identification and historical memory. *Personality and social psychology bulletin, 33*, 384–395.

104. *Ibid.* Experiment 2.

105. Glick, P. (2002). Sacrificial lambs dressed in wolves' clothing: Envious prejudice, ideology, and the scapegoating of Jews. In L.S. Newman & R. Erber (Eds.), *Understanding genocide: The social psychology of the holocaust* (pp. 113–142). New York: Oxford University Press, Inc.

106. Chalk, F., & Jonassohn, K. (1990). *The history and sociology of genocide: analyses and case studies.* New Haven, CT: Yale University Press.

107. See page 169 in: Sampson, *Dealing with differences.*

108. Meissner & Brigham, Thirty years of investigating the own-race bias in memory for faces.

109. Fiske, Controlling other people.

110. Cited in: Walsh, The Abu Ghraib files.

111. Maner *et al.* Functional projection.

112. Ebenbach & Keltner, Power, emotion, and judgmental accuracy in social conflict.

113. Gorham, News media's relationship with stereotyping.

114. Schnake & Ruscher, Modern racism as a predictor of the linguistic intergroup bias.

115. Sahdra & Ross, Group identification and historical memory.

116. For a longer discussion of these four factors see: Jones, *Social psychology of prejudice.*

117. Grove, L. (1994, July 28). Barry Goldwater's left turn. *The Washington Post.* Retrieved April 29, 2008, from www.washingtonpost.com/wp-srv/politics/daily/may98/goldwater 072894.htm

118. President Bush, Colombia President Uribe discuss terrorism.

119. Roccas, S., & Brewer, M.B. (2002). Social identity complexity. *Personality and social psychology review, 6*, 88–106.

120. Whitley & Kite, *The psychology of prejudice and discrimination.*

121. Aronson, E. (2004). Reducing hostility and building compassion: Lessons from the jigsaw classroom. In A.G. Miller (Ed.), *The social psychology of good and evil* (pp. 469–488). New York: The Guilford Press.

122. Bridgeman, D.L. (1981). Enhanced role taking through cooperative interdependence: A field study. *Child development, 52*, 1231–1238.
123. Aronson, Reducing hostility and building compassion.
124. For a review of work in the area of stereotype suppression, see: Jones, *Social psychology of prejudice.*
125. Monteith, M.J., Spicer, C.V., & Tooman, G.D. (1998). Consequences of stereotype suppression: Stereotypes on AND not on the rebound. *Journal of experimental social psychology, 34*, 355–377.
126. Devine, P.G., Monteith, M.J., Zuwerink, J.R., & Elliot, A.J. (1991). Prejudice with and without compunction. *Journal of personality and social psychology, 60*, 817–830.
127. Son Hing, L.S., Li, W., & Zanna, M.P. (2002). Inducing hypocrisy to reduce prejudicial responses among aversive racists. *Journal of experimental social psychology, 38*, 71–78.
128. Batson, C.D., Chang, J., Orr, R., & Rowland, J. (2002). Empathy, attitudes, and action: Can feeling for a member of a stigmatized group motivate one to help the group? *Personality and social psychology bulletin, 28*, 1656–1666.

TWO

"They must be guilty of something": Myths of criminalization

But the thing is, you don't have many suspects who are innocent of a crime. That's contradictory. If a person is innocent of a crime, then he is not a suspect.
Former Attorney General of the United States, Edwin Meese[1]

In the early morning hours of July 23, 1999, law enforcement officers raided homes and arrested 46 residents on drug charges in the small west Texas town of Tulia. Forty of those arrested were African Americans, representing about 10% of the town's African American population. Local television stations were alerted in advance of the raids, and cameras rolled as suspects, many of whom were not allowed to get fully dressed, were led out of their homes into squad cars. The arrests were based on white undercover officer Tom Coleman's 18-month investigation. And while no drugs, weapons, or large sums of cash were found at any of the residences, 38 of the 46 were convicted, based, in most cases, solely on Coleman's testimony that the suspects had sold him drugs. Coleman did not wear a wire or take notes during the purported transactions, and there were no eyewitnesses or video records.

Judges ruled information about Coleman's checkered past inadmissible at the trials. No African Americans served as jurors on any of the cases. The first trial concluded with resident Joe Moore being sentenced to 90 years in prison. Another suspect got 300 years. These exorbitant sentences prompted many suspects who were awaiting trial and who saw the inevitability of conviction, to plea bargain in order to receive less jail time. Undercover officer Coleman was rewarded for his work by being named Law Enforcement Officer of the Year by the Texas State Attorney General. Over the next four years, the cases against the Tulia residents began to unravel. It was discovered that undercover officer Tom Coleman had a history of racism, perjury, and intimidation and harassment of informants. Eventually, the work of *New York Times* journalist Bob Herbert, the National Association for the Advancement of Colored People, and the American Civil Liberties Union turned up the true story of Tulia and Tom Coleman. Eventually, 35 of the 38 convictions were overturned and Tom Coleman was indicted for perjury by a grand jury.

How does such a grave injustice happen in a country where one is presumed innocent until proven guilty? Some say it's the failed drug war. Local drug task forces are financed by the federal government in such a way that the more arrests they make, the more funding they get. Racism and classism surely played a role. Those who were arrested were black and poor. They could not afford expensive defense attorneys. And for many of the television viewers who watched the arrests on television and read about the arrests in their local papers, it just made sense that the disheveled African American suspects could be up to no good. After the arrests, one local newspaper headline read "Tulia streets cleared of garbage."[2] To many, the suspects just looked as though they were *guilty of something*.

This chapter examines the sociocognitive mechanisms that lead many to believe that those who are accused of crimes are probably guilty of something. There are many excellent analyses of the US drug war,[3] and racism and classism in the criminal justice system at the policy level (e.g. prisons).[4] But my analysis focuses on thinking at the *individual* level, thinking which can lead many to believe that criminal suspects are guilty until proven innocent (and in some cases, even when suspects are exonerated via DNA testing, prosecutors continue to resist the seemingly conclusive evidence of the new outcome).[5] While my focus is on individual thinking, cognition at the individual level affects and is affected by procedures, policies, laws, and engrained values inherent to the criminal justice system. Therefore, the connection between the micro-level thinking that psychologists are concerned with, and macro-level issues should also be clear in this chapter. The organization of this chapter does take the reader through the stages of the criminal justice process, but I begin even earlier with people's mental associations of people of color with crime, this being present even before a crime is committed. The research presented in this section demonstrates many people's proclivity toward assuming that ethnic minorities are associated with crime. Next, the ways in which bias and bigotry can affect each stage of the criminal justice process are examined. Each stage of the process can produce both errors in thinking and mythical assumptions that set in motion a trajectory of injustice from suspicion through sentencing. Finally, as in all chapters in this book, the last section deals with strategies for preventing many of the errors and injustices described in this chapter.

Crime and color

My youngest son was arrested last year. Police came to my house looking for an armed robbery suspect, 5-foot-8 inches with long hair. They took my son, 6-foot-3 with short braids. They made my daughter, 14, fresh from the shower and dressed for bed, lie facedown in wet grass and handcuffed her. They took my grandson, 8, from the bed where he slept and made him sit on the sidewalk beside her.

Leonard Pitts, Jr.[6]

The above quote is the beginning of an article, entitled, "Black's presumed guilt hits a little too close to home," written by Leonard Pitts, Jr., an African American. The experience faced by his son is typical for African American families but not for white families. Pitts' son, who obviously did not fit the description of the robbery suspect, save for the fact that both are black, spent two weeks in jail before the charges were dropped. When it comes to criminal sus-pects, the sentiments often seem to be that any black man will do.[7]

It is simply easier and more automatic to associate crime with blackness or brownness than with whiteness.[8] This is especially true for violent crime. For many, when they hear about a drug bust or a shooting, they spontaneously conjure up an image of an African American man more often than that of a white man. That's why, in 1994, when Susan Smith drowned her two sons, to cover up her crime she fabricated a story about a black man abducting the children. Or why, in 2005, "runaway bride" Jennifer Wilbanks concocted a story about being kidnapped and raped by a Latino man. Or why, in 1989, Charles Stuart shot his wife in the head and shot himself in the abdomen, but attempted to blame the incident on an African American man.[9] Or why, in October, 2008, shortly before the US presidential election, a white campaign worker for presidential candidate John McCain concocted then recanted a story that a 6-foot-4 black man attacked her and carved a "B" (for "Barack") in her face showing his support for African American candidate Barack Obama.[10]

Crime coverage in the news media and in reality shows like *Cops* help viewers make these quick and easy associations. In her review of studies on media portrayals of ethnic minorities, Mary Beth Oliver[11] found several disturbing patterns: African American men are *overrepresented* as criminal suspects and *underrepresented* as victims of crime in comparison to actual crime statistics. The opposite is true for whites: they are *underrepresented* as perpetrators and *overrepresented* as victims. African American men, like those arrested in Tulia, Texas, are also more likely to be portrayed in the media as threatening and menacing (e.g. handcuffed, physically restrained by police officers, poorly dressed, etc.) than white suspects. Oliver found that when whites have been exposed to these racist portrayals, they can easily call to mind negative racial attitudes later. What's worse, crime stories reported on the news that did not reveal the race of the suspect still prompted negative racial attitudes among white viewers. In other words, there is a tendency for whites, when thinking about crime, to conjure up stereotypes about crime and blackness, even when a particular crime does not involve African Americans. Oliver found that when white readers were exposed to a newspaper story about a violent crime, they were more likely to attribute the suspect's behavior to his *disposition* (e.g. violent personality), than to situational factors (e.g. suspect recently lost his job) if the suspect was black rather than white. This suggests that there is a perceived stability and permanence to black crime – *"that's just how those people are"* – whereas white crime is assumed to be more transient and situational. Once viewers' conceptual frameworks about the "violent black male" are in place, exposure to violent crime alone is sufficient to evoke these schemas and to influence subsequent judgments.

Mental association of race with crime leads people to judge the same behavior by African Americans and whites differently. A study of white American university students by Eaaron Henderson-King and Richard Nisbett[12] found that observing or even hearing about an African American man's negative actions caused whites to avoid contact with a different black man later. The same respondents who saw an African American man behave negatively, subsequently perceived African Americans in general as more hostile. In other words, the behavior of one member of a minority group is generalized to other members of that same group – individual people of color are stand-ins for their entire group. In contrast, participants in Henderson-King and Nisbett's study did not base their judgments of white men on the negative behavior of one white man. Whites were viewed as *individuals*, not as representative members of an ethnic group. In fact, in their study, when the student participants observed a *white* man behaving negatively, they subsequently avoided an *African American* man! Perhaps just witnessing a negative interaction, regardless of the race of the interactants, made the white participants want to be more comfortable, associating only with "their own" versus "others." As we found in the "They all look alike" chapter, and Mary Beth Oliver's work described above, people tend to attribute the negative actions of outgroup members to dispositional rather than situational factors, whereas similar actions by ingroup members are more often assumed to be the result of situational factors.[13] Henderson-King and Nisbett further found that those who witnessed or heard about a black man doing something negative minimized the existing power difference between whites and African Americans in the US, compared to those who witnessed or heard about a black man doing something neutral or positive, or a white man doing something negative. In other words, when a single African American man does something bad, whites tend to generalize that to all African American men, and then the threat they feel when they witness this negative behavior makes them less sympathetic to the struggles of African Americans in the United States.

Automatic associations and the police officer's dilemma

How do these automatic associations linking ethnic minorities with violence and crime actually relate to real crimes and real suspects? The 1999 shooting death of Amadou Diallo[14] by four New York City police officers provides a good illustration of that relationship. Diallo, a West African immigrant with no criminal record, fit the general description of a serial rapist being sought by the police. When the four officers approached Diallo and ordered him to stop, he began reaching into his pocket for his wallet, but the officers, believing that he was reaching for a gun, fired forty-one shots at the unarmed man, killing him instantly.

We do not know exactly what went through the minds of those NYPD officers who had to make the split decision to shoot or not to shoot. But there are simulation studies that give us a glimpse into the patterns of the quick decisions law enforcement officers make based on race, what has been referred to as the *police officer's dilemma*. Joshua Correll and his colleagues[15] had African American and white participants play a video game simulation in which they had to decide whether or not to shoot a "suspect" holding an ambiguous looking object. If the suspect was holding a cell phone, the respondent had to refrain from shooting but if the suspect was holding a gun, the respondent had to shoot. Participants were faced with either a black or white suspect. Monetary awards were provided to the participants to encourage speed and accuracy. Results of the study revealed that participants fired at an armed target more quickly if he was African American than if he was white, and they decided *not* to shoot an unarmed white target more quickly than an unarmed African American target. The tendency to make more false alarms (shooting the unarmed person) than misses was more pronounced when the target was black than white. That is, they tended to shoot unarmed African Americans more often than unarmed whites. If a target was African American, respondents required less certainty that he was, in fact, holding a gun, before they decided to shoot him. Thus, race (or ideas about race) interfered with the ability of the respondents to be accurate. This pattern occurred among both white and black participants – that is, African American participants were quicker to shoot at the black unarmed suspect than the white unarmed suspect. Surely respondents could have performed perfectly on the task by simply focusing on the object in the target's hand, completely ignoring race. But participants were overwhelmed by their associative link between violence and black men. After Correll's main experiment, white participants were measured on their ability to recognize the faces of the African American and white targets they had seen. White participants were less accurate at recognizing the faces of African American targets than white targets when they were subsequently asked if they'd seen the face before – in other words, for whites, African Americans *all look alike*.

While Correll's study is only a video simulation study, it demonstrates the automatic and non-conscious link for many people between African American men and violence and may be a glimpse into the reactions of the NYPD officers who shot and killed Amadou Diallo. The finding in the Correll study about the inability of white respondents to distinguish the faces of African Americans as accurately as those of whites finds further support in a study, also on crime, conducted by Mary Beth Oliver and Dana Fonash.[16] In their study, white US college students read about either a violent or non-violent crime that involved either a white or black suspect. They were later shown photographs of white and black men and asked whether or not they had seen the men before in the stories they had read. Readers were more likely to misidentify the (wrong) black man as the suspect than the (wrong) white man but only when the crime was a violent one. For white respondents, violent black suspects again tended to *all look alike*. It was easier for a white person to misidentify African American suspects, especially when they were suspects in violent crimes. These findings suggest that there could be problems in identifying suspects in police photos or lineups. There are significant implications here for relying upon the accuracy of the eyewitness testimony of white witnesses in cases involving black suspects.

Bias during investigations and arrests

Contrary to one of our most cherished American ideals – the assumption that a suspect is considered innocent until proven guilty – bias operates in forceful ways from the early stages in the criminal justice process. Once a suspect has been identified, police tend to stop searching for other suspects and stop pursuing other leads. This narrowed focus is due, in part, to the lack of resources departments have to maintain investigations of several individuals simultaneously. Perhaps as important as the constraints of material resources, however, is the operation of specific cognitive processes. Once investigators and prosecutors have targeted a suspect and have justified the massive amount of time required for a thorough investigation, there is a tendency to close off alternatives to further justify their pursuit of the main suspect. The reasoning runs some-thing like this: *How can I try so hard to identify and build a case against a suspect if there might be other suspects out there?*

Part of the reason the public believes that those who are sus-pected of a crime are actually guilty is due to the belief that there are many "safety nets" during the sequence of events of the criminal justice process that protect the innocent from wrongful suspicion and conviction. Many believe that if a suspect is truly innocent, the truth will come out at some time during the process. In his compilation of the literature that unites psychology and law, Saul Kassin[17] finds, in fact, *innocence* actually puts *innocents* at specific risk for being found guilty. In other words, suspects who are actually innocent of a crime are at more risk than those who are actually guilty, when it comes to assumptions of guilt. According to Kassin, there are five critical points in the judicial process that are espe-cially risky for innocent suspects.

Risk #1: Police overconfidence and the presumption of guilt

The first risk to innocent suspects is law enforcement officers' overconfidence in their ability to track the correct leads, and the fact that narrowing the pool of suspects actually tends to lead those involved in pursuing criminal investigations to presume guilt prematurely. For people in general, once we form an impression, we unwittingly seek, interpret, and create observational data that verify that impression. This tendency reveals an inversion of the conventional wisdom: "*I wouldn't have believed it if I hadn't seen it.*" In the criminal justice process, after the early stages of investigation and identification of a suspect, the wisdom is perhaps captured in this way: "*I wouldn't have seen it if I hadn't believed it.*" Across many studies, trained professionals, compared to naïve controls, exhibit a proclivity to judge targets as being deceptive. An assumption for many police officers seems to be: "*You can tell if a suspect is lying by whether he is moving his lips.*"[18]

Once suspects are identified, gaining accurate information about their whereabouts at the time of the crime and alibi can be difficult because as soon as an individual becomes a suspect, he or she becomes *the* suspect. This motivates investigators to look at the circumstances and facts of the case only in terms of their particular suspect – as if there are no other possible suspects. Once investigators put together a story in which the circumstances fit the suspect, it's difficult to perceive alternatives. This creates a (sometimes false) sense of confidence for the investigators and puts them on a track that seems to inevitably point to the already identified suspect.

Two studies on interrogations and confessions conducted by Saul Kassin illustrate how investigators' assumptions can hamper their ability to detect deception accurately. In one study, Kassin and his colleagues[19] tested the accuracy of law enforcement officers and students in judging confessions, both true and false. Kassin showed the mostly white American students and police officers either video or audiotapes of male prisoners giving either a true confession (of the crime they actually committed) or a scripted false confession. One might expect that police officers, with their training and experience, would be able to detect subtle clues or the common *tells* in a suspect that reveal deception – lack of eye contact, stammering and stuttering speech, nervous fidgeting, perhaps. The results were surprising. Neither students nor law enforcement performed better than would be predicted by chance. Rolling dice to decide who was telling the truth and who was lying would have yielded about the same results. But there were surprising results between groups. First, law enforcement officers actually performed worse than did students – students were accurate 59% of the time and law enforcement officers 48%. How can this be? The most likely explanation is that law enforcement training, instead of facilitating accuracy, possibly hinders it by introducing systematic bias that reduces overall judgment accuracy. Police training entails the use of many visual cues such as gaze aversion, non-frontal posture, slouching, and grooming gestures that are supposedly typical of deception. It appears that law enforcement officers develop schemas that are more elaborate and extreme versions of the common-sense evaluative schemas already used by civilians in everyday life.

Police officers, compared to students, presume guilt more often. In this study, the officers guessed that 65% of the confessions were true compared with students who guessed that 55% were true (half of the confessions were true). What's more, police officers were more confident in their assessments than were college students and confidence was negatively correlated with accuracy! That means the more confident the observer, the less accurate the judgment. Finally, raters (regardless of whether they were students or law enforcement officers) made more accurate judgments when they listened to the confessions on audiotape rather than when they watched video in addition to listening to the audiotape. It seems that the visual cues people use to determine guilt or innocence actually contribute to their inaccuracy – judges are better off just listening.

Bias and the tendency to "see guilt" affect all stages of the criminal justice process, even after the investigation, arrest, and interrogation. A dramatic example of the effects of this type of bias was revealed in the 2002 scandal that drew national attention and forced the Houston, Texas, Police Department Crime Lab to close its doors because of widespread fraud and incompetence.[20] Crime analysts were found to have acted as a kind of "rubber stamp" for the police department, tailoring lab reports to fit the theories of the prosecution, and ignoring exculpatory evidence that would have excluded defendants.[21] It is unclear whether or not these serious mistakes were the result of conscious efforts or non-conscious thinking, although the mistakes always favored the prosecution.[22]

The implications for fairness and accuracy in the criminal justice system are widespread. Police officers are, in effect, trained to presume guilt. Their confidence in lie detection blinds them to accurate evaluation of evidence. When officers have been asked whether or not they are worried that they might be interrogating innocent people and presuming they are guilty, a common response from police is: "*No, because I do not interrogate innocent people.*"[23] That people were more accurate when they listened to confessions without video has implications for training because many law enforcement investigators believe the way they detect characteristics about a suspect is visual – body language, visibly detectable nervousness, etc.

Despite training, professional standards, and popular notions, there is no group of people (e.g. police, FBI, psychotherapists) that reliably differentiates lies from truths at levels that are better than by chance. People from fields that provide lie detection training usually do not perform better than do civilian college students.[24]

Risk #2: Innocents waive crucial rights

Naively believing that truth and justice will prevail, innocent suspects often waive their rights to be questioned and have an attorney present. This is the second risk described by Kassin.

Innocent suspects overestimate their ability to prove their innocence. They think that because they have nothing to hide, they would look guilty if they didn't waive their Miranda rights. The Miranda warning was established in 1966 to protect suspects against coerced confessions and self-incrimination. Ever since the landmark US Supreme Court decision, *Miranda vs. Arizona*, police must warn suspects of certain rights before starting an interrogation. These rights include the right to remain silent when in police custody. Suspects do not need to talk or answer any questions law enforcement may ask. Suspects also have the right to an attorney, either hired or court-appointed if they cannot afford one.

Relevant to the discussion here, innocent individuals and those who have no prior felony record are more likely to waive their Miranda rights than those with a history of criminal justice experience. The waiving of these crucial rights means that suspects allow police to interrogate them with no protection from an attorney. Those with criminal justice experience seem to better know their rights and protect themselves in ways that innocent people do not. In one of Kassin's[25] studies, some participants (mostly white American college students) committed a mock theft and some did not, but all were suspects. Those who were innocent were much more likely to sign a waiver giving up important protections than those who were guilty (81% vs. 36%). Those who were innocent were also more likely to waive a regular police line up and instead agreed to a one-on-one "show-up" with the victim – a procedure that put them in more danger of being identified by the victim. Among guilty participants, only 47% waived the line up; but among the innocents, 100% waived the line up.

Why do innocent people waive these important rights, while those who are guilty tend not to? According to Saul Kassin, there are at least two reasons. First, innocent people tend to believe in an *illusion of transparency*, which is the tendency to overestimate the extent to which people's true thoughts, emotions, and motivations can be seen by others. Their thinking seems to be, *If I am honest and show that I have nothing to hide, they will see that I am not guilty.* In terms of waiving a line up, the innocent suspect figures, *I didn't commit the crime so a witness cannot identify me.*

A second reason why innocent suspects put themselves at risk by waiving important rights is because they tend to believe in a just world.[26] *Belief in a just world* is a construct that explains a host of phenomena from why people tend to blame rape victims for being raped (e.g. *"What was she doing drunk at a fraternity party?"*) to why the guilty-of-something myth persists. The belief in a just world is the belief that good things happen to good people and bad things happen to bad people. It's the notion that if we are good, decent, hard-working individuals who pull ourselves up by our bootstraps, good things will come our way. If something bad happens to us, we must have done something to deserve it. The belief produces the idea that when people are accused of a crime, *they must be guilty of something.* Believing in a just world is functional in that it makes people feel better. It allows people to believe that the world is a just and predictable place. For the purposes of our discussion here, innocent people's belief in a just world contributes to their sometimes faulty belief that the truth will come out in the end. From the perspective of those judging others, the *belief* contributes to the myth that if someone is accused of a crime, he or she must be guilty of something because it would be too difficult to cope with the fact that sometimes an innocent person is railroaded into being found guilty. People want to believe that the legal system is just.

Risk #3: Police interrogate innocents more aggressively

The third risk to innocent suspects is that, in spite of or because of their plausible and vigorous denials, they trigger highly confrontational interrogations by interrogators. Kassin's study described earlier comparing students' and law enforcement officers' ability to detect true and false confessions only looked at the judgments of *confessions*, not the interactive dynamics of interrogations. Do police question innocent and guilty suspects differently? Are there techniques that interrogators use that put innocent people at risk for prosecution and even conviction? Another set of studies conducted by Kassin[27] addresses these questions.

Once an interaction transitions from *interview*, gathering information from witnesses and potential suspects, to *interrogation*, investigators believe they have gotten the correct suspect. The interrogation is a guilt-presumptive process. While innocent suspects might hope that interrogators will remain open-minded enough to hear them out, once an interrogation begins, the focus for investigators becomes narrowed to the point that investigators have a set of beliefs that they are committed to and now they just need to obtain a confession. What happens when Risk #2, which often involves waiving the right to counsel, and the presumption of guilt of Risk #3, combine? Kassin refers to a three-step chain of events: "a perceiver forms a belief about a target person; the perceiver behaves toward the target in a manner that conforms to that belief; and the target responds in turn, often behaving in ways that support the perceiver's belief."[28] Thus the interrogation itself amounts to a process that confirms guilt in the interrogator's mind. And again, because innocent suspects tend to waive their rights to an attorney, these interrogations tend to occur without the presence of counsel.

A laboratory study can tell us how the interrogation process might be different, depending on whether the interrogator approaches the procedure presuming guilt or innocence. Kassin performed such a study in which he could control relevant variables, such as the type of crime, and actual innocence or guilt. In this two-phase study, Kassin and his colleagues[29] instructed mostly white American college students steal $100 (other students were placed in a similar situation but were instructed not to steal the $100). After the theft, the stealers and the non-stealers were interviewed. Other students served as investigators and were divided into two groups: those who were told that most suspects were innocent and those who were told that most suspects were guilty. The "investigators," girded with the assumption of either guilt or innocence, were instructed to interrogate one of the suspects. Did the presumption of guilt or innocence affect how the investigators behaved toward the suspects? Yes. Investigators who were led to expect guilt rather than innocence asked more guilt-presumptive questions (e.g. "How did you find the key that was hidden behind the VCR?") and exerted more pressure (e.g. repeated accusations) to get a confession. In the second phase of the experiment, audiotapes of the interrogations were played to independent observers during which they judged the presumed guilt or innocence of the suspects they heard being interrogated. According to the neutral observers, the suspects judged to be the most anxious, defensive, and *guilty*, were the suspects who were actually innocent (as opposed to those who stole the $100) and who were paired with guilt-presumptive (as opposed to innocence-presumptive) investigators. According to observers, the suspects who told the most plausible denial stories, yet brought out the worst in the interrogators, were innocent suspects. Thus, the most pressure-filled sessions occurred when innocent suspects were paired with guilt-presuming investigators! Again, the police interrogation is a guilt-presumptive process that sets into motion a set of assumptions and biases on the part of investigators when hearing an innocent person resisting guilt and telling a plausible story of denial, instead of carefully weighing the information and adjusting their judgments of the suspect, denials seem to make interrogators work doubly hard at obtaining a confession.

Risk #4: Coercive interrogations and false confessions

Certain interrogation techniques, such as isolation and the presentation of false evidence, increase the fourth risk to innocent suspects, the risk of a false confession. But certainly, truly innocent people would never confess to a crime they didn't commit, right? Before the students in my "Psychology and the Law" course read the article that describes the next study, I ask if any of them would ever confess to a crime they did not commit. At first, they all confidently answer "no." After some discussion, a few students admit that if they were being tortured under threat of death, they *might* make a false confession. People simply do not believe someone would make a false confession. Many believe that under no circumstances would they give a false confession. If they didn't do it, they didn't do it. But another study performed by Saul Kassin shows that getting people to make false confessions involves a lot less pressure than torture. Kassin and Katherine Kiechel[30] asked mostly white American college students to type letters on a keyboard in what was supposedly a study on reaction time – participants had to keep up with typing a fast-paced reading of information on a keyboard. At one point, participants were accused of causing the experimenter's computer to crash by pressing on the keyboard the ALT key they had been instructed to avoid. Subsequently, the students were asked to sign a confession. All participants were actually innocent and all "suspects" initially (correctly) denied that they pressed the ALT key. In some sessions, a planted accomplice of the experiment told the experimenter that she had witnessed the participant hit the forbidden key; in others she said she had not seen what happened. Thus, in some versions of the procedure there was an eyewitness. This false eyewitness evidence significantly increased the number of students who eventually agreed to sign a written confession, from 65% (when there was no witness) to 100% (when there was a witness). The presentation of false evidence also increased the number of participants who eventually believed they were truly responsible for this outcome to 100%. That is, while no one initially admitted to hitting the dreaded key, after some questioning by the experimenter and the presentation of a witness, *everyone* signed the confession. Furthermore, when the participants were asked how the accident happened, 35% made up details consistent with their confession that they pressed the ALT key. That is, they confabulated details that were in line with their (false) confessions. For instance, they stated, "I hit it with the side of my right hand after you called out the 'A'." Again, all participants were actually innocent.

While the Kassin and Kiechel study was a laboratory experiment whose participants were college students and the study did not mimic the high stakes and extreme stress involved in being falsely accused of an actual crime, it does illustrate how susceptible one can be to influence. In Kassin and Kiechel's study, there really was no motivation to confess, but with the presentation of (false) incriminating evidence in this moderately stressful situation (fast-paced key strokes), eventually all "suspects" did confess. Replications of this study have been conducted with similar results in conditions which include financial consequences,[31] and also with juveniles,[32] who are especially vulnerable to making false confessions.

Three processes commonly used in interrogations and taught in interrogation training manuals are: *isolation, confrontation,* and *minimization.* These three processes can lead to false confessions. Prolonged periods of *isolation,* coupled with fatigue and sleep deprivation, can heighten susceptibility to being influenced and can impair one's ability to make complex decisions. Interrogations producing confessions that are later found to be false tend to be longer than other interrogations. As Kassin reports, typical interrogations last 3 to 4 hours, but interrogations that produce confessions that are later found to be false averaged 16 hours. Once a suspect is isolated, interrogators can *confront* suspects with false DNA evidence supposedly linking them to the crime, they can present phony eyewitnesses, and they can claim that the suspect failed a polygraph. All of these techniques are legal and admissible in US courts.[33] That's right, an interrogator can lie to a suspect about evidence, eyewitnesses, and polygraph data. As we saw in Kassin and Kiechel's "ALT key" study, false evidence greatly increases the risk that innocent people will confess to acts they did not commit. The third step in interrogations is a process called *minimization*. To ensure a confession, the interrogator uses minimizing techniques such as providing a moral justification for committing the crime such as, "I'm sure she had it coming," face-saving excuses, explaining that the crime was accidental, or saying that the suspect was provoked or impaired by drugs. Minimization techniques can also include promises of leniency by the court. All along, the interrogator implies that as soon as the suspect confesses, he or she can go home.

Risk #5: How could anyone give a false confession?

Again, police, judges, jurors, and lay people have extreme difficulty believing anyone would confess to a crime they hadn't committed. The fifth risk to innocent suspects then, according to Kassin, is the resistance to believing that people would actually confess to a crime they did not commit. It has already been established that law enforcement officers are no better (and are, in some cases, worse) than college students at differentiating true confessions from false.

For juries, confessions carry more weight than eyewitness testimony. People do not fully discount a confession, even when it is logically and legally appropriate to do so. The belief that suspects are guilty of something is so powerful that prosecutors sometimes continue to deny innocence even after DNA tests unequivocally clear the wrongfully convicted confessor. Their gut tells them the person is still guilty. Kassin states three reasons why innocence is not often detectable: first, people tend to take "facts" at face value. If people confess, we believe them. People also tend to discount the extent to which situational factors (e.g. a stressful interrogation) impacts behavior. Second, people are not very good at deception detection. It has already been established that law enforcement officers are no better at distinguishing true confessions from false than are college students who do so at the rate of chance. Third, police-induced false confessions often contain content cues, such as vivid details, that people associate with truth-telling. To conclude this section, Kassin states:

> Reflecting a fundamental belief in a just world and in the transparence of their own blameless status, however, those who stand falsely accused also have faith that their innocence will become self-evident to others. As a result, they cooperate with police, often not realizing that they are suspects, not witnesses; they waive their rights to silence, counsel, and a lineup; they agree to take lie-detector tests; they vehemently protest their innocence, unwittingly triggering aggressive interrogation behavior; and they succumb to pressures to confess when isolated, trapped by false evidence, and offered hope via minimization and the leniency it implies.[34]

Kassin's studies were conducted with white participants and white convicts. From what we have learned about race and the criminal justice system, this process for a person of color could be even more risky.

An ancillary to falsely confessing to a crime not committed is the occurrence of pleading guilty to a crime not committed. While it may seem unimaginable, if a suspect is faced with overwhelming evidence, or, like in the Tulia case, sees peers convicted on similar evidence, suspects might plead guilty to a crime they did not commit in order to ensure a shorter prison term.

Bias in the courtroom: How jurors perceive defendants and interpret evidence

This next section deals with sociocognitive processes that are relevant after a criminal defendant has been arrested and indicted.

It addresses how juries interpret information and how their interpretations influence the decisions they make.

Inadmissible evidence as an opportunity for bias

The area of inadmissible evidence is another area that holds great potential for the study of subtle bias. Inadmissible evidence is information that is presented by an attorney or a witness during a trial, but is then struck from the record by the judge for any number of reasons. Inadmissible evidence is often incriminating evidence that was obtained without a search warrant. When this information is presented, the judge has the discretion to have the information struck from the official court record and informs the jury that it should not use this information in its deliberations. Essentially, jurors are instructed to forget they ever heard the information. Disregarding the information is easier said than done. There is a saying among trial lawyers; *"You can't unring a bell."* There are many studies that find that when you ask someone *not* to think about an object, they can think only about that object! The consensus among social psychologists, therefore, is that jurors do tend to allow inadmissible information to influence their decisions.[35] The differential use of inadmissible information based on race or gender of a defendant or witness is a good way to assess subtle prejudice because a juror doesn't have to admit she is using inadmissible evidence in her decision. She may not even know she is relying on it.

Sometimes jurors are capable of obeying a judge's order to dismiss evidence, but sometimes jurors are not, and are instead influenced by disallowed evidence. For instance, jurors are more likely to disregard inadmissible evidence that is unreliable than inadmissible evidence that seems reliable but was obtained improperly (e.g. obtaining drugs by an illegal search).[36] Jurors seem motivated to make what they believe to be the correct (what they perceive as a "just") decision even if it means not complying with a judge's instructions.

Gordon Hodson and his colleagues[37] investigated whether subtle bias may be a factor in jurors' handling of inadmissible evidence. They found that the harshest treatment was for black defendants in cases where some evidence had been ruled inadmissible. In a jury simulation study, white college students in the United Kingdom were presented with legal documents based on an actual legal case and were asked to make decisions, such as a recommended sentence, about the case. The students read about either a white or black defendant in a case that either contained inadmissible evidence or did not. Those students assigned to a case with inadmissible evidence were told in advance: *"in the documents there may be evidence that has been ruled to be inadmissible by the judge. In the interest of ensuring realism/validity, please disregard the information that has been ruled inadmissible."* In other words, there were four different versions of the case: students read about either a white or black defendant with documents containing admissible evidence, or about a white or black defendant with documents containing inadmissible evidence. The details of the case in each condition were otherwise identical. The case was one of robbery and the inadmissible evidence was improperly obtained DNA evidence. Note that the inadmissible information, although highly reliable scientific evidence, was illegally obtained. Participants read the information and were asked about the defendant's guilt, a recommended sentence, the likelihood that the defendant would re-offend, whether the defendant was rehabilitatable, and whether his sentence should be reduced later for good behavior. Results were consistent with the dynamics of subtle racism. The students judged the black defendant in the *admissible* condition as less guilty than they judged the white defendant, recommended shorter sentences for the black person than the white, and tended to perceive the likelihood of re-offending to be lower for the black than the white defendant. In stark contrast, when the evidence was ruled *inadmissible*, participants rated the black defendant as more likely to be guilty than the white, recommended longer sentences than those recommended for the white, and perceived the likelihood of re-offending to be significantly greater for the black defendant than for the white defendant. Overall, the harshest ratings against the defendant came when a black defendant was judged and there was inadmissible evidence.

Why does this particular combination of *black defendant* and *inadmissible evidence* produce such harsh judgments? In other words, why do jurors tend to weigh inadmissible evidence more heavily when the defendant is black? The inadmissible condition presents an opportunity allowing presumably non-racial motives, such as the juror's desire to avoid letting a guilty person go free, to influence a juror's decision. In other words, the participant could defend her judgment by stating that she did not want to let a guilty person go, so she "used" inadmissible evidence to make what she believed was a just decision. The finding that people are able to adjust for this influence when judging white defendants, thus eliminating the impact of an important piece of incriminating evidence in their judgments of whites and leading to weaker perceptions of guilt, is consistent with previous studies showing that whites are inclined to give the benefit of the doubt to other whites. In this study, the participants did not extend the same benefit to black defendants. When the evidence was admissible, the only reason for judging a black defendant harshly (compared to a white) was race – the research participants in this condition likely did not want to appear racist so they did not judge the black defendant harshly in the admissible condition – they were actually more lenient toward the black defendant than the white in this condition. However, the inadmissible condition gave white participants an excuse to judge the black defendant more punitively than the white defendant. Discriminatory behavior was rationalized on non-racial grounds – participants can reason, *It's not because the defendant is black that I believe he's guilty, I just don't want a guilty person to go free.*

Another study[38] found similar responses among white US college students with the additional finding that they felt they were less affected by the inadmissible information when the defendant was black than when he was white. The authors speculated that research participants encountering a black defendant may have been reluctant to admit that their verdicts would have been different if they had not been exposed to the inadmissible evidence. Because participants were instructed to disregard the evidence, failure to comply with this instruction could have been perceived by others and themselves as racist.

So inadmissible information is "useful" to participants judging a defendant's guilt or innocence, even when they are admonished by a judge to not use it. One area of research we do not yet know about is the way in which exculpatory evidence – information that could lead to acquittal – is considered by jurors depending on the race of the defendant. Social psychology studies have not yet addressed the use of exculpatory information.

Bias in convictions and sentencing

Several aspects of sentencing can reveal bias. For instance, it has long been known that in the US, the typical sentence for the possession or sale of crack cocaine is significantly longer than the typical sentence for the possession or sale of powder cocaine. Pharmacologically identical, crack cocaine is manufactured simply from powder cocaine. Crack is made from a mixture of powder cocaine, baking soda, and water that is cooked and cooled until a solid "rock" is formed that can be broken and sold in small quantities. Many allege that differences in the penalties associated with rock and powder cocaine exist because whites and middle- and upper-class users and sellers deal with powder, while non-whites and lower-class users deal with crack.[39] This section explores the differential treatment in convictions and sentencing, based on race and other demographic factors.

There are two ways to explore bias in convictions and sentencing: by examining decisions from actual cases based on archival
research and by examining decisions made in experimental or
simulation studies using mock jurors. In addition to the wealth of
information that can be derived from archival studies on sentences
resulting from actual convictions, data can also be gleaned using
results of simulation studies conducted by social psychologists
in which mock jurors (often college students or jury-eligible
community samples) are utilized.

Archival studies of actual decisions

In archival studies, court records are analyzed to determine whether
or not there is a relationship between sentencing decisions and, say,
the race of the defendant. David Mustard[40] examined the sentencing disparities of forty-one offenses outlined by the United States
Sentencing Commission. Mustard examined all of those who were
sentenced in the US federal court system over a three-year period, a
total of 77,236 cases. African Americans and Latina/os with the
same criminal history received longer sentences than did whites for
committing the same offense in the same district. Offenders who
did not graduate from high school received longer sentences than
did offenders with college degrees. Low income offenders received
longer sentences than did higher income offenders. US citizens
received lower sentences than did non-US citizens.[41]

When Mustard examined the six most frequently committed
crimes, there were specific racial discrepancies. Drug trafficking
and bank robbery figures indicate the largest black–white differences. For instance, regarding drug trafficking, blacks are assigned
sentences that are 14% longer than those for whites. There are also
differences in terms of who is assigned prison time, rather than
probation. Whites are more likely than Latina/os and African
Americans to be assigned no prison term. Citizens are less likely
to receive a sentence than non-citizens.

Upward or downward departures from recommended sentencing guidelines can be made by a judge. Non-whites are much less likely than whites to have their sentences adjusted down, and African Americans are more likely than whites to receive upward departures from the guidelines. Offenders without a high school degree are less likely to receive a downward departure and more likely to receive an upward departure, while college graduates are more likely to receive a downward departure and less likely to receive an upward departure. And lower income offenders are less likely to get their sentences reduced while higher income offenders are more likely to have their sentences reduced. Mustard concluded that the large differences in lengths of sentences are the result of race, education, income, and citizenship. These disparities occur despite explicit statements in the guidelines that these characteristics should not affect sentence length.

A review of the literature by The Sentencing Project[42] also found that, in the United States, young African American and Latino men receive harsher sentences for the same crime than similarly situated white men. Differences exist in terms of employment status. Unemployed black men are sentenced more harshly than unemployed white men. African Americans even pay a higher *trial penalty* than similarly situated whites. A trial penalty occurs when defendants are given harsher sentences for going to trial and being found guilty rather than initially pleading guilty, thereby avoiding a trial. The trial penalty may be a specific punishment for African Americans who might be perceived by the judge as "uppity" and resisting rather than admitting guilt and taking their lumps.

One study reviewed by The Sentencing Project found that unemployed African American defendants were more likely than unemployed whites to be detained pending trial. Again, there's an assumption that an unemployed African American man presents more of a threat to society than an unemployed white man.

African Americans who victimize whites tend to receive more severe sentences than both African Americans who victimize other African Americans and whites who victimize either African Americans or whites. For instance, African Americans who kill whites, as opposed to people of color, are more likely to be executed.[43] In Florida, African Americans who kill whites are nearly forty times more likely to be sentenced to death than those who kill African Americans.[44] In addition to the discrimination this finding reveals, it also speaks to the value of African Americans as victims – the life of an African American is worth less than the life of a white American. What accounts for the differences in sentencing between people of color and whites? African American and Latino men are sentenced more harshly than white men because blacks and Latinos are seen as particularly dangerous and problematic and so are given longer sentences for public safety concerns and for the perceived antisocial and incorrigible nature of young black and Latino men. Experimental research supports the existence of these assumptions about African Americans and Latina/os.[45] Also, when an African Americans kills a white person, that case is more likely to have publicity associated with it than a case where a person of color kills another person of color.[46]

Archival studies are limited by the types of conclusions that can be drawn from them. Because the data lend themselves to correlational analysis, potentially significant variables other than race must be statistically controlled to ensure that factors covarying with race have not produced what appear to be race effects. For instance, when examining archival data, it is often impossible to separate whether or not there is differential treatment based on race, or on race and class, or just on class, because many criminal defendants are poor and are ethnic minorities. Are they being treated differently because they are poor or because they are minorities? Archival studies cannot be utilized to analyze the independent contributions of these factors.

Simulation studies with mock jurors

Simulation studies (experiments) also have their limitations. They can lack external validity, meaning that they tend to be conducted in artificial environments that seem too controlled and unrealistic to produce data that can be adequately generalized to a real court-room and a real trial.

Even though there are limitations, some simulation studies can be quite realistic. They can take place in a courtroom where participants/jurors hear scripted cases and are then instructed to deliberate. There are important benefits to simulation studies. As they are experiments, researchers can control for factors that might distort findings. Additionally, the use of experiments may allow for determination of causality. This is not possible when utilizing correlational archival studies of actual cases. Laboratory research permits variables to be specified clearly and untangled in a precise fashion, adding clarity to the inferences that can be drawn from such data. This control over variables in experiments is crucial in the study of subtle forms of prejudice, as we will see in this section. Experimental jury simulation studies can also explain some of the *whys* of these sentencing disparities.

But first, the findings on race from simulation studies have been mixed in terms of whether there is racial discrimination in convictions and sentences. One study[47] found that racial bias influenced sentencing decisions, while another[48] concluded that African American defendants were no more likely than white defendants to be found guilty, and still another[49] found a same-race preference with whites showing bias against blacks and blacks showing bias against whites. However, most previous studies looked at overt or "old-fashioned" racism and only more recent studies have explored subtle manifestations of racial prejudice. When subtle prejudice is taken into account, we find bias with more complicated patterns than what old-fashioned bias would suggest.

Samuel Sommers and Phoebe Ellsworth[50] used an aversive racism framework to examine whether there is white bias against African Americans when race is made salient versus when race is not made salient. They conducted an experiment in which white mock jurors rated various aspects of a defendant's case. Respondents were presented with a trial summary of an interracial battery case. One version had a white defendant and black victim, the other version had a black defendant and a white victim. Half of the versions were "race-salient" (a racial slur was made toward the defendant, either white or black, during an earlier altercation) and half just specified the race of both the defendant and the victim. The defendant and victim were part of the same high school basketball team and the defendant was accused of attacking the victim. One might predict that when race was made obvious (in the race-salient condition) there would be anti-black bias among white jurors. But this prediction comes from an old-fashioned racism perspective – whites feeling fairly comfortable showing overt bias against African Americans. A prediction based on the assumptions of subtle racism, benign bigotry, would suggest that if race were made salient, whites would not feel comfortable showing bias against African Americans because they would be afraid that they would appear racist. If race was merely implied, however, but was not an overtly significant aspect of the study, whites might feel that they could appear as though they were responding to the conditions of the crime, not to the race of the defendant or victim. Study results were consistent with Sommer and Ellsworth's assumptions. White jurors demonstrated a significantly higher conviction rate for the African American defendant in the non-race-salient condition than in the race-salient condition. Also, white jurors were more likely to convict the black defendant than the white defendant; the case against the African American defendant was judged to be stronger than the case against the white defendant; respondents rated the white man's defense as stronger than the African American man's; and jurors recommended a more severe sentence for the African American than the white. In contrast, when race was made salient, the conviction rates for whites and blacks were comparable.[51] Sommers and Ellsworth conclude that the assumption that race-salient trials are most likely to elicit white juror prejudice is incorrect. Instead, when race is salient, white jurors tend to make an effort to appear unbiased toward black defendants. When race is only an underlying factor, white jurors are likely to demonstrate bias. This paradoxical finding may be responsible for the apparent lack of social psychological research on finding racial bias in the courtroom, mentioned at the beginning of this section.

Capital punishment and death qualification

The United States is one of a few countries left in the world that sanction state-sponsored executions. Eighty-eight percent of worldwide executions are carried out by just five countries: China, Iran, Pakistan, Saudi Arabia, and the United States.[52] The US federal government and 38 state governments can execute their citizens. Capital punishment remains controversial for two main reasons. First, many opponents of the death penalty argue that killing, in any form is wrong – if murder is a crime, then the government should not sanction murder under any condition. Second, capital punishment, known as the *ultimate punishment*, is not reversible, thus the risk of convicting and then killing an innocent person is a risk not many people want to take.

With many high profile exonerations having taken place across the United States, in 2000, Illinois Governor George Ryan declared a moratorium on executions in his state. In a press release, the governor stated, "I cannot support a system, which, in its administration, has proven to be so fraught with error and has come so close to the ultimate nightmare, the state's taking of innocent life.

Thirteen people have been found to have been wrongfully convicted." Governor Ryan noted that since the death penalty was reinstated in Illinois in 1977, 12 Death Row inmates have been executed while 13 have been exonerated.[53]

On the other hand, some see the risk of executing the innocent as being analogous to vaccination – i.e. vaccines are necessary to save lives even if occasionally a child dies from an adverse reaction.[54] Proponents of the death penalty argue that capital punishment serves as a deterrent to criminal activity. Obviously, the person executed will not commit future crimes, but does capital punishment deter others from killing? Studies consistently conclude that the death penalty does not affect the rate of violent crimes. Proponents of the death penalty also maintain that murderers are such dangerous people that allowing them to live increases the risk of injury or death to inmates or correctional officers. However, systematically performed studies find that capital murderers (those who have been convicted and are on death row) are no more violent than life-without-parole and parole-eligible inmates.[55]

The death penalty is administered only in a minority of eligible cases, and its determinants often seem inconsistent and arbitrary. One factor accounting for the inconsistency regarding who is actually executed is race – both the race of the victim and the race of the perpetrator. While the percentage of victims of homicide are similar for African Americans (47%) and whites (51%),[56] the death penalty is meted out at a much greater rate to African Americans than to whites, and to those who kill whites compared to those who kill African Americans. Specifically, death sentence rates of black-defendant/white-victim far exceed any other combination of perpetrator and victim.[57]

"Death-qualification"

In most criminal cases in the United States, a jury decides to convict or acquit, while a judge makes sentencing decisions. In capital cases, however, the jury determines both the verdict and whether or not to impose a death sentence. The jury's decision is based on the weighing of aggravating evidence (which could influence jurors to consider the death penalty) or mitigating evidence (which could sway jurors to spare the life of the convicted). When jurors are empanelled to serve on cases in which the death penalty is being sought, during *voir dire* – the process by which judges and attorneys ask potential jurors questions to attempt to uncover any biases – potential jurors are required to answer questions about their attitudes toward capital punishment. Cases involving the death penalty have to have a jury that has been "death-qualified," meaning jurors are willing to consider death as a punishment. Those who strongly oppose capital punishment are explicitly and systematically removed from the jury by the judge, while those in favor of, or at least willing to consider, the death penalty are retained for service. The result of this process is that a "death-qualified" jury is empanelled.

The death-qualification procedure in capital cases is unlike that in any other kind of trial. It is the only situation in which the possible outcome of the case and potential sentencing issues are brought to the attention of the jurors prior to the jury's hearing of the case. This procedure introduces a major source of bias against the defendant in death penalty cases. Potential jurors are required to think in terms of a guilty verdict even before they hear opening arguments. Therefore, another hidden bias produced by the death-qualification process is the juror's *a priori* belief in the possible (and perhaps probable) guilt of the defendant prior to hearing the case. In this way, *guilt*, not *innocence*, is the frame with which jurors on capital cases view the case and testimony. The implication here is that jurors go into a case with the presumption of guilt. This flies in the face of the American legal system's assumption of *innocence until proven guilty*.

Important questions among defense attorneys and social scientists have been, by excluding potential jurors who strongly oppose the death penalty, what kind of jurors are left? Is the death-qualified jury different from a jury made up of those who oppose the death penalty? Phoebe Ellsworth and her colleagues conducted a series of studies that address these questions.[58] They found that death-qualified jurors exhibit more bias against the defendant than juries composed of jurors who have a range of attitudes toward capital punishment. Specifically, death-qualified jurors are more inclined to favor the prosecutor's viewpoint, are more likely to mistrust criminal defendants and their counsel, sympathize more with a punitive approach toward offenders, are more concerned with crime control than with due process, and are more likely to find a defendant guilty.

One of Ellsworth's experiments with jury-eligible adults in the US compared the deliberations and decisions of juries that were death-qualified with juries that included some jurors who were "excludables" (those who strongly oppose the death penalty and therefore would not be eligible to serve on actual capital juries). In contrast to death-qualified juries, juries that included some excludables were more skeptical of witnesses (regardless of whether they were for the defense or prosecution), were more likely to take the deliberation process seriously, and were better at remembering evidence.[59] One reason a death-qualified jury is more likely to impose the death penalty than a jury comprised partly of excludables is that death-qualified jurors are more likely to be swayed by aggravating circumstances and to be less sympathetic to mitigating circumstances.[60]

So the process of death-qualification certainly puts the defendant at a disadvantage by stacking the jury against the defense. In addition to the death-qualification procedure and its impact on each particular case, the process may actually influence jurors' attitudes toward the death penalty. The death-qualification procedure takes place in the presence of all prospective jurors. Psychologist and attorney Craig Haney[61] wanted to see whether or not people are influenced by the *process* of death qualification itself. He constructed two versions of a videotape of a court proceeding. A sample of non-college student adults in the US were shown one of two versions of the tape. In one condition, viewers saw the typical death-qualification procedure in which prospective jurors were asked their opinions of the death penalty and were dismissed from service if they expressed strong opposition to it. In the control condition the death-qualification procedure did not appear. Compared to people in the control condition, those who viewed the death-qualification segment were more convinced of the defendant's guilt, were more likely to believe that the judge thought the defendant was guilty, and were more likely to impose the death penalty if the defendant was convicted. Thus, merely witnessing the death-qualification procedure can have an effect on how jurors judge the defendant.

Again, capital *voir dire* is the only *voir dire* that requires the penalty to be discussed before it is actually relevant to the case at hand. The US Constitution is designed such that there is a presumption of innocence. Guilt has to be proven beyond a reasonable doubt; the defendant is considered innocent until proven guilty. So we err on the side of acquittal. But in capital cases, the focus of jurors' attention is drawn away from the presumption of innocence and toward post-conviction events.[62] These proceedings can literally have life-and-death consequences.

Finally, attitudes about race and attitudes toward capital punishment interact to form the following patterns: Among whites, those who score high on racial prejudice are more likely than others to support capital punishment and are also more likely to support convicting innocent persons than acquitting guilty ones. Thus, racial prejudice is a strong predictor of support for the death penalty.[63] Even though evidence demonstrates that death-qualified jurors are more likely than others to vote for conviction, the US Supreme Court has ignored or dismissed this social science evidence apparently because these empirical studies speak only to cumulative tendencies of juries and not to bias related to specific cases.

Putting it all together

The belief that those who have been accused of a crime are probably guilty is a taken-for-granted assumption rooted, in part, in people's belief that the world is a just place, that good things happen to good people and bad things happen to bad people. The world feels like a more understandable and predictable place if we believe that bad people get locked up and good people remain free. In addition to one's belief in a just world, the idea that some people seem to matter less than others, as we found in the last chapter, is likely a reason for the guilty-of-something belief. Thus, the belief that those accused of a crime are probably guilty especially harms people of color. The research presented in this chapter demonstrates people's proclivity toward assuming that ethnic minorities are associated with crime. Television news crime coverage and reality shows like *Cops* reinforce the link in many people's minds between race and crime. On television, men of color are *overrepresented* as criminal suspects and *under-represented* as victims of crime in comparison to actual crime statistics, and the opposite is true for white representations.[64] Research on attributions reveals the belief that blacks are more naturally criminal than are whites. Whites are more likely to make situational attributions about white criminal suspects ("*I wonder what made that man steal?*") and dispositional attributions about black suspects ("*Some people act like animals*"), suggesting the belief in the proclivity toward and permanence of criminality in black communities.[65] The same behavior of blacks and whites produces wholly different judgments about each group. The fictional equation of blackness with danger is why people, both black and white, are more likely to shoot an unarmed black person than an unarmed white person as demonstrated in the *police officer's dilemma*.[66]

The police officer's dilemma may be a proxy for real life as we have seen in police shootings of unarmed black men.

The cognitive shortcuts described throughout this book that play such a significant role in subtle prejudice can play a serious and even deadly role in criminal investigations. These not-so-innocent short-cuts, along with police investigators' predisposition to presume guilt, over-confidence in their ability to detect innocence and guilt, innocent suspects' naïveté about the criminal justice system, interrogators' impatience with innocent suspects' protests of innocence, and coercive interrogations combine to railroad some innocent suspects.[67] Racial and ethnic bias impacts the frequency of convictions and severity of sentencing. African Americans and Latina/os receive longer sentences than whites with the same criminal history for the same type of offense. Bias occurs along class lines as well, with low-income offenders receiving longer sentences than higher income offenders.[68]

The United States is one of the few countries that practices state-sponsored executions, sharing this distinction with countries such as China, Iran, Pakistan, and Saudi Arabia. The procedure for drawing a "death-qualified" jury adds yet another layer of bias stacked against the defendant. Death-qualified jurors (those who agree to be willing to vote to execute the defendant who has not even been proven guilty yet) tend to be pro-prosecution, more punitive, and simply more likely to find a defendant guilty than are jurors that are not death-qualified.[69] Death-qualified juries are even less likely to take the deliberation process seriously, and are less accurate at remembering evidence than are juries that are not death qualified.[70] Given the proof of bias in every stage of the criminal justice process, capital punishment requires a confidence in one's justice system that is simply unwarranted in the United States.

Finally, regardless of one's political orientation, one's opinion of the death penalty, and one's view of whether or not the world is a just place, few people want an innocent person to go to prison or to the death chamber. In addition, every time an innocent person is convicted, a guilty person goes free to commit more crimes. If we are truly concerned with public safety, minimizing bias and respecting due process should be everyone's goal.

Strategies for change

Several strategies for reducing the operation of racial bias in the criminal justice process address the erroneous belief that criminal suspects must be guilty of something. In addition to strategies affecting people's thought processes and behaviors, like those discussed in other chapters in this book, many of the strategies for racial bias reduction involve the changing of guidelines, policies, and laws, reaching all the way to the US Supreme Court. These strategies, therefore, are less about individual thought processes and behavior change than the strategies outlined in other chapters. In concrete terms, this means that the reader must pressure lawmakers to make structural changes in the United States criminal justice system that are designed to increase fairness.

Saul Kassin[71] makes several suggestions to reduce the likelihood of coercive interrogations, false confessions, and the railroading of innocent suspects. Kassin's suggestions should also help secure meaningful due process whether or not a suspect is innocent or guilty. This first section has to do with reducing bias during the investigative stage of a case and includes Kassin's recommendations, as follows.

Reducing bias during investigations

Suspects should not waive rights

A suspect's right to refuse to speak to investigators without an attorney present is fundamental and extremely important. There are really no circumstances under which individuals should waive this right. As was indicated in the discussion of Saul Kassin's studies, innocence may not set you free.

Lie detection training for law enforcement

Given the dismal performance of law enforcement officers in dis-tinguishing true confessions from false, training for law enforcement might need to focus more on attending to audio, rather than behavioral cues. Recall that raters performed worse at differentiat-ing true from false confessions when they viewed video than when they listened to audio-only recordings.[72]

Videotape all confessions

All interviews and interrogations should be video recorded in their entirety. Great Britain mandated that all sessions be taped in their entirety and a few US states have mandatory video recording requirements. There are several advantages to this: First, the pres-ence of a camera will likely deter some of the more egregious coercive tactics. Second, having a video record will deter frivolous defense claims of coercion where none exist. Third, video record-ings provide an objective and accurate account of all that tran-spired. Questions about whether rights were administered or waived, or whether promises or threats were made, can be resolved. The recording should show both the accused and the interrogators.

Excessive interrogation time

Guidelines should be set regarding the amount of continuous time a suspect can be detained and questioned and still produce a state-ment deemed voluntary. Interviews with confessions that were later found to be false lasted on average 16 hours, much longer than true confessions lasted.

Presentation of false evidence

Currently, in the United States it is legal for police to lie to suspects about DNA evidence or eyewitness testimony that might implicate the suspect. In light of studies showing that the presentation of the false evidence draws confessions from the innocent and the numerous false confession cases in which this tactic was employed, lawmakers should reconsider police presentation of false evidence.

Offers of leniency

Minimization tactics, such as offers of leniency in return for a confession, currently used by police, contribute to false confessions.

Defense strategies to minimize bias against defendants

In addition to changes at the investigation stage of a crime, changes in the jury selection process and in the presentation of jury instructions may make trials more fair.

Making race salient to jurors

Earlier in the chapter I discussed a study conducted by Samuel Sommers and Phoebe Ellsworth[73] on jury decisions in which white jurors read about a case involving either a white or black defendant in an interracial battery case. Half of the versions were made race salient (by explicitly referring to the defendant's race), while the other versions had information about the defendant's race, but did not make race salient. Sommers and Ellsworth found that when race was made salient, jurors did not want to appear racist, so they made similar judgments about the black and white defendant. However, when race was not made obvious, they were much more likely to convict the black than the white defendant. In these times of benign bigotry, whites tend to be cautious and try not to appear biased, however, when race is not an obvious issue and when whites are not concerned about appearing biased, they are more likely to act in a discriminatory manner.

So what is the lesson for actual attorneys with defendants who are African American or are from other marginalized groups?

The implication of the Sommers and Ellsworth study is that by making race salient to the jury, jurors may feel self-conscious about appearing racially biased so they may be on guard against discrimination and therefore be more cautious about jumping to conclusions about an African American defendant. Obviously there are other factors involved in a jury's verdict, but Sommers and Ellsworth's proposition is intriguing.

In 1995, former football star and actor, O.J. Simpson was tried for the killing of his ex-wife and frrend friend. Simpson is African American. During the trial Simpson's attorney, Johnnie Cochran, was accused of playing the "race card," meaning he accused the prosecution and some witnesses of racism. Simpson was found not guilty. The strategy of making race a focus of a trial could backfire, however, if jurors think charges of racial bias are trumped up. Making race the focus in the Simpson trial did not appear to backfire, but nonetheless, it can be a risky strategy.

Jury instructions

Inadmissible evidence and juror instruction

Recall the earlier discussion on jurors' handling of evidence that is provided during a trial but that later becomes inadmissible. The impact of inadmissible evidence on the jury can be lessened if the judge tells the jurors in advance of trial proceedings that they may hear information that will be ruled as inadmissible and that they must disregard that information. This kind of forewarning by the judge allows jurors to muster up cognitive defenses against inadmissible evidence. Forewarning is more effective in having the jury *truly* disregard the information than if the judge only tells the jury *after* they have heard inadmissible evidence. An early warning, along with a later reminder, may permit jurors both to suspend the processing of evidence and to think more critically about information that may later be discounted. Jury instructions that come before the evidence are more effective than instructions that come after the evidence.[74]

The impact of inadmissible evidence can be so powerful that some have even suggested that trials be videotaped without a jury, edited, and then shown to the jury. This suggestion does not seem logistically feasible, but is an intriguing idea.

Judicial instructions prior to verdict

When a judge provides instructions to jurors prior to their rendering a verdict, there is less racial bias than when a judge does not provide instructions.[75]

Discourage early voting in jury deliberation

Judges can discourage juries from early voting. A study by Phoebe Ellsworth[76] found that those juries who *begin* their deliberations by voting spend the rest of the deliberation time defending their original positions and foreclosing on understanding the facts of the case and the laws pertaining to the case. Juries who postponed voting spent more time talking about the relevant issues in the case. Once having arrived at a story or explanation of a sequence of events, many people find it difficult to entertain a different way of interpreting the same events.[77]

Provide clear sentencing guidelines to juries

Because sentence guidelines can be ambiguous and confusing to jurors, there is room for subtle bias in jury deliberation of the appropriate sentence. Benign bigotry often emerges in ambiguous conditions. Jurors can discriminate against minority defendants when sentencing guidelines are ambiguous. Making sentencing guidelines more clear to judges and/or to jurors may reduce bias at this stage of the judicial process.

Policy changes

Make biological evidence testable

For those convicted of a crime for which biological evidence exists, that evidence should be made available for testing. The evidence should be retained throughout the duration of an offender's sentence.[78]

Crime labs should be independent from the police
and district attorney

Crime labs should be independent bodies not under the supervision or organizational structure of law enforcement.[79] There is too much of a temptation for DNA analysts who work for the prosecution to arrive at results consistent with prosecution theories.[80] Also, if a crime laboratory, as in the case of the Houston Police Department Crime Lab, has been found to have made serious mistakes or engaged in misconduct over a period of time, decisions about re-tests for those convicted on biological evidence should not be left to the district attorney's office, which is the usual practice.[81] The decision to re-test biological evidence should be taken out of the hands of the district attorney and should be automatic at the request of the defense, or decided by an independent body.

Revoke or revise the death-qualification procedure

The research on death qualification is conclusive: the procedure creates juries that are stacked against the defendant. Death-qualified juries are more conviction-prone than juries that include those who are excluded from serving because of their opposition to the death penalty.[82] Make lawmakers aware of the research on death qualification.

Abolish capital punishment

All sentences, except for capital ones, are reversible. Given the data presented in this chapter, it is obvious that capital punishment should be abolished in favor of long-term sentences including life in prison without parole, and rehabilitation. This would bring the US in line with similar nations. Even Russia has had a moratorium on state executions since 1996.[83] In fact, the US has become so isolated from comparable nations on this issue, many countries will not extradite their citizens accused of violent crime in the US because the US still has the death penalty.

NOTES

1. Ed Meese interviewed in: Reagan seeks judges with "traditional approach." (1985, October 14). *US news and world report*, 99, 67.
2. *Cited in:* Heyman, J.D., Brass, K., & Perry, B. (2002, September 30). Trouble in Tulia. *People*, 58, 79–81.
3. Drug policy and the criminal justice system. (2001). Retrieved March 20, 2006, from www.sentencingproject.org/pdfs/5047.pdf
4. Davis, A.Y. (2003). *Are prisons obsolete?* New York: Seven Stories Press. Reiman, J. (2007). *The rich get richer and the poor get prison: Ideology, class, and criminal justice.* Boston: Pearson-Allyn & Bacon.
5. See the following documentaries for instances of prosecutors' resistance to accepting exculpatory evidence: Bikel, O. (Producer). (2004). *The Plea* [Frontline]. Arlington, VA: PBS; Roker, A. (Producer). (2004). *Al Roker investigates: Faulty forensics.* [Court TV]. New York: Court TV.
6. Pitts, L., Jr. (2007). Blacks' presumed guilt hits a little too close to home. In P.S. Rothenberg (Ed.), *Race, class, and gender in the United States* (7th edition, pp. 287–288). New York: Worth.
7. *Ibid.*
8. Racial stereotypes influence readers' memories of crime stories, study finds. (2004). *Black issues in higher education*, 21, 16.
9. Robinson, E. (2005, June 28). Runaway racism. Retrieved September 2, 2008, from www.washingtonpost.com/wp-dyn/content/article/2005/06/27/AR200506 2701320.html
10. Cops: McCain worker made up attack story (2008, October 24). Retrieved October 27, 2008, from www.cbsnews.com/stories/2008/10/24/politics/main4544204.shtml
11. Oliver, M.B. (2003). African American men as "criminal and dangerous": Implications of media portrayals of crime on the "criminalization" of African American men. *Journal of African American studies*, 7, 3–18.
12. Henderson-King, E.I., & Nisbett, R.E. (1996). Anti-black prejudice as a function of exposure to the negative behavior of a single black person. *Journal of personality and social psychology*, 71, 654–664.

13. Hewstone, M., Jaspars, J., & Lalljee, M. (1982). Social representations, social attribution and social identity: The intergroup images of "public" and "comprehensive" schoolboys. *European journal of social psychology, 12*, 241–269.
14. Bandele, A. (2000, November). 41 bullets. *Essence, 31*, 137–138, 184, 186, 190.
15. Correll, J., Park, B., Judd, C.M., & Wittenbrink, B. (2002). The police officer's dilemma: Using ethnicity to disambiguate potentially threatening individuals. *Journal of personality and social psychology, 83*, 1314–1329.
16. Oliver, M.B., & Fonash, D. (2002). Race and crime in the news: Whites' identification and misidentification of violent and nonviolent criminal suspects. *Media psychology, 4*, 137–156.
17. Kassin, S.M. (2005). On the psychology of confessions: Does *innocence* put *innocents* at risk? *American psychologist, 60*, 215–228.
18. *Ibid.*, page 217.
19. Kassin, S.M., Meissner, C.A., & Norwick, R.J. (2005). "I'd know a false confession if I saw one": A comparative study of college students and police investigators. *Law and human behavior, 29*, 211–227.
20. Bromwich, M.R. (2006, May 11). Fifth report of the independent investigator for the Houston Police Department Crime Laboratory and Property Room. Retrieved October 16, 2007, from www.hpdlabinvestigation.org/reports/0605 11report.pdf
21. *Ibid.* In addition, William Thompson, professor at University of California at Irvine, made the same observation on the Court TV documentary: Roker, A. (Producer). (2004). *Al Roker investigates: Faulty forensics*. [Court TV]. New York: Court TV.
22. Thompson, *Al Roker Investigates*.
23. Kassin, On the psychology of confessions, page 216.
24. Bond, C.F., Jr., & DePaulo, B.M. (2008). Individual differences in judging deception: accuracy and bias. *Psychological bulletin, 134*, 477–492.
25. Kassin, S.M., & Norwick, R.J. (2004). Why people waive their *Miranda* rights: The power of innocence. *Law and human behavior, 28*, 211–221.
26. Lerner, M.J. (1980). *The belief in a just world: A fundamental delusion*. New York: Plenum.
27. Kassin, On the psychology of confessions.
28. *Ibid.*, page 219.
29. Kassin, S.M., Goldstein, C.C., & Savitsky, K. (2003). Behavioral confirmation in the interrogation room: On the dangers of presuming guilt. *Law and human behavior, 27*, 187–203.
30. Kassin, S.M., & Kiechel, K.L. (1996). The social psychology of false confessions: Compliance, internalization, and confabulation. *Psychological science, 7*, 125–128.

31. Horselenberg, R., Merckelbach, H., & Josephs, S. (2003). Individual differences and false confessions: A conceptual replication of Kassin and Kiechel (1996). *Psychology, crime, and law, 9*, 1–8.
32. Redlich, A.D. & Goodman, G.S. (2003). Taking responsibility for an act not committed: The influence of age and suggestibility. *Law and human behavior, 27*, 141–156.
33. Levine, M., Wallach, L., & Levine, D. (2007). *Psychological problems, social issues, and law* (2nd edition). Boston: Pearson.
34. Kassin, On the psychology of confessions, page 224.
35. For a review, see page 195 in: Bartol, C.R., & Bartol, A.M. (2004). *Psychology and the law: Theory, research, and application.* Belmont, CA: Thomson-Wadsworth.
36. Sommers, S.R., & Kassin, S.M. (2001). On the many impacts of inadmissible testimony: Selective compliance, need for cognition, and the overcorrection bias. *Personality and social psychology bulletin, 27*, 1368–1377.
37. Hodson, G., Hooper, H., Dovidio, J.F., & Gaertner, S.L. (2005). Aversive racism in Britain: The use of inadmissible evidence in legal decisions. *European journal of social psychology, 35*, 437–448.
38. Johnson, J.D., Whitestone, E., Jackson, L.A., & Gatto, L. (1995). Justice is still not colorblind: Differential racial effects of exposure to inadmissible evidence. *Personality and social psychology bulletin, 21*, 893–898.
39. For a discussion on differences in sentencing, see: Coyle, M. (n.d.). Race and class penalties in crack cocaine sentencing. Retrieved March 20, 2006, from www.sentencingproject.org/pdfs/5077.pdf
40. Mustard, D.B. (2001). Racial, ethnic, and gender disparities in sentencing: Evidence from the US federal courts. *The journal of law and economics, 44*, 285–314.
41. *Ibid.* Mustard also found that women receive shorter sentences than do men.
42. Kansal, T. (2005, January). Racial disparity in sentencing: A review of the literature. *The sentencing project.* Retrieved November 13, 2007, from www.sentencingproject.org/pdfs/disparity.pdf
43. See interview of David Jacobs in: Conant, E. (2007, August 1). Study finds racial disparity in executions. *Newsweek.* Retrieved August 7, 2007, from www.fadp.org/news/msnbc-20070801/
44. For a review, see page 145 in: Reiman, *The rich get richer and the poor get prison.*
45. Bridges, G.S., & Steen, S. (1998). Racial disparities in official assessments of juvenile offenders: Attributional stereotypes as mediating mechanisms. *American sociological review, 63*, 554–570.
46. Jacobs in: Conant, Study finds racial disparity in executions.

47. Sweeney, L.T., & Haney, C. (1992). The influence of race on sentencing: A meta-analytic review of experimental studies. *Behavioral sciences and the law, 10,* 179–195.

48. Mazzella, R., & Feingold, A. (1994). The effects of physical attractiveness, race, socioeconomic status, and gender of defendants and victims on judgments of mock jurors: A meta-analysis. *Journal of applied social psychology, 24,* 1315–1344.

49. Mitchell, T.L., Haw, R.M., Pfeifer, J.E., & Meissner, C.A. (2005). Racial bias in mock juror decision-making: A meta-analytic review of defendant treatment. *Law and human behavior, 29,* 621–637.

50. Sommers, S.R., & Ellsworth, P.C., (2001). White juror bias: An investigation of prejudice against black defendants in the American courtroom. *Psychology, public policy, and law, 7,* 201–229.

51. When Sommers and Ellsworth conducted a similar study with African American mock jurors, they found that the jurors tended to be more lenient toward African American defendants in both race-salient and non-race-salient conditions. See: Sommers, S.R., & Ellsworth, P.C., (2000). Race in the courtroom: Perceptions of guilt and dispositional attributions. *Personality and social psychology bulletin, 26,* 1367–1379.

52. Amnesty International. (2008, April 15). *Secrecy surrounds death penalty.* Retrieved November 17, 2008, from www.amnesty.org/en/news-and-updates/report/secrecy-surrounds-death-penalty-20080415

53. Governor Ryan declares moratorium on executions, will appoint commission to review capital punishment system (2000, January 31). Retrieved June 3, 2006, from www.illinois.gov/PressReleases/PrintPressRelease.cfm?SubjectID=3&Rec Num=359

54. Greene, E., Heilbrun, K., Fortune, W.H., & Nietzel, M.T. (2007). *Wrightsman's psychology and the legal system* (6th edition). Belmont, CA: Thomson.

55. See, for instance: Cunningham, M.D., Reidy, T.J., & Sorensen, J.R. (2005). Is death row obsolete? A decade of mainstreaming death-sentenced inmates in Missouri. *Behavioral sciences and the law, 23,* 307–320. Also see: Edens, J.F., Buffington-Vollum, J.K., Keilen, A., Roskamp, P., & Anthony, C. (2005). Predictions of future dangerousness in capital murder trials: Is it time to "disinvent the wheel?" *Law and human behavior, 29,* 55–86.

56. US Department of Justice, Office of Justice Programs, Bureau of Justice Statistics. (n.d.). Racial differences exist, with blacks disproportionately represented among homicide victims and offenders. Retrieved August 9, 2006, from www.ojp.usdoj.gov/bjs/homicide/race.htm

57. Blume, J., Eisenberg, T., & Wells, M.T. (2004). Explaining death row's population and racial composition. *Journal of empirical legal studies, 1,* 165–207.

58. Fitzgerald, R., & Ellsworth, P.C. (1984). Due process vs. crime control: Death qualification and jury attitudes. *Law and human behavior*, 8, 31–51; Cowan, C.L., Thompson, W.C., & Ellsworth, P.C. (1984). The effects of death qualification on jurors' predisposition to convict and on the quality of deliberation. *Law and human behavior*, 8, 53–79. See also: Thompson, W.C., Cowan, C.L., Ellsworth, P.C., & Harrington, J.C. (1984). Death penalty attitudes and conviction proneness: The translation of attitudes into verdicts. *Law and human behavior*, 8, 95–113.
59. Cowan *et al.* The effects of death qualification on jurors' predisposition.
60. Butler, B.M., & Moran, G. (2002). The role of death qualification in venirepersons' evaluations of aggravating and mitigating circumstances in capital trials. *Law and human behavior*, 26, 175–184.
61. Haney, C. (1984). On the selection of capital juries: The biasing effects of the death-qualification process. *Law and human behavior*, 8, 121–132.
62. Haney, C. (1984). Examining death qualification: Further analysis of the process effect. *Law and human behavior*, 8, 133–151.
63. Young, R.L. (2004). Guilty until proven innocent: Conviction orientation, racial attitudes, and support for capital punishment. *Deviant behavior*, 25, 151–167.
64. Oliver, African American men as "criminal and dangerous."
65. *Ibid.*
66. Correll *et al.* The police officer's dilemma.
67. Kassin, On the psychology of confessions.
68. Kansal, Racial disparity in sentencing.
69. Fitzgerald & Ellsworth, Due process vs. crime control. Cowan *et al.* The effects of death qualification on jurors' predisposition to convict and on the quality of deliberation. See also: Thompson *et al.* Death penalty attitudes and conviction proneness.
70. Cowan *et al.* The effects of death qualification on jurors' predisposition.
71. Kassin, On the psychology of confessions; Kassin, S.M., & Gudjonsson, G.H. (2005). True crimes, false confessions: Why do innocent people confess to crimes they did not commit? *Scientific American mind*, 16, 24–31.
72. Kassin *et al.* "I'd know a false confession if I saw one".
73. Sommers & Ellsworth, White juror bias.
74. For a discussion, see: Greene *et al.* *Wrightsman's psychology and the legal system*.
75. Mitchell *et al.* Racial bias in mock juror decision-making.
76. Ellsworth, P.C. (1989). Are twelve heads better than one? *Law and contemporary problems*, 52, 205–224.
77. Griffin, D., Dunning, D., & Ross, L. (1990). The role of construal processes in overconfident predictions about the self and others. *Journal*

of personality and social psychology, 59, 1128–1139. Also cited in: Ellsworth, P.C. (1989). Are twelve heads better than one? *Law and contemporary problems, 52*, 205–224.

78. Huff, C.R. (2002). Wrongful conviction and public policy: The American Society of Criminology 2001 Presidential Address. *Criminology, 40*, 1–18.

79. Thompson, in *Al Roker investigates*.

80. Bromwich, Fifth report of the independent investigator for the Houston Police Department Crime Laboratory and Property Room; Thompson, in Roker, *Al Roker investigates*.

81. David Dow, from the Texas Innocence Network, made a similar point on Court TV documentary: Roker, *Al Roker Investigates*.

82. Haney, On the selection of capital juries.

83. See page A18 in: Murphy, K. (2006, May 18). Russia's bar on the death penalty questioned. *Los Angeles times*, p. A18.

THREE

"Feminists are man-haters": Backlash myth-making

The feminist agenda is not about equal rights for women. It is about a socialist, anti-family political movement that encourages women to leave their husbands, kill their children, practice witchcraft, destroy capitalism, and become lesbians.

Reverend Pat Robertson[1]

Feminism. The very word evokes strong feelings in most people. Strong feelings and, too often, a world of misconceptions. The real meaning of feminism and what it actually means to call oneself a feminist has become mired in and obscured by an array of prejudices, preconceptions, and mechanisms that serve to maintain the existing distribution of power and inequality. Structured inequality based on gender – much like inequalities based on race, ethnicity or sexual identity – has been an established way of doing things for centuries. For some, the question begins and ends with women's right to vote. For others, a belief exists that gender inequality is, in large part, a thing of the past, and that women now enjoy social and economic equality in terms of access to resources and prestige. Still others believe that feminism is a somewhat antique effort, a passing fad the necessity of which has been satisfied by progress. In any event, many women and many more men resist identifying themselves as feminists. A number of factors are at work here, but, in the final analysis, it amounts to this: feminists are thought to be man-haters.

As we try to separate fact from fiction and reason from prejudice, let's first examine what is really at stake when we talk about feminism. At its core, feminism is the belief in certain fundamental principles of equality. In a society in which women and men have traditionally received unequal treatment, feminism seems a reasonable and long-overdue corrective to the historical lack of access women continue to experience. *Merriam-Webster* defines feminism as: (1) the theory of the political, economic, and social equality of the sexes; and (2) organized activity on behalf of women's rights and interests.[2] The *Encyclopedia Britannica* defines it as: the belief in the social, economic, and political equality of the sexes.[3] And bell hooks[4] defines feminism as "a movement to end sexism, sexist exploitation, and oppression." On the face of it, it would seem that all women, and most men, would identify with the goals of feminism. In spite of this democratic imperative, in spite of the widely agreed-upon philosophical desire for guarantees of equality, today, few women call themselves feminists. Even in settings in which we might expect to find fairly enlightened thinkers, and among young people and students, survey research shows that the percentage of respondents who actually call themselves feminists is strikingly small. In surveys of university women, the percentage who identify as feminists ranges from 8%[5] to 44%[6] depending on the demographic makeup of the students. What accounts for these low numbers? When you consider the misconceptions we carry around with us because of the way in which feminism is portrayed in popular culture and politics, it is not surprising that relatively few women call themselves feminists. Anti-feminists blame feminists for a variety of social problems: for young men entering college at a lower rate than that of young women;[7] for the decline in "manliness" in American culture;[8] and even for the attacks of September 11, 2001.[9] Surveys find that women hold feminist beliefs but are hesitant to describe themselves as feminists because they know that feminism is viewed by some as anti-male.[10]

If most people – men and women – endorse the fundamental principles of feminism, it should stand to reason that most people would actually support feminism. Instead, we find that many people, including women themselves, resist applying this label. In fact, rather than evoking the ideals of equality, the word "feminist" is linked in people's minds with distasteful concepts such as man-hating. We are left with a significant question then: How can it be that most people support the principles of feminism but run from the word itself? Part of the answer lies in understanding the ways that distortions, stereotypes, and prejudices accumulate and engulf a term or concept like feminism. In this case, the insights of social psychology aid our inquiry. We are able to explore, for example, whether there is any truth to the claim that feminists hate men. Using the tools of social psychology, we can seek to determine whether there is any truth to this claim, and we can examine feminists' attitudes in a systematic and objective way. We can separate reality from fantasy and fear, and we can begin to understand the underlying sexism that produces such damaging stereotypes. This chapter examines the myth that feminists dislike men, and the deployment by anti-feminists of this myth. The empirical literature regarding women's attitudes toward men is analyzed for evidence of man-hating, and the cultural function of the man-hating myth is analyzed as well.

This chapter is broken into four broad parts, beginning with a section that discusses stereotypes about feminists, including individuals' beliefs about feminists, and stereotypes that exist in popular culture and politics. Second, a direct examination of the man-hater myth is undertaken by analyzing feminists' actual attitudes about men.

Third, explanations for the persistence of this myth are explored. Referring back to the definitions of feminism, feminists desire equality for women. Why is this desire so threatening to anti-feminists? And, finally, strategies for reducing the man-hater myth are suggested.

Stereotypes about feminists and beliefs about feminism

I have long thought that if high-school boys had invited homely girls to the prom we might have been spared the feminist movement.

Kate O'Beirne[11]

The anti-"feminist agenda"

Feminists are described as "angry women"[12] with "persecution fantasies,"[13] who "shame men"[14] and are "chronically dissatisfied."[15] The conservative talk show host and self-proclaimed anti-feminist Rush Limbaugh has coined and popularized his description of feminists and, in conservative popular media, made it legendary: "Feminism was established so as to allow unattractive women easier access to the mainstream of society."[16] In his book, Manliness, Harvey Mansfield describes feminists as "anti-male" and states that feminists are "none too pleased with men and not shy about letting them know it."[17] In 2005, when the Pentagon attempted to establish the Office of the Victim Advocate to handle hundreds of claims of sexual assault by men in the military against women soldiers, Elaine Donnelly,[18] the president of the Center for Military Readiness, described the effort as establishing an "Office of Male-Bashing." The creation of an office to investigate rape and harassment, and to support victims, was predicted to "create a new job market for 'women's studies' graduates schooled in man-hating ideology."[19]

Why is it that feminists supposedly hate men, according to anti-feminists? In her book, *Women who Make the World Worse: How their Radical Feminist Assault is Ruining our Schools, Families, Military, and Sports*, conservative commentator Kate O'Beirne[20] suggests that feminists are man-haters either because of their upbringing or because they have an ax to grind – they have, as individuals, bad experiences with men and this makes them become feminists who dislike men. In an article entitled "Male Bashing," Judy Markey[21] answers the question of why women (not feminists per se) bash men: "Is it because taking on an entire gender is less risky than examining what's lacking in our *personal* intimate relationship?"[22] Feminists are constructed as scorned women. I argue in this chapter that anti-feminists have a conscious agenda for demonizing feminists, not because feminism is outlandish, but because feminist goals resonate with people. Anti-feminists are left with unfounded and illogical name-calling.

Anatomy of the anti-feminist

Who is likely to hold anti-feminist beliefs? First, people, especially men, who have authoritarian personalities, tend to dislike feminism. *Authoritarianism* is marked by rigid adherence to conventional values and categorical (stereotypical) thinking. Authoritarians are those who are likely to demonstrate unquestioning obedience to authority. Authoritarians believe that feminists have fundamentally different values than they have.[23] For similar reasons, political conservatives are more likely to harbor negative attitudes toward feminism than are liberals.[24]

Dana Truman and her colleagues[25] examined the relationship between specific aspects of masculine ideology, including attitudes toward feminism, and attitudes about rape, in male college students. Truman found that the men's attitudes toward feminism were the most consistent predictor of attitudes that support date rape. In other words, men who rejected the goals of feminism were also more likely to believe that, "*Being roughed up is sexually stimulating to many women*" and "*When women go out on dates bra-less and wearing short skirts and tight tops, they are just asking for trouble.*" Truman concludes that less favorable views about feminism were linked to the belief that women should be subordinate to men. In a similar vein, another study[26] examined various factors that might relate to rape callousness in mostly white, US college students. Rape callousness taps into one's (false) belief in rape myths such as "*Many women have an unconscious wish to be raped,*" and "*The reason most rapists commit rape is for sex.*" The relationship between several variables that one might assume would be related to rape callousness, including sexual socialization, sexual experience, political liberalism, male dominance, and attitudes toward feminism, was examined.[27] What was the strongest predictor of rape callousness? *Male dominance*, that is, the belief that women should be subordinate to men, and *attitudes toward feminism*. These two factors were stronger predictors than any of the other measures. These two studies suggest that men (and women) who are socialized to believe that women are subordinate to men are more likely to believe that rape is justifiable.

Feminism yes, feminist label no: Individuals' attitudes about feminism and feminists

One might assume that the image of feminists portrayed in the mass media reflects individuals' beliefs about feminists – feminists are portrayed negatively in the media because individuals have negative feelings about them. Instead, there is something of a disjuncture between what popular culture and mass media portray about feminists and what people actually think. Sure, there are negative stereotypes about feminists, but individuals tend to have more positive feelings toward feminism than is reflected in mass media.

The literature on people's beliefs about feminists presents a more complicated picture than what is presented in mass media and by anti-feminists.

Let us look at some surveys of people's attitudes toward feminists. One study of Canadian college students found that feminists were evaluated more positively than negatively when students were asked to rate feminists on a 0 to 100 "feeling thermometer," ranging from extremely unfavorable to extremely favorable. Feminists were rated between 75 and 80, with women rating feminists somewhat higher than did men.[28] In another study,[29] white women at an all-women's Catholic college were asked about their assumptions regarding feminists and the degree to which they identified themselves as feminists. Students' attitudes toward feminism were mixed. Many of the women surveyed possessed positive attitudes such as the belief that feminists are confident and willing to take a stand, while others believed that feminists go overboard in their activism, and can be aggressive and manly. An interesting finding from this study was that the women sampled tended to agree with the principles of feminism but were hesitant to call themselves feminists because of the bad rap feminism gets, including allegations of man-hating. Another study[30] also produced mixed responses when college students at two universities in Ohio were asked to evaluate feminists on the basis of 54 adjectives. Overall, characterizations of feminists were neutral to positive. These characterizations included: independent, career-minded, activist-oriented, knowledgeable, logical, and intelligent. Also, feminists were thought to be heterosexual, rather than lesbian, which contradicts another popular stereotype that feminists are lesbians (and that lesbians are feminists). The negative characterizations of feminists tended to consist of descriptions commonly attributed to men, including descriptions such as aggressive and dominant. This suggests that feminists are believed to violate traditional gender roles.

One study found that women's self-identification as feminists can be influenced by the positive or negative stereotypes about feminism they are exposed to. In one experiment[31] mostly white American undergraduate women read paragraphs about feminists containing either positive stereotypes (e.g. *intelligent, confident*), negative stereotypes (e.g. *stubborn, anti-male*), or neither. The students were later asked whether they were feminists. Those women who were exposed to positive stereotypes about feminists were twice as likely to identify as feminists as those in the negative and control conditions. The fact that the women in the negative stereotype and control conditions were equally unlikely to self-identify as feminists suggests that the negative stereotypes did not provide participants with any new stereotypic information beyond what the control group had. Negative stereotypes about feminists are so prevalent that further exposure to them may not be necessary for women to avoid identifying themselves as feminists.

Most women endorse feminist principles

The mass media's power to influence is demonstrated in the disconnect between women's views and women's willingness to call themselves feminists. As I said above, among college students, between 8% and 44% of women identify as feminists. A study with a large national sample of non-college students found that 29% of women and 12% of men self-identify as feminists.[32] However, most women endorse feminist principles. For instance, one study of mostly white American women who were college students found that of the women who did not consider themselves feminists, 81% agreed with some or all of the goals of the feminist movement.[33] What prevents women from embracing the feminist label? As discussed above, women are hesitant to call themselves feminists because of the success of the anti-feminist agenda in popular media. There are also other reasons that cause women to shy away from the term "feminist" even though they share the ideals of feminism.

The threat of activism

One barrier to identifying as a feminist has to do with how feminist activism is viewed. Being in favor of gender equality, just like being in favor of most kinds of equality, is the norm. As I discussed in the Introduction to this book, unlike half a century ago, today there is an assumption that people are not (overtly) sexist. Apparently, what differentiates those who do and those who do not identify as feminists is activism. Feminists are more likely to believe in collective action (political activism, community organizing) as a remedy to gender inequality.[34] African American women and men who prefer the label *feminist* to *pro-feminist, anti-sexist,* or *womanist,* are more likely to be activists.[35] Israeli-Palestinian and Israeli-Jewish women's studies graduates who did not identify as feminists believed that feminists are more activist-oriented than they felt comfortable with.[36] Many who acknowledge the prejudice of the past, and who favor equality presently, do not admit that inequality and prejudices persists. A person who is an activist, in this case a feminist, is saying there is still a problem with gender inequality. This challenges those people who no longer think gender inequality is a problem and who resent those working on behalf of women's rights. Sarah Riley,[37] who conducted interviews with Scottish professional men in the fields of accounting, architecture, and law, found this disconnect between feminist values and feminists. The men were resentful of feminists while purporting adherence to feminist principles. Their sentiments imply that although today people should and do believe in gender equality, feminists are trouble makers who create conflict where there shouldn't be any.

Feminism as a white women's movement

Another barrier to identifying as a feminist is that the US women's movement has been thought by women of color to be a white women's movement of white women's concerns. Some black feminist women and men have shied away from the feminist label out of concern for appearing too "white."[38] Women of color are less likely to embrace the feminist label than white women. For instance, one study[39] found that 8% of African American women, 12% of Asian American women, and 19% of Latinas identified as feminists. The same study found that 33% of white women identified as feminists. Issues such as abortion rights, that have been emphasized by the US women's movement, are more relevant to white middle-class women, whereas issues such as forced sterilization have been a concern for poor women.[40] Likewise, empirical research in the social sciences has focused on surveys developed with white women as respondents. When surveys include women of color as respondents, their numbers are often too few to analyze meaningfully.

In her examination, Evelyn Simien[41] found that both black women and men recognized that black women are discriminated against and that race and gender discrimination are linked. Black men were equally likely and, in some cases, more likely, than were black women, to support black feminism, with one exception. When respondents were asked whether or not they agreed with the statement: "*Black women have suffered from both sexism within the black movement and racism within the women's movement,*" men were less likely than women to agree with this statement. Simien suggests that in identifying with black women as a marginalized group, black men are willing to support the interests of black women, as long as they do not jeopardize the movement for black civil rights.

Attitudes of women who are feminists

How are women who identify as feminists different from those who are not feminists? First, do feminists differ demographically from non-feminists? In large-scale national studies in the United States, feminists are more likely to be white,[42] although, as we saw from the discussion above, this might have more to do with women of color trying to avoid the term "feminist" than disavowing the sentiments of feminism. More women than men identify as feminists[43] and feminists tend to have more formal education,[44] and tend to live in cities rather than in rural areas.[45] One of the most powerful factors differentiating feminists from non-feminists is conservatism – non-feminists are more likely to have conservative political beliefs than feminists.[46] Feminists and non-feminists can also be distinguished by their beliefs about the link between feminism and lesbianism. Non-feminists are more likely than feminists to believe that feminists are lesbians.[47]

Not surprisingly, feminists and non-feminists tend to have different gender-role orientations and attitudes about gender roles. Gender-role orientation is the degree to which you believe you adhere to feminine (e.g. sensitive, nurturing) and masculine (e.g. assertive, rational) stereotypes. Masculine-stereotyped men are less likely to identify as feminists than are men who are feminine-stereotyped or androgynous (possessing both feminine- and masculine-stereotype characteristics). Men who are not feminists see feminism as incompatible with masculinity. Feminine women are hesitant to identify as feminists. They perceive feminists as non-traditional in terms of gender roles.[48] American Latina/os tend to be less egalitarian in terms of gender roles than whites or African Americans, and therefore are less likely to identify as feminists.[49] In terms of gender-role attitudes, feminists have been found to be more consistent in their gender-related attitudes than non-feminists. For instance, non-feminists may support egalitarianism in the labor market and political arena, but may be reluctant to challenge existing norms concerning interpersonal relationships with men.[50] Feminists are also less likely to believe that gender differences are inborn and biological and more likely to believe that differences are due to socialization.[51]

Another feature distinguishing feminists from non-feminists is feminists' belief in *systemic* gender inequality, and then, as an extension, their belief that something should be done about it (activism). Feminists tend to have broad, societal explanations for gender inequality.[52] Also, feminists, compared to non-feminists, are much more likely to believe in collective action as a method of reducing gender inequality.[53] For instance, Alyssa Zucker examined the differences between feminists and those who believe in the tenets of feminism but do not identify as feminists – what Zucker referred to as *egalitarians*. A significant difference between feminists and egalitarians was that feminists were more likely to be activists than were egalitarians. Zucker's research suggests that perhaps some women shy away from calling themselves feminists because they are not ready to be, or are reluctant to become, activists.

Is feminism good for women?

Is a feminist identity good for women's psychological well-being? Kendra J. Saunders and Susan Kashubeck-West[54] addressed this question in a study designed to explore the relationship between feminist identity development, gender-role orientation, and psychological well-being. Psychological well-being was assessed using surveys measuring autonomy, mastery of one's environment, personal growth, relations with others, and self-acceptance. Survey participants included an ethnically and socioeconomically diverse group of women including college students, faculty, and staff. Saunders and Kashubeck-West found that those who identified as feminists had higher levels of psychological well-being than did non-feminists. This study is correlational, meaning that it is unclear whether feminism contributes positively to women's psychological well-being, or whether women who are psychologically well-off are more likely to become feminists. The findings from these studies are intriguing nonetheless.

Laurie Rudman and Julie Phelan[55] directly tested the assumption that feminism conflicts with heterosexual romantic relationships, as some anti-feminists suggest. In two studies, one with a mostly white US college sample and the other with mostly white US residents, Rudman and Phelan examined relationship health (e.g. stability, sexual satisfaction, etc.) and feminism of romantic partner. First, contrary to stereotypes about feminists, feminist women were more likely to be in a heterosexual romantic relationship than non-feminist women. Women who thought their partners were feminists reported better relationship quality, equality, and stability than those women who did not believe their partners were feminists. Men were found to have better relationship stability and sexual satisfaction if they believed their partners were feminists than if they did not believe their partners were feminists. These findings stand in stark contrast to anti-feminist stereotypes asserting that feminist women are "chronically dissatisfied"[56] as set forth by Kate O'Beirne in her book, Women who Make the World Worse.

Do feminists dislike men? What is the evidence?

So now let us address the common belief that feminists are man-haters. While there are plenty of examples in the mass media and popular culture supposedly illustrating feminists' attitudes toward men, there is a minuscule amount of empirical studies on the subject.

In addition to my own empirical study that I will describe shortly, Anthony Iazzo's 1983 study is the only study I know of that links self-identified feminists with positive and negative attitudes toward men. Iazzo[57] developed the Attitudes Toward Men scale as a complement to the litany of studies on men's attitudes toward women. In his study in which the scale debuted, Iazzo measured the degree to which women agreed with 32 statements regarding men that included the following topics: Marriage/Parenthood (e.g. "Men consider marriage a trap"), Sexuality (e.g. "A man cannot get enough sex"),

Work (e.g. "A man's job is the most important thing in his life"), and *Physical/Personality Attributes* (e.g. "An athletic man is to be admired"). Women expressed their agreement on a 1 to 4 scale with 1 representing *Agree Strongly* (most negative attitude) and 4 representing *Disagree Strongly* (most positive). A score of 80 would indicate a neutral attitude toward men.

The "control group" sample was 104 mostly white women recruited from a university, department stores, and other places of business. They were compared with battered wives, rape victims, lesbians, and feminists from a local chapter of the National Organization for Women. The control group mean score was 89.93, above the neutral midpoint of 80.00, suggesting slightly positive attitudes toward men. The average score of feminists was 79.54, not statistically distinguishable from the 80.00 midpoint, suggesting neutral attitudes toward men. So feminists did not have negative attitudes toward men. What about lesbians, a category that is often conflated with feminists? Lesbians scored, on average, 70.97, so somewhat lower than neutral but hardly a score indicative of man-hating. Further inspection of the statements that make up the Attitudes Toward Men survey may shed light on why lesbians scored lower than both feminists and the "control group" of women. Some of the statements may not be relevant to lesbians. For instance, some of the items are: "*Male sex organs are attractive*" and "*The male body is visually unappealing,*" "*The sight of a penis is repulsive.*" These are questions from the Sexuality subscale. It would have been interesting to have analyzed how feminists and lesbians scored on each separate subscale. For instance, perhaps lesbians had relatively "anti-male" attitudes on the 7 items that made up the Sexuality scale because they do not find men's body parts attractive. Conversely, their scores on the other subscales could have been neutral or positive. The limitation Iazzo's survey used to measure attitudes toward men is that statements might be irrelevant to lesbians because the statements assume that women have had intimate relationships with men.

With British college students, John Maltby and Liza Day[58] examined various psychological characteristics as they correlate with attitudes toward women and men. For women, a feminine-stereotyped gender-role orientation – the degree to which people see themselves in terms of feminine stereotypes – was found to be correlated with negative attitudes toward men. In other words, the more women saw themselves as feminine, the less they liked men. While Maltby and Day's study did not measure *feminists'* attitudes toward men, their results imply that perhaps it is *non*-feminists who do not like men because feminists tend to have relatively more masculine-stereotyped and androgynous gender-role orientations than do non-feminists. Another way to put it is that, in this study, women with traditional gender-role orientations (who tend to be non-feminists) had more negative attitudes toward men than did women with non-traditional gender-role orientations (who are more likely to be feminists). Another study[59] with an ethnically diverse sample of women university students found that those women who perceived large value and belief differences between women and men tended to like men less than did those women who did not perceive large value and belief differences. Again, this study did not examine feminists' attitudes per se; however we can extrapolate from the data. Other studies have found that feminists tend to think women and men are not very different,[60] whereas non-feminists are more likely to think that women and men are fundamentally different.[61] Therefore, perhaps non-feminists, who see women and men as fundamentally different, have more negative attitudes toward men than do feminists.

Ambivalence toward men: Two aspects of attitudes toward men

The most recent method of measuring attitudes toward men has been the Ambivalence toward Men Inventory, developed by Peter

Glick and Susan Fiske.[62] Their work found that there are two aspects of women's (and to a somewhat lesser extent men's) attitudes toward men. *Hostility toward men* represents overtly negative attitudes toward men. It characterizes men as inferior in ways that are safe to criticize, such as men are babies when they are sick. *Hostility toward men* also taps into resentment about men's power relative to women, men's aggressiveness, cultural attitudes that portray men as superior, and the way men exert control within heterosexual intimate relationships. Individuals with high hostility toward men scores tend to agree with statements such as, "*When men act to 'help' women, they are often trying to prove they are better than women,*" and "*Most men pay lip service to equality for women, but can't handle having a woman as an equal.*" The second aspect of attitudes toward men is *benevolence toward men*. *Benevolence toward men* represents overtly positive or affectionate attitudes toward men. It is a set of beliefs that includes the idea that just as women are dependent on men, so too are men dependent on women. *Benevolence toward men* suggests that a woman's role is to take care of a man, but only in the domestic context. Experiencing subjectively positive feelings of affectionate protectiveness, admiration, and connection with men in intimate relationships represents benevolence toward men. Those who score high on benevolence toward men agree with statements such as, "*Women are incomplete without men,*" and "*Even if both members of a couple work, the woman ought to be more attentive to taking care of her man at home.*"

Attitudes of hostility and benevolence toward men are correlated with other kinds of attitudes. For instance, *benevolence toward men* is correlated with sexist attitudes toward women. So those who believe that men should protect women, and that women should take care of men at home, also tend to believe that women *need* protection because they are weaker than men. Interestingly, women's *hostility toward men* and *benevolence toward men* scores correlate, indicating that some women simultaneously hold beliefs that actively support and justify male dominance (*benevolence toward men*) at the same time as they resent the consequences of this dominance (*hostility toward men*). So a question relevant to this chapter is, which women are resentful? Feminists or non-feminists? Glick and Fiske speculate that the greater the dependence a woman has on men, the more she is likely to experience both benevolence and hostility toward men; the former because of her recognition of her investment in men and the latter because of resentment over her dependence.

While Glick and Fiske do not directly answer the question of where feminists fall in terms of their benevolent or hostile attitudes toward men, they do explore the relationship between gender inequality and *hostility toward men* and *benevolence toward men*, which has implications for feminism and attitudes toward men. In a massive study across sixteen nations, Glick and Fiske,[63] along with several colleagues around the world, used translated versions of the Ambivalence toward Men Inventory (AMI) to investigate attitudes toward men. They gathered individual responses to the AMI as well as a measure of attitudes toward women. In addition, they utilized two United Nations indices of gender inequality: The Gender Empowerment Measure, which is a measure of women's representation in powerful occupational roles and government; and the Gender Development Index, which measures how women fare on development measures such as life expectancy, literacy rates, schooling, and standard of living.

Glick and Fiske found that, in most nations, hostility toward men was higher among women than among men. *Hostility toward men* scores correlated with the national measures of gender inequality. Specifically, hostility toward men was higher in traditional than in egalitarian nations. Also, benevolence toward men was higher in traditional than in egalitarian nations. Glick and Fiske reason that women in traditional nations may be more resentful toward men for what they view as abuses of power, but that this resentment is not necessarily a challenge to gender hierarchy because it coexists with benevolent beliefs about men's roles as protectors and providers. The more hostile men are toward women, the more women resent and show hostility toward men. Heightened resentment of men's hostility may explain why women's *hostility toward men* scores increasingly outstrip men's in more traditional cultures.

It is worth noting that there were many more gender similarities than differences across nations – women and men in the sixteen nations tended to have similar attitudes toward women and men. In terms of addressing the myth of feminists and man-haters, Glick and Fiske's study on attitudes toward men imply that man-hating is linked more to *anti*-feminism and gender *in*equality, than it is to feminism and gender equality.

Anthony Iazzo's study, described earlier, is the only study available that measured self-identified feminists' attitudes toward men, although only 28 feminists were included in his study. He found that feminists' attitudes toward men were neutral and not significantly different from his "control" group of women. While the Ambivalence toward Men Inventory is widely used, it had not been used with feminists until my colleagues, Melinda Kanner and Nisreen Elsayegh, and I[64] conducted a study that examined feminists' and non-feminists' attitudes toward men. We surveyed an ethnically diverse sample of 488 university women and men and asked them to respond to statements about gender roles including the items from the Attitudes toward Men Inventory. Students were also asked whether or not they are feminists. Only 14% of the sample of women and men identified as feminists, which is consistent with an ethnically diverse sample. Contrary to popular stereotypes, self-identified feminists had lower levels of hostility toward men than non-feminists. Interestingly, women overall did tend to have higher levels of hostility toward men than did men, but again, the hostility was not among the feminists. Feminists also tended to have lower levels of *benevolence toward men*. Low levels of *benevolence toward men* does not mean one has malevolence toward men, it just means that the respondent does not agree with traditional gender roles – for instance that women should take care of men in the home, and men should be the main wage earners. Thus, based on our study results, it appears that feminists, compared to non-feminists, do not have negative attitudes toward men. Feminists do tend to reject traditional gender roles that put women in less powerful positions than men.

Taken together, systematic empirical studies do not find evidence that feminists dislike men. In contrast, there is some suggestion that non-feminists, those women who adhere to traditional gender stereotypes, dislike, or at least, resent, men. We must ask, then, why does the myth of feminist man-haters persist?

Why does the myth of the feminist man-hater persist?

The myth of the feminist man-hater exists at least in part because feminists do not behave themselves. Feminists tend to violate gender-role expectations, and that makes people uncomfortable. There are stiff sanctions for women who violate gender roles, and thus there are somewhat similar reactions to feminists, lesbians, and even women leaders. Now that we have established the lack of empirical support for the notion that feminists are man-haters, we are left with explaining why the myth persists and what we can do about it. This section begins by examining individuals' reactions to conventional and non-conventional women by first examining a form of benign bigotry known as ambivalent sexism. This concept is related to, but different from, hostility toward and benevolence toward men. Next, we will look at people's perceptions of another type of gender violator, women leaders. Then the supposed link between feminism and lesbianism is examined, and the function of lesbian-baiting as a strategy to keep women in their place is discussed. Finally, the empirical research presented in this chapter is put in its larger cultural context by tying it to the "battle of the sexes" and the "boy crisis" rhetoric that are currently popular.

Women are wonderful but feminists are not: Rewarding traditional and penalizing non-traditional women

Understanding people's negative attitudes toward feminists requires an examination of more general attitudes toward women. Just as people's attitudes toward men are ambivalent – with a mix of respect and admiration along with resentment of their power and privilege – attitudes toward women are ambivalent as well. At first glance, however, attitudes toward women seem positive relative to attitudes toward men. And attitudes toward women *are* more positive in terms of *affect* – the emotional feeling of positive or negative. Even though men hold higher status in most societies, women seem to be *liked* more. Alice Eagly and Antonio Mladinic[65] have coined the phrase "women-are-wonderful" to illustrate this. The global category "woman" is viewed more positively than the global category "man." The women-are-wonderful effect occurs on explicit attitude surveys as well as with implicit attitude measures such as when positive words such as "good" and "happy" are associated more with women than with men.[66]

There are two important points about the positive feelings people have about women compared to men that relate to the negative reaction some have to feminists. Just because a group is liked does not mean that it is treated fairly and taken seriously. Also, just because the global category "women" is liked more than "men," does not mean that particular *subcategories* of women are liked. These important caveats to the women-are-wonderful effect are elaborated in this section.

Discrimination and disrespect

Gender-based discrimination is widespread and well documented.[67] Take, for example, the disparities in pay between women and men.

Women college graduates in the US who work full time make only 80% of what comparable men make.[68] In the US, girls and women are more likely to live in poverty than are boys and men.[69] And while women in the US held half of all management and professional positions in 2004, only 14% of architects and engineers, and 29% of physicians and surgeons are women, while 86% of paralegals and legal assistants are women.[70] In terms of representations of women in popular culture in the US, men are overrepresented on prime time television shows,[71] and in television commercials,[72] in feature films,[73] in music television,[74] in children's television cartoons,[75] and in newspaper comics.[76] In terms of political representation, women make up only 17% of the members of the US House of Representatives and Senate.[77]

As Alice Eagly's work on the women-are-wonderful effect revealed, women may be *liked*, but they are not necessarily *respected*. Susan Fiske and her colleagues[78] have found that groups that are targets of discrimination are judged along two dimensions, *warmth* and *competence*. Historically, social psychologists have tended to assume that prejudice involves simultaneous dislike and disrespect for an outgroup, but Fiske finds that prejudice results from dislike *or* disrespect, but not necessarily both. Stereotype content may not reflect simple evaluative antipathy but instead may reflect separate dimensions of warmth and competence. For instance, some people think Jews are highly competent, but lack warmth – they are respected but not liked. People tend to view old people as warm, but do not respect them – they are high on warmth, low on competence. As you might guess, women are viewed as warm and therefore likeable, but they are less likely to be seen as competent and are therefore less respected. Men, relative to women, are less liked but are viewed as more competent.

If women are liked more than respected, where do feminists fit in? Geoffrey Haddock and Mark Zanna[79] found that people have different views of two categories of women that are seen as opposites: *housewives* and *feminists* (although these categories could overlap). Like Alice Eagly's work on the women-are-wonderful effect and Susan Fiske's work on warmth and competence, Haddock and Zanna found that when Canadian college students were asked to form a mental image of the typical woman and typical man, women were evaluated more favorably than were men. However, when *subcategories* of women were considered, different attitudes emerged. Feminists tend to be evaluated more negatively than housewives, even though feminists and housewives are both part of the larger category of women. Haddock and Zanna further found that those who dislike feminists believe that feminists violate traditional values and customs. In other words, feminists are seen as a threat to the status quo in a way that housewives are not. Therefore, women are wonderful as long as they fulfill traditional roles.

Ambivalent sexism: the carrot and the stick of patriarchy

Because there are differing views of different *types* of women, *sexism*, the prejudice and discrimination against women, is not a single, unitary concept. Peter Glick and Susan Fiske[80] developed *ambivalent sexism* as a measure of sexism that captures subjectively positive and negative feelings toward women. Glick and Fiske's concept of ambivalent sexism is similar to, but different from, their concept, *ambivalence toward men* discussed earlier in this chapter. Ambivalent sexism captures people's attitudes toward women, while ambivalence toward men captures people's attitudes toward men.

Racial/ethnic groups may, and often do, avoid kinship ties (or almost any kind of contact) with other racial/ethnic groups; however, heterosexual women and men have to be intimate. For instance, one might object to marrying someone of another race, but it is unlikely that a heterosexual man will decide not to be involved with a woman. And although men may wish to exclude women from certain activities and roles, few (even among the most rabidly sexist) wish to banish women completely from their lives. You can avoid another ethnic group but it's hard to avoid another gender.

Glick and Fiske find that men's (and people's, generally) attitudes toward women can be broken down into two kinds of sexism, *hostile* sexism and *benevolent* sexism. Hostile sexism is what most people think of when they think of sexism. It consists of overtly hostile feelings toward women, with negative feelings toward, and stereotyping of, non-traditional women in particular. Hostile sexism seeks to justify male power, traditional gender roles, and men's exploitation of women as sexual objects through derogatory characterizations of women. Hostile sexists would agree with statements such as, "*When women lose to men in a fair competition, they typically complain about being discriminated against,*" and "*Most women fail to appreciate fully all that men do for them.*" Benevolent sexism is a trickier concept because it involves subjectively positive attitudes toward women. Women are characterized as pure creatures who need protection from men. It is the view that women are adored by men and are necessary to make men complete. Benevolent sexism relies on kinder and gentler justifications of male dominance and prescribed gender roles; it recognizes men's dependence on women and takes a romanticized view of heterosexual relationships. Ideologies of what Glick and Fiske refer to as benevolent paternalism allow members of dominant groups to characterize their privileges as well deserved, even as a responsibility they must bear (similar to the "white man's burden"). Men are willing to sacrifice their own needs to care for the women in their lives. Benevolent sexists agree with statements such as, "*No matter how accomplished he is, a man is not truly complete as a person unless he has the love of a woman,*" and "*Women should be cherished and protected by men.*" For women, benevolent sexism undermines women's resistance to male dominance: benevolent sexism is disarming because it is subjectively favorable and also promises that men's power will be used to women's advantage, as long as they can secure a high-status male protector. Benevolent sexism is classic benign bigotry. People do not immediately recognize benevolent sexism as sexist and many women are even flattered by the attitudes of benevolent sexism.[81]

While hostile sexism and benevolent sexism are separate and contradictory concepts, people can, and often do, experience hostile and benevolent sexism simultaneously. People can have loving and hating attitudes toward women. People tend to feel hostile sexism towards women who violate traditional gender roles (e.g. feminists, sexually active women) and benevolent sexism toward conventional women (e.g. homemakers). Benevolent sexism can result in the women-are-wonderful effect because traditional women are considered to be wonderful because of their purity and nurturance. The way Glick and Fiske describe the workings of ambivalent sexism, benevolent sexism is the "carrot" – the reward of positive feelings toward and protectiveness given to women who embrace traditional roles; and hostile sexism is the "stick" – the hostility directed at women who reject traditional roles. Punishment (through hostile sexism) alone is not the most effective means of shaping behavior because that might result in only resentment and resistance. However, punishment for some and reinforcement for others maintains patriarchy and the gender status quo.[82]

Benevolent sexism, then, is insidious for three reasons. First, it doesn't seem like prejudice to male perpetrators because men do not view it as something negative. Second, women may find its "sweet allure difficult to resist."[83] Praising women's nurturing traits is part of expressing the belief that women are especially suited to domestic roles. Furthermore, stereotypes of women as nurturing and communal justify their subordinated status.[84] Third, benevolent sexism can drive a wedge between women. Women (e.g. feminists) who reject the overtly negative aspects of hostile sexism as well as the cloaked negative aspects of benevolent sexism are at odds with traditional women who are rewarded by benevolent sexism and reject feminism because they want to hold on to the little power they get as a result of benevolent sexism. So while feminists and traditional women should be working in solidarity to fight gender discrimination, they are split by being on two opposite sides of benevolent sexism.

Like their work on ambivalence toward men, Glick and Fiske have analyzed patterns of hostile and benevolent sexism in a variety of cultures.[85] In general, men's hostile sexism is higher than women's, and women are more receptive to benevolent sexist beliefs than hostile sexist beliefs. In nations where hostile sexism was endorsed, women were especially likely to embrace benevolent sexism, in some cases even more so than the men. Glick and Fiske point out the irony of women who are forced to seek protection from members of the very group that threatens them. The greater the threat, the stronger the incentive to accept benevolent sexism's protective ideology. This explains the tendency for women in the most sexist societies to endorse benevolent sexism more strongly than do men. Furthermore, the countries in which women rejected both benevolent and hostile sexism were the ones in which men had low hostile sexism scores. As sexist hostility declines, women may feel able to reject benevolent sexism without fear of a hostile backlash.

Ambivalent sexism addresses the question, *is chivalry good for women?* By excluding women from the outside world of work and from positions traditionally held by men, benevolent sexists exclude women from roles that offer more status in society. Thus, some women (specifically traditional women) are protected to some extent by chivalry, but at great cost. Women are protected but patronized. Ambivalent sexism is correlated with other objectionable attitudes. Hostile sexism is correlated with having a *social dominance orientation*.[86] Those who have a social dominance orientation believe in maintaining social hierarchies and in preventing the redistribution of societal resources. When a group that is discriminated against, in this case women, attempts to gain access to societal resources, those with a social dominance orientation will react negatively. Benevolent sexism is correlated with authoritarianism.[87] As we saw earlier in this chapter authoritarians tend to dislike feminists, so it would be expected that authoritarians like those who adhere to traditional roles. But benevolent sexism is correlated with *paternalistic chivalry* – the belief that while women should be treated with courtesy and consideration, they should be restricted to traditional roles within an intimate relationship.[88] Feminists, who may reject chivalry for good reason, get an angry, defensive response from men who feel that feminists are ungrateful.

In a study of Spanish women's reactions[89] to discriminatory scenarios (e.g. losing a promotion), the same acts of discrimination were perceived as less serious when the perpetrators expressed a benevolent, protective justification than when they expressed a hostile one. Furthermore, women who scored higher in benevolent sexism were more likely to excuse both hostile treatment from a husband and benevolently justified discrimination by non-intimate men (e.g. a boss). But this pattern of response only occurred among women participants who did not work outside the home. This finding suggests that women who are highly dependent on men are prone to forgive even hostile acts, perhaps reinterpreting them as signs of the husband's passionate attachment. One study with Turkish and Brazilian respondents (college students and a community example), found that individuals (both women and men) with high levels of hostile sexism found wife abuse more acceptable than those with low levels of hostile sexism.[90] Benevolent sexism has been linked to attributions of blame against women for acquaintance rape. Individuals high in benevolent sexism attributed less blame to perpetrators and recommended shorter sentences for an acquaintance rape perpetrator than did those low in benevolent sexism.[91] A study of Zimbabwean male college students found that those men with higher levels of hostile sexism reported that they were more likely to commit acquaintance rape than men with lower levels of hostile sexism.[92] Thus, hostile sexism rationalizes mistreatment of women who violate traditional roles, while benevolent sexism provides a framework for what is acceptable (i.e. traditional) behavior for women.

The work on ambivalent sexism demonstrates that while traditional women tend to elicit positive feelings from people, non-traditional women such as feminists have hostile reactions directed toward them. Even though the supposed protective qualities of benevolent sexism are alluring to some women (namely, traditional women), that protection comes with the price of restricted options and strong sanctions against women who appear to violate traditional roles.

Penalties for non-traditional women

A central feature of negative attitudes toward women is the dislike of women who do not fit into the traditional feminine role (e.g. feminists, lesbians, women athletes). From the discussion of Glick and Fiske's work on ambivalent sexism and Fiske's work on warmth and competence as a relevant dimension of judging social categories, it should be clear that what makes feminists threatening is that they violate (or appear to violate) and reject traditional gender norms for women.

Women leaders also violate people's expectations about women and therefore threaten the gender status quo. While women who are leaders are not necessarily feminists, and feminists are not necessarily women in leadership positions, both produce similar reactions. Think of the strong reactions toward Hillary Clinton, Martha Stewart, and Condoleezza Rice. A brief discussion, therefore, on people's reactions to women leaders, will shed light on the negative reactions that feminists sometimes receive. While women in leadership positions in the work domain have gradually increased, expectations about what women are like have not kept pace with women's changing roles. Research has indicated that women who behave in ways typically reserved for men are found to be less socially appealing than men who behave similarly or women who behave in ways that are more in line with normative prescriptions. When a woman is acknowledged to have been successful at performing male gender-typed work, she is, by definition, thought to have the attributes necessary to effectively execute the tasks and responsibilities required. But it is these same attributes that are in violation of gender-prescriptive norms. So, although there is a good fit between what the woman is perceived to be like and what the work entails, there is a bad fit between what the woman is perceived to be like and what she *should* be like.[93]

A study by Madeline E. Heilman and her colleagues[94] illustrates the subtlety with which judgments about women who violate gender expectations get played out. Heilman gave US college students packets that contained a profile of a clearly successful or ambiguously successful woman or man in a male-dominated job (Assistant Vice President in mechanics and aeronautics). All information about the worker was identical except for gender. Students were asked to rate the candidate on *competence*, *likeability*, and *interpersonal hostility*. The results reveal the operation of subtle prejudice. When students rated the candidate's competence, successful women and men were evaluated equally – they were both given credit for their successes. However, as theories of subtle prejudice would predict, gender played a role when the candidates' qualifications were ambiguous. When information about the candidate's performance was ambiguous, the woman was rated as less competent than the man. There were results associated with liking ratings as well. When there was ambiguity about the person's performance, there was no significant difference between the liking ratings of women and men targets. But when there was clear evidence of success, the woman was liked less than the man. In other words, the clearly successful woman was liked significantly less than the clearly successful man, the unsuccessful woman, and unsuccessful man. A similar finding emerged in terms of judgments of hostility. The woman candidate was rated as less hostile than the man in the ambiguous performance outcome condition but was rated as more hostile than the man in the clearly successful condition. These results demonstrate the double standard used when judging women in male-dominated occupations: Women were viewed as less competent than men only when there was ambiguity about how successful they had been; when the women's success was made explicit, there were no differences in these characterizations. However, when success was explicit, women were viewed as less likeable than men. Women, although rated less competent than men when information about them was ambiguous, were at least rated as less hostile interpersonally. But the switch when success was clear is dramatic: women who are acknowledged as successful were viewed not merely as indifferent to others but as downright uncivil. And these patterns held for both women and men raters, so these gender stereotypic norms and the tendency to penalize women who violate them are meaningful for both women and men. Heilman conducted another study[95] and found that dislike was associated with not being recommended for promotions and salary increases. Heilman concludes that while there are many things that lead an individual to be disliked in the job setting, it is only women who are disliked when they are successful.

The gender double standard for women who are viewed as violating gender rules exists not only in the male-dominated domains of mechanics and aeronautics, but also in the teaching profession, when women violate students' gender-role expectations. Gabriel Smith and I[96] conducted a study to see whether or not teaching style would affect students' preconceptions of a hypothetical professor. We gave an ethnically diverse sample of undergraduate students a syllabus for a proposed social science course. Each syllabus portrayed one of two teaching styles: strict (male-stereotyped) and lenient (female-stereotyped). While the requirements were the same for both types of teaching styles, the lenient professors allowed for tardiness, provided make-up exams, and their syllabi were written with conciliatory language. The lenient professors were pushovers. The strict style was conveyed by emphatic language about *no* exceptions to any of the requirements and lacked warmth and conciliation. In addition to the two teaching styles, we also varied each syllabus according to the professor's gender and ethnicity (Latina/o or Anglo) via the professor's name. Students read a syllabus and rated the professor on warmth, competence, and knowledge. We found that students' expectations of professors were based on teaching style, ethnicity, and gender. Students used different criteria for ratings based on these factors. Latina professors earned both the highest and lowest ratings – contingent upon their teaching styles: Latina professors who conformed to the female stereotype and taught with a lenient approach were rated more positively than any other type of professor (e.g. Anglo men, Anglo women, or Latino men who taught with the same style). However, the very lowest ratings of professors were also reserved for Latinas – those who had the strict style. Thus, for Latinas, students' ratings were contingent upon their teaching style, whereas ratings of Anglo men were similar regardless of whether they had a strict or a lenient style. The strict teaching style, which is uncharacteristic of stereotypes about Latinas, violated students' expectations, resulting in a penalty for Latinas. Our study results epitomize benign bigotry: Latina professors earned the highest (best) student ratings, higher than Anglo women and men, which would seem to be complimentary or flattering to Latina professors. But the Latina professors only earned such positive marks when they conformed to gender and ethnic stereotypes and performed from a weak position. When they violated stereotypes, performing from a position of strength, they earned the very lowest ratings.

How prevalent is people's discomfort with competent women? Melissa C. Thomas-Hunt and Katherine W. Phillips[97] wanted to see how women and men who were experts on a task would be judged by members of their work group. Women and men college student participants completed a survival task individually. (The task involved choosing the most important items necessary to survive an Australian bushfire.) Their answers were compared to survival experts' responses on the same task. Thus each participant was categorized as an "expert" or "non-expert" (but was not told so) according to the comparison of their answers to the experts. Next, the women and men were put into small work groups that had one expert (either a man or woman) in each group. The group was asked to complete the same task, and afterward, each group member was asked to evaluate how knowledgeable and influential on the group decisions each member was.

The results are remarkable because of their consistency and breadth. First, there were no actual differences between women and men on their performance, even though the task was male-stereotyped. That is, women were just as likely to be experts as men. However: (1) women were *perceived* to be less expert than men; (2) women exerted less actual influence within their groups than did men; (3) correspondingly, women reported feeling less confidence in their ability to influence the group than did men. Thus, while there were no actual differences in women's and men's expertise, women were perceived as less expert, just because they were women, and therefore were less influential on the group, and the women themselves recognized this. Also compared were the perceived competence and influence of experts and non-experts: (4) women experts were actually perceived as *less* expert than women non-experts, while there was no difference in how men experts and non-experts were viewed; (5) women experts were actually *less* influential than female non-experts, whereas men who were experts were more influential on the group than men who were not; and, (6) women experts reported having *less* influence on their group than did women non-experts, while there was no difference between men experts' and men non-experts' perceptions of their own influence. So women were actually accurate in their assessment, whereas non-expert men thought they were influential but were not, and, finally, (7) groups with men who were experts actually outperformed groups with women experts, even though there was no prior performance difference between women and men who were experts. The implications of Thomas-Hunt and Phillips' study are vast. Not only do men have a greater impact on group interactions than do women, but also possessing expertise can actually be a liability for women. Being an expert for women actually hindered their influence. Such lower performance expectations held for women may result in their being labeled as ill-informed when they contribute information that is unique but that lacks consensual validity. Women were initially no less confident in their own abilities than were men. But over time in the group, they became less confident.

Lesbian-baiting

Understanding the link between feminism and lesbianism reveals some of the fundamental sources of the discomfort and antagonism toward feminism we have explored so far. Indeed, in casual contexts and in mass media, *lesbian* is, erroneously, often portrayed as interchangeable with *feminist* where the presumption is made that lesbians are, by definition, feminists, and feminists are presumed to be lesbians. Both lesbians and feminists are understood as women who disrupt and threaten gender rules, and both terms describe non-traditional women. Both feminists and lesbians seem inherently unladylike, assertive, and outspoken, and women like this threaten the gender status quo.[98]

Homophobia, in addition to sexism, creates an additional set of tactical opportunities to discredit and marginalize feminism's efforts to achieve comprehensive equality for women. Like the accusation of male-bashing, the framing of lesbianism as the inevitable result of feminism or as a necessary dimension of feminism, is a scare tactic designed to frighten people away from associating with feminism and feminist activism. The very positioning of lesbianism as a source of discrediting reveals the underlying layer of homophobia that often joins with sexism to maintain systems of oppression and retain privilege. Women who have worked actively against sexual assault and rape are often the target of lesbian-baiting. Framed as insults and debasement, accusations of lesbianism, along with descriptions of feminists as angry, unladylike, and unfeminine, are employed to make feminists, and by extension the goals of feminism, unattractive and repellent. Ali Grant,[99] who has studied community responses to anti-violence activists, argues that these slurs are the result of people feeling as though women are acting out of their place by complaining too much about men's violence against women. It's as though it is okay to believe that rape is wrong, but that women should not complain about it, or at least if they complain, they should not complain loudly. Battered women's shelters and rape crisis centers have been vandalized with graffiti such as "No Means Dyke," or "No means tie her up."[100] Rape crisis centers have been charged with "turning women into lesbians" or "being man-hating."[101] Women's activism is seen as a threat. "Lesbian," as much as it is an expression of sexual identity, also functions as a regulatory term.[102] It refers to women who are independent from men. That is why it can be used when a woman refuses sexual advances from a man. Since *lesbian* is often conflated with *feminist*, and because of homophobia, feminists are often required to prove they are not lesbians.

Lesbian-baiting can also be a form of sexual extortion, especially in the military. Kelly Corbett, a staff attorney at Servicemembers Legal Defense Network, has written about lesbian-baiting since the emergence of the US military policy of *Don't Ask, Don't Tell, Don't*

Pursue.[103] *Don't Ask* is a policy directed at lesbian and gay service members. The policy was established in 1993 with the goal of allowing lesbians and gay men to serve in the military as long as they did not discuss their sexual orientation openly or engage in homosexual acts. According to Corbett, accusations of lesbianism are a threat to all military women, regardless of their sexual orientation. The anti-gay policy gives harassers and rapists tools of sexual extortion. Allegations of lesbianism often ruins a soldier's career. It doesn't matter whether or not the allegations are true. Women soldiers who refuse sexual advances from men may be accused of being lesbians and subjected to investigation for homosexual conduct. Thus, the *Don't Ask* policy is being used as a weapon of retaliation against women who report sexual harassment or rape, against those who rebuff sexual advances, or against those who succeed in their careers. Obviously, if lesbians and gay men could serve openly in the military, this would be a less effective weapon against service members. It is no wonder that many women do not identify as feminists because they are afraid of a potential allegation of lesbianism.[104]

Although lesbians, like feminists, are viewed by some as man-haters, there is no empirical evidence suggesting this link in reality. Judy Markey begins her Redbook article, "Male Bashing," with, "I used to be a rather accomplished male-basher. After all, I was married to a man."[105] Magazines from the popular press imply that male-bashers are heterosexual women with traditional gender roles: women complain about men's infidelity,[106] inept husbands,[107] and men who are not "domesticable."[108] Lesbians likely have different relationships with men and therefore do not have the complaints, disappointments, and frustrations that some heterosexual women have. Ali Grant interviewed lesbian feminist activists who reported that, rather than disliking men, they felt that men were either neutral players (e.g. male relatives) or just not relevant to their lives. One lesbian interviewee reported that men are not a major part of her life and that heterosexual women complain about men "all the time."[109] More systematic research needs to be done in the area of lesbians-as-man-haters. I suspect another stereotype will be debunked, just as the feminists-as-man-haters stereotype has been.

Confusing the unit of analysis: "Battle of the sexes" vs. patriarchy and privilege

Feminists are accused of man-hating when they object to gender discrimination because some interpret the objection as being anti-man (as complaints about *particular, individual* men, or even *all men*) rather than as a protest against the patriarchal system that gives power and privilege to men relative to women. Other people may be more deliberate and cynical in their attempts to demonize feminists and feminism and may seek the use of those efforts to drive a wedge between feminist and non-feminist women. Feminists see sexism as part of a *system* of inequality.[110] Those who do not understand the systemic nature of gender inequality translate feminists' activism as complaints directed at particular men or at men as a *category*, as if feminists blame each man or all men. For instance, in his book, *Manliness*, Harvey Mansfield describes feminism as women being "none too pleased with men and not shy about letting them know it."[111] The incorrect notion that feminists hate men (rather than feminism being understood as a critique of a patriarchal system) does more than make women reluctant to call themselves feminists. It also makes invisible the roles that women play in contributing to gender inequality. In the studies I have reviewed in this chapter that revealed gender discrimination, nearly all found that men *and* women participants discriminate against women. Sexism and gender discrimination is not just something men do to women. Everyone participates in a sexist system, although it is certainly true that men benefit through the male privilege inherent in a sexist system. Ignoring the systemic nature of gender inequality also leads men to feel stuck in a defensive response rather than being able to see that men too are confined by gender expectations. Trivializing feminists' resistance to inequality as anger at men insults the women's liberation movement that fights for the right to vote, for equal pay, for educational equity, and for reproductive freedom – efforts focused on changing the system, not on "bashing" men.

One manifestation of the focus on individual men versus the focus on systemic gender discrimination and male privilege is the "battle-of-the-sexes"[112] rhetoric that is prevalent in popular culture. Battle-of-the-sexes rhetoric produces false neutrality and false parallelism of the advantages/disadvantages of women and men and suggests that both women and men are equally advantaged and disadvantaged – just in different ways.[113] For instance, in the *Time Magazine* article, "Men: are they really that bad?" Lance Morrow[114] takes on what he describes as the "overt man bashing of recent years."[115] He says, "both men and women have been oppressed by the other sex, in different ways,"[116] and "American men and women should face the fact that they are hopelessly at odds."[117] Judy Markey[118] says in her *Redbook* article, "Male-bashing," "How can we gripe that they put us down as a group, if we do the same thing to them?"[119] and, "We'll wind up sounding like squabbling children crying, 'He started it!' 'No, she did!'"[120] This popular discourse that women-and-men-are-at-odds suggests that women's and men's complaints are parallel and equal. The rhetoric of the "sex wars"[121] trivializes genuine critiques about patriarchy and male supremacy and reduces discrimination to a he-said-she-said dynamic in which there are no real winners and no real losers, but only miscommunication between the sexes. Feminists, then, are merely "chronically dissatisfied"[122] with men.

This view of individual-based gender debates can reduce things such as rape and sexual harassment to miscommunication that can leave *men* victims. For instance, in his book, *The Myth of Male*

Power, Warren Farrell[123] writes that "Feminism has taught women to sue men for creating a 'hostile environment' or for date rape when men initiate with the wrong person or with the wrong timing."[124] Similarly, Lance Morrow claims that a successful approach to a woman is called romance and courtship. Sexual harassment, according to Morrow, is simply an unsuccessful approach, and, in his view, is unfairly treated as a crime.[125] The real victims of sexual harassment and rape are not women, but men who are victimized by women's flirtations and mixed messages. Women are teases who "elaborately manipulate and exploit men's natural sexual attraction to the female body, and then deny the manipulation and prosecute men for the attraction – if the attraction draws in the wrong man."[126] So the problem lies with individual women who cannot take a joke or who tease men; or the problem lies with individual men who misread women's signals, rather than considering a system that sexualizes women and girls and creates an environment in which women are meant to be subordinate to men.[127]

These writers imply that male chivalry should be highly valued in our culture but that it is misinterpreted by feminists. And that we need to go back to a time of "knightly solicitude for the sake of women's safety . . . and men's honor"[128] because "Male chivalry protected women far better than feminist lawsuits over girlie calendars and dirty jokes."[129] But is male chivalry really better for women than feminism? We've already seen how a feminist identity is positively correlated with well-being.[130] Should a woman be flattered when a man opens a door for her? Glick and Fiske's research, reported earlier in this chapter, suggests that male chivalry entails patronizing and condescending attitudes toward women which imply that women are suited only for the domestic role of wife and mother. As we saw earlier, benevolent sexism, which includes chivalrous attitudes toward women, is correlated with hostile sexism, a social dominance orientation, authoritarianism, and even victim-blame.

Center-stealing: Boy crises and threats to privilege

Why is it that whenever women start to get anywhere in this fallen world the big question is: what about men?

Katha Pollit[131]

In recent years, another manifestation of the accusation of man-hating is in the popular discourse on the "boy crisis." Beginning in the 1980s there was an increase in awareness regarding the male-centered psychological theories that treated girls like deviants and boys as the norm, with books such as Carol Gilligan's[132] *In a Different Voice* and Mary Pipher's[133] *Reviving Ophelia*. Part of this focus was a critique of the educational system that is more geared toward the benefit of boys. Myra and David Sadker's[134] book, *Failing at Fairness: How America's Schools Cheat Girls*, as well as a report from the American Association of University Women,[135] generated headlines in the popular press. As these works grew in popularity, a backlash in the form of a recovery effort for boys supposedly wounded by the alleged disproportionate attention given to girls and women during the 1980s and early 1990s began to grow as well. Several anti-feminist pop psychology books on boys' development[136] became best sellers. Christina Hoff Sommers' book, *The War Against Boys*, and now more recently, Kate O'Beirne's book, *Women who Make the World Worse and how their Radical Feminist Assault is Ruining our Schools, Families, Military, and Sports*, accompanied hundreds of books, newspaper and magazine articles published in the US, Europe, and Australia about the "boy crisis." This particular brand of backlash against feminism – the supposed "boy crisis" – argues that feminism has supposedly taken its toll most notably in American schools that have become "anti-boy,"[137] and they perpetuate a "myth of boys' toxicity"[138] with a climate that is "rigged against boys."[139] Writers cite the disproportionate numbers of women entering and graduating from college compared to men as their evidence of women getting one up on men. Typical newspaper and magazine articles of this type are entitled "At colleges, women are leaving men in the dust,"[140] "Silence of the lads,"[141] and "How boys lost out to girl power."[142] The facts about the boy crisis have not matched the hype and there have been detailed critiques of both the hyperbolic rhetoric and the evidence cited in these articles and books.[143]

The American Association of University Women's 2008 report[144] on the status of gender and educational achievement during the past 35 years has found that standardized test performance has improved for both girls and boys and that more men *and* women are graduating from college today than ever before. The proportion of young men graduating from high school and earning college degrees is at an all-time high. While older/non-traditional women college students outnumber their counterparts who are men, the gender gap is almost absent among those entering college directly after high school. Why do older women outnumber older men as college students? It is likely due, at least in part, to the fact that women college graduates earn less than men even after controlling choice of field.[145]

Christina Accomando and I[146] analyzed the literature on the "boy crisis", the claims that girls have myriad advantages over boys. We find that this literature reveals a panic reaction that amounts to *center-stealing*.[147] Center-stealing occurs when members of a privileged group imagine a threat when attention, even temporarily and briefly, is directed away from them and towards members of a marginalized group. Center-stealing occurs when the privileged group steals back attention from the subordinate group, putting the focus back on the dominant group. While books and articles which focus on how the educational system has been biased against girls assume that it is necessary to redress past wrongs including sexism, discrimination, and exclusion, "boy crisis" authors see the focus on girls as a takeover by girls and women. The "boy crisis" authors assume that the playing field for girls and boys (and men and women) was level before this relatively brief focus on girls, rather than seeing the decades of disadvantage of girls. The brief moment of academic, educational, and popular focus on the inhospitable nature of classrooms for girls and of the workplace for women has been perceived as a conquest by girls and women.

This backlash against feminism may account for the disconnect between those who, while claiming to support egalitarianism, think that feminists have gone too far. Sarah Riley's[148] transcripts from Scottish men, discussed earlier in this chapter, reveal these sentiments among the men she interviewed. *I'm all for equal rights but don't try to get me to change.* Also, *women claim to want equality but they actually want to put themselves ahead of men.* The result of this reaction to feminism is that when feminists come along and complain about gender discrimination, they are seen as trying to get special advantages and to get ahead of men. And Judy Markey,[149] in her article on "Male-bashing," says, "in our search for equality, it seems we've also begun to assert our superiority. Which, of course, is precisely what male-bashing is all about – putting men down so we can feel superior."[150] In the present day, it is men who are the supposed victims of sexism, who are "gang-pecked"[151] by women.

Who is bashing whom?

What is the significance of using the term "male bashing?" What is "male bashing" and why is that particular term deployed to quiet feminism? Sue Cataldi[152] discusses the irony of this term. To *bash* means to violently strike with a heavy crushing blow. *Bash* connotes an indiscriminate, random, confused lashing out. *Bash* suggests that the striking of the blow is part of an attack rather than a fight, unfair, undeserved, or prejudiced – similar to how the word "gay-bashing" is used – violently beating someone because of their presumed homosexuality. "Male bashing" is doubly poignant because of both its misleading and its obfuscating meanings: first, the actual "bashing" is overwhelming in the form of battery of women by men. The hardened expression in mass media fails to accurately represent the actual facts. Second, the expression "male bashing" diverts attention from this stark reality, replacing our ability to understand genuine violence with a fear fantasy about women who simply fail to cooperate with strict gender-role expectations.

"Bashing" itself has become an all-too-commonly heard word, and some of the specific and horrifying nature of bashing is easily folded into a "just another statistic" mentality. Bashing occurs in several forms and happens in a variety of relationships, to a variety of already marginalized people and groups. Verbal bashing appears to involve unjustly denouncing the members of a group, people who are innocent victims. As Cataldi reminds us, women (in general) are not bashers, they are *bashed*. In the UK, 77% of domestic violence victims are women. On average two women are killed every week by a current or former male partner.[153] In fact, women are more likely than men to be victims of every category of sexual and intimate violence: non-sexual partner abuse, sexual partner abuse, non-sexual family abuse, sexual family abuse, sexual assault, and stalking.[154] In the US, one study of more than five thousand American women college students found that 28.5% had experienced an attempted or completed sexual assault either before or since entering college. One fifth of the college women reported experiencing an attempted or completed sexual assault since entering college.[155] Sexual assault is also common in already-physically abusive relationships. Sixty-eight percent of physically abused women are also sexually assaulted by their intimate partners.[156] One out of every 12 American women will be stalked at some point in their lives, and 87% of the stalkers will be men. Four out of five stalking victims are women.[157]

The underlying gender relationships and expectations for women and men are revealed in these small bits of linguistic customs.

There is, for example, no formulaic expression that describes battery or abuse of women by men such as "female-bashing," nor is there a similar expression designed to describe comments intended to be humor launched by men about women. The point is this: we do not have an expression like "female-bashing" because men "bashing" women, whether in the form of verbal or physical assault, is the expected, or normative, case. Why aren't physical assaults on women characterized as "female-bashing?" Sue Cataldi[158] argues that conjuring up images of abused men bashed by women and casting women in the role of bashers reverses what actually happens. This table turning can then operate, perniciously, as a form of victim-blaming and as a means of exaggerating the severity of any harm done to men who are, supposedly, verbally bashed by women. Another function of co-opting the expression "male-bashing" and its brutality is to lead us into thinking that what the "male-bashing" women supposedly engage in is equivalent to what men do to women. Those who use the expression may also be attempting to siphon attention and support away from women and from those who are physically harmed by men. Calling feminists "male-bashers" shifts the focus from the systemic problem of men's violence against women to a focus on men who have gotten their feelings hurt by feminists and feminism. The feminist critique of patriarchy may be disconcerting to men and some women. It might hurt men's feelings, it might seem unfair, and it might seem to disregard men's good intentions. This may make men feel uncomfortable but it is not male-bashing. Feminists are not critical of men simply for being men. The target of feminist critique is sexism and misogyny in a male-dominated society.

Putting it all together

This chapter has examined the myth that feminists are man-haters. We have seen that there is no evidence, no real basis, that supports this erroneous belief, but it still persists, and has the power to shape attitudes and behavior. Feminists are described by many in the mass media as angry[159] and anti-male.[160] Many women who embrace the principles of feminism are reluctant to identify as feminists. They often cite the negative reputation, particularly the man-hating stereotype that feminism has in the mass media, popular culture, and politics, as one of their reasons for their hesitation in identifying as a feminist. This false but persistent view of feminists as man-haters is so strong, in fact, that it actually prevents people from correctly identifying themselves as feminists. Individuals surveyed about feminism and feminists reveal that they actually hold neutral to positive attitudes of both feminist ideals and the people who identify with these ideals. We have seen that there is no empirical evidence to support the notion that feminists' attitudes toward men are more negative than non-feminists'. In fact, in one of the only empirical studies on the topic, feminists reported lower levels of hostility toward men than non-feminists.[161] The work in the area of ambivalent sexism and ambivalence toward men suggests that women who adhere to traditional gender roles, those we might expect are unlikely to be feminists, may resent men's relative power, while endorsing the paternalistic chivalry that benevolent sexism is composed of.[162]

Anti-feminism and the behavior that results from such sentiments, particularly in men, tend to be associated with an authoritarian worldview. Authoritarianism requires adherence to conventional roles and values and inflexibility in thinking. Also, anti-feminist men are more likely than feminist men to adhere to rape myths and victim blame. Given these associations and ways of thinking about women, it might be more accurate if anti-feminism had the nasty reputation that feminism has. In contrast to the negative and anti-social correlates of anti-feminism, feminism, as a set of principles and a way of looking at the world, tends to be positively correlated with psychological well-being for women.

Correspondingly, men were found to have better relationship stability and sexual satisfaction if they believed their partners were feminist than if they did not believe their partners were feminist. These findings stand in stark contrast to anti-feminist stereotypes asserting that feminist women are "chronically dissatisfied"[163] as set forth by Kate O'Beirne in her book, *Women Who Make the World Worse*.

Feminists, like other non-traditional women, such as lesbians, women athletes, and women leaders, are viewed negatively because they transgress traditional expectations of women being docile and behaving themselves. Feminists upset the status quo. Part of the threat of feminism is that feminists are more likely to see gender inequality as systemic, not as a problem between individual women and men. So while anti-feminist women might resent men, as we have seen in the work on women's ambivalence toward men, feminists resent the unfairness of the system of gender inequality. Some people mistake feminists' fight against patriarchy as a fight against particular men.

Finally, the whole enterprise of feminists-as-man-haters needs to be deconstructed and dismantled. Women are not bashers, they are more often the bashed, the targets of men's violence. Framing feminism as male-bashing shifts the focus from *real* violence against women perpetuated by some men onto the *fictional* man-hating feminists who hurt men.

Strategies for change

While it's not our fault that sexism exists, it is our responsibility to make active and progressive changes in our own attitudes and behavior, and to influence those around us. Confronting and challenging sexism presents slightly different issues than our discussions of anti-racist innovations discussed in other chapters. Many people believe that the perceived differences between women and men indicate real, underlying biological differences that, in themselves, have significance and meaning. Compared to our contemporary understanding of race, the apparent visible differences that distinguish human beings on gradients of observable characteristics, such as pigmentation, hair type, stature, and other physical features, do not reflect meaningful underlying biological differences, nor are such surface characteristics linked to personality, temperament, or culture. Many people in the twenty-first century, and most education from elementary school through college training, no longer hold that race and ethnicity are biological categories. Our understanding has progressed sufficiently to reflect the reality of these categories, that these are fundamental social, not biological, categories, and our casual (and, fortunately, now historical) belief that race and ethnicity reflect essential properties has been largely displaced by more sophisticated and more accurate understanding.

Such is not, unfortunately, the case with our understanding of sex and gender. For instance, many of my students believe that the different roles assigned to women and men are natural rather than social, most likely due to the fact that women give birth to children. In contrast, the roles assigned to people on the basis of ethnicity or race are believed to be due to a variety of factors such as discrimination, social class, or, in unfortunate and stereotypical attributions, based on stereotypes such as supposed laziness or initiative. I find a stronger sense of political outrage and higher levels of motivation to make progressive social change among the students who take my "Psychology of Prejudice" course – which deals primarily with ethnicity, race, and gender peripherally, whereas the students who take my "Psychology of Women" course – which deals primarily with gender, and race and ethnicity peripherally, seem more resigned to the well-worn path of gender roles, no matter how restrictive and oppressive such roles might be.

It is this perception of the stability of gender differences that I have in mind as I make suggestions for change. The initial strategies for change in this chapter deal with loosening the clenched fist of people's beliefs about the *essential* nature of gender differences. The first strategies for change deal with the entrenchment of gender roles. They are probably closer to *rationales for change*, rather than strategies per se.

Challenging masculine gender roles

In many parts of the chapter, traditional gender roles, such as the beliefs that women are, by nature, nurturing caregivers, while men are, by nature, aggressive and competitive, have been discussed.

In this section, I want to discuss some of the hazards, to men, to women, and to society overall, of traditional masculine gender roles. The beliefs men learn concerning the inferior role of women encourage insensitivity toward and degradation of women. Men with traditional gender-role attitudes also tend to endorse a range of negative beliefs about gender. For instance, men who endorse traditional gender roles tend to believe that there is a place for violence and coercion in relationships, they believe that sexual relationships between women and men are inherently adversarial, and these men also tend to subscribe to rape myths (e.g. the idea that women secretly want to be raped, or could stop a rape from happening if they really wanted to). *Anti-femininity* in men – the need to avoid anything perceived as feminine – is also associated with acceptance of interpersonal violence.[164] Men who believe that men should adhere to traditional male gender roles are more likely to be psychologically aggressive with their female partners.[165] Men who perceive stress and threat associated with their masculinity are more likely to use verbal and physical violence in their relationships.[166] Finally, male-dominated marriages have been shown to contain more male-to-female violence than egalitarian marriages.[167] This cursory review of harm inflicted on women, on relationships, on men, and, ultimately, on society in general traces back to the injurious nature of strict and unthinking adherence to conventional gender roles.

The association between traditional masculinity and date rape supportive ideology suggest that masculine gender roles be addressed in rape education and prevention programs and in the public sphere in general. A starting point for many men to personalize the ways in which gender socialization shapes their lives might be to discuss ways in which traditional gender roles may be harmful not only to women but also to men. The scope could then be narrowed to address directly the ways in which such traditional learning may sanction sexual assault against women. Attempts to derogate feminism may also serve to downplay the seriousness and prevalence of date rape.[168]

Promoting cross-gender interaction with children

One of the hallmarks of childhood in many cultures is the emergence of gender segregation. Gender segregation, the voluntary preference to interact and play with members of the same gender, begins around the age of 3 in the United States and Europe. Gender segregation, which is vigorously enforced by other children, remains until heterosocial and heterosexual relationships begin to emerge in adolescence. Campbell Leaper and I[169] reviewed the research on childhood gender segregation and the potential consequences of the phenomenon for adults. While there are many toys and games that appeal to both girls and boys, when children play in gender-segregated groups, they tend to develop different skills and corresponding social norms. For instance, girls' gender-stereotyped play may involve dolls and kitchen sets that provide them with opportunities to practice the social–relational skills that are typically beneficial in the private world of intimate relationships. Boys' gender-stereotyped play may involve construction toys or sports that give them opportunities to practice skills related to competition and assertiveness. These divergent pathways are encouraged and maintained by parents, teachers, and peers.[170] By the time they reach adolescence, boys are more likely to have prepared to view relationships in terms of greater independence and dominance, whereas girls have prepared to view them in terms of nurturance and support. Boys' gender-segregated play is more likely to prepare them for success in the workplace, while girls' segregated play is more likely to prepare them for success at home. The typical trajectory of development from same-gender interactions teaches girls and boys only one half of what they need to know for life. Encouraging cross-gender (also called mixed-gender) play teaches a broader range of skills that benefit adult women and men in the workplace and also in intimate relationships. Egalitarian relationships are associated with high degrees of satisfaction in both lesbian and gay relationships, heterosexual relationships, and same-gender friendships.[171]

Gender in the classroom

Women's and gender studies coursework

Gender studies courses can play a promising role in disrupting the view that gender differences are biological and natural. First, undergraduate students who have taken a gender studies course are more likely to correctly view gender differences as a result of socialization than as biological.[172] In one study[173] comparing mostly white and mostly women college students who had taken gender studies courses with those who had not, the experience of taking women's studies courses had several benefits. Compared to those who had not taken gender studies courses, gender studies students were more likely to report that the class affected their life outside the classroom. Gender studies students were more likely to increase their egalitarian attitudes toward women and other stigmatized groups; their awareness of sexism and other forms of discrimination increased, and their level of activism for social change increased as well. Another study found that gender studies experience increases awareness of male privilege.[174] Perhaps the most robust result of taking gender studies courses are the students' belief in the importance of activism. Women who take gender studies courses are more likely to show commitment to feminist activism by the end of the semester compared to the beginning. Activism is important for meaningful societal change because it involves personal, direct, grassroots efforts on the part of individuals. Students have increased feelings of empowerment and feel as though they can have a role in social change.[175] Men who take women's/ gender studies classes tend to benefit to the same extent as women.[176] One limitation of most of the studies on the impact of gender studies is that we do not know much about the long-term effects of taking such classes, although one study found that students' lessons from the courses were sustained over a 9-month period.[177] Also, while much of the research on feminist attitude change has been on women's/gender studies classes, there is no reason to think similar work cannot be done in psychology courses.

Teaching girls about discrimination

Should children learn about discrimination? There is some intriguing research on the effects of children learning about gender and racial discrimination. This area of research is still new and underdeveloped, probably because of concerns that children learning about discrimination as part of curricula might cause them distress. Or just as some fear that sex education research might put the forbidden ideas in children's heads, will talking to children about prejudice poison them or make them feel bad? Rebecca Bigler and her colleagues have conducted two studies on the effects of children learning about gender and racial discrimination. Bigler's study on teaching children about racism is discussed in Chapter 5, but the gender study is relevant here. Erica Weisgram and Rebecca Bigler[178] examined the effects of girls who are interested in science learning about gender discrimination in science fields. American girls (mostly white) aged 11–14 years attended a conference specifically for girls interested in careers in science. Half of the girls attended a one-hour session about gender discrimination in scientific fields. The session included ways in which gender discrimination has affected women scientists and biographies of notable scientists who have faced discrimination in their careers. The other half of the girls attended sessions not including information on discrimination. All girls responded to surveys before and after the conference on their interest in science, and perceptions of gender discrimination. The two groups of girls did not differ in their level of interest in science after the conference, however, compared to the girls who did not attend the session on gender discrimination, those who did showed increases in self-efficacy within science and were more likely to believe that science is a worthwhile subject of study. Therefore, exposure of girls to frank discussions about gender discrimination in science had a net positive effect on them. The authors reasoned that perhaps the explicit discussion of gender discrimination explained why there are fewer women in science fields and provided an alternative to the stereotype that men are inherently superior to women in their aptitude for science. Most girls who participated in the gender discrimination lesson believed that discrimination can be overcome by having more women in the sciences. And moreover, many girls indicated that learning about gender discrimination made them feel that they should enter the field to fight discrimination. Weisgram and Bigler discovered another important finding from their study. They asked girls to estimate the percentage of women in scientific professions. On average, the girls estimated that 40% of scientists are women – much larger than the actual percentage. Weisgram and Bigler suspect that girls who prepare to enter scientific fields that are unbeknownst to them highly male dominated become disillusioned at some point and lose interest in the field. This study included girls that were already interested in science. We do not know what the influence of a discussion about gender discrimination would be with girls who don't express overt interest in science. Nonetheless, their results are intriguing and suggest frank talk about discrimination, rather than traumatizing young people, could benefit them.

Cooperative learning and status

In Chapter 1, "Those people all look alike," I described the jigsaw classroom,[179] a collaborative learning strategy that not only facilitates learning, but also promotes empathy and social reciprocity between classmates. Much of the research on the effectiveness of the jigsaw method has been done with children from different ethnic backgrounds. Cooperative learning strategies similar to the jigsaw method have shown promise for gender relations as well. In one study,[180] cooperative learning groups of 11- and 12-year-olds were compared to an individualist condition and found that cooperative learning resulted in greater retention of the material and higher level learning than did individualistic learning. Although there were initial performance differences favoring boys, at the end of the study in the cooperative conditions there were no gender differences in performance and verbal participation. Also, while there were status differences favoring boys, at the end of the study there were no differences in perceived leadership and status in the cooperative conditions but there were in the individualistic conditions.

Resist gender labeling

Teachers of young children play an important role perpetuating gender stereotypes and maintaining gender boundaries. Teachers often use gender as a way of organizing students in a classroom. For instance, a teacher might create girls' and boys' lines to leave for recess or lunch, or might inadvertently foster competition between girls and boys by saying things such as, "the girls are sitting quietly, now we are waiting for the boys." In one experiment, Rebecca Bigler[181] examined the use of gender labeling in the classroom. She trained teachers of 9-year-old white American children to either use gender as a way of organizing the classroom, or to not refer to gender during lessons and instead refer to students only by their individual names and treat the classroom as one unit. The children were assessed before and after the 4-week experimental period on a range of skills and attitudes. Bigler found that the use of gender as an organizing method in the classroom increased children's gender stereotyping in those classrooms, compared to children in the control classroom in which gender was not an organizing principle. When gender was made salient, children showed greater stereotyping of occupations, for instance, believing that there are some careers appropriate for "only women" and "only men." These children also had exaggerated beliefs about gender-related traits for females and males – they believed females and males were more different than did the classrooms that were not organized according to gender. Children with less sophisticated cognitive skills were especially influenced by the gender organization of the classroom – their stereotypes were particularly rigid. Bigler's data suggest that to reduce stereotyping classroom teachers and other adults should refrain from grouping children on the basis of gender and this may be particularly important for younger children who are still in the process of forming stereotypes. Why is it that many people feel comfortable using gender as an explicit way to organize children, whereas most people refrain from organizing children according to race or ethnicity?

Promoting women's success in the workplace

The studies on people's perceptions of "non-traditional" women, and by non-traditional, I mean feminists, lesbians, athletes, and women leaders in the workplace, are consistent. People, both women and men, are uncomfortable with women who are perceived to violate gender-role norms. Virginia Valian[182] argues that the workplace can be a challenging environment for women because femininity is incompatible with workplace success. Masculinity, those stereotyped characteristics associated with men such as competitiveness and assertiveness, is required for success in the workplace. For women, feminine behavior (outside the work place) is encouraged and rewarded. Therefore, in work settings, women face the bind of feeling pressured to conform to feminine stereotypes, but recognize that masculine characteristics are required for success. Valian has some suggestions for this area in which women can be seen as out of place – the workplace.

Challenging hypotheses

When we hear about an individual's success or failure we can examine our own reactions to discover and state explicitly what we implicitly see as its causes. *Why did X not get promoted? Why did the people at this morning's meeting not discuss Y's suggestion?* If we negatively evaluated a woman in some situation, we can try to find a comparable behavior by a man to test whether we see his behavior in the same light. Valian suggests conducting thought experiments in which we switch the genders. Think about how you would rate someone who is undependable or lazy. How would we judge a man/woman for the same behavior? Are there situations in which people are more or less likely to rely on gender stereotypes to evaluate women and men? With regard to stereotyping, when people have more time to devote to thinking about someone else's behaviors and motivations, they are less likely to rely on gender stereotypes. When we can give more thorough attention, we are less likely to rely on gender stereotypes. Also, if evaluators know that their judgments will be reviewed by an unbiased, higher authority, they are more likely to form accurate judgments, and not judgments solely based on gender stereotypes.

1. Robertson letter attacks feminists. (August 26, 1992). *The New York times.* Retrieved February 19, 2008, from http://query.nytimes.com/gst/fullpage.html?res=9E0CE7DC1430F935A1575BC0A964958260&scp=1&sq=robertson+letter+attacks&st=nyt
2. *Merriam-Webster Online Dictionary.* Retrieved December 15, 2007, from www.m-w.com/dictionary/feminism
3. *Encyclopedia Britannica Online.* Retrieved December 15, 2007, from www.britannica.com/eb/article-9343946/feminism
4. See page viii in: hooks, b. (2000). *Feminism is for everybody.* Cambridge, MA: South End Press.
5. Myaskovsky, L., & Wittig, M.A. (1997). Predictors of feminist social identity among college women. *Sex roles, 37,* 861–883.
6. Bullock, H.E., & Fernald, J.L. (2003). "Feminism lite?" Feminist identification, speaker appearance, and perceptions of feminist and antifeminist messengers. *Psychology of women quarterly, 27,* 291–299.
7. Sommers, C.H. (2000). *The war against boys.* New York: Simon & Schuster.
8. Mansfield, H.C. (2006). *Manliness.* New Haven, CT: Yale University Press.
9. Falwell apologizes to gays, feminists, lesbians. (2001, September 14). *CNN.com.* Retrieved July 8, 2009, from http://archives.cnn.com/2001/US/09/14/Falwell.apology/
10. For instance, see: Alexander, S., & Ryan, M. (1997). Social constructs of feminism: A study of undergraduates at a women's college. *College student journal, 31,* 555–567; and see: Aronson, P. (2003). Feminists or "postfeminists"? Young women's attitudes toward feminism and gender relations. *Gender and society, 17,* 903–922.
11. Quoted in: Lopez, K.J. (2005, December 29). Interrogatory, NRO's Q&A: Women who make the world worse. *National review online.* Retrieved October 9, 2008, from www.nationalreview.com/interrogatory/obeirne200512290819.asp
12. See page xviii in: O'Beirne, K. (2006). *Women who make the world worse: And how their radical feminist assault is ruining our schools, families, military, and sports.* New York: Sentinel.

13. *Ibid.*, page xvi.
14. Mansfield, *Manliness*, page 11.
15. O'Beirne, *Women who make the world worse*, page xv.
16. Limbaugh, R. (2005, August 12). *The Rush Limbaugh Show* [Radio Show Broadcast] Retrieved February 21, 2008, from http://mediamatters.org/mmtv/200508160001
17. Mansfield, *Manliness*, page 5 and page 4, respectively.
18. See page 7 in: Donnelly, E. (2005, Week of December 5). Pentagon doesn't need an office of male-bashing. *Human events, 61*, 7.
19. *Ibid.*
20. O'Beirne, *Women who make the world worse*.
21. Markey, J. (1993, May). Male-bashing. *Redbook, 181*, 104–107.
22. *Ibid.*, page 105.
23. Haddock, G., & Zanna, M.P. (1994). Preferring "housewives" to "feminists": Categorization and the favorability of attitudes toward women. *Psychology of women quarterly, 18*, 25–52.
24. Smith, S.M., & de Man, A.F. (1996). Selected personality characteristics and attitudes toward feminism. *Social behavior and personality, 24*, 273–278.
25. Truman, D.M., Tokar, D.M., & Fischer, A.R. (1996). Dimensions of masculinity: Relations to date rape supportive attitudes and sexual aggression in dating situations. *Journal of counseling and development, 74*, 555–562.
26. Bell, S.T., Kuriloff, P.J., Lottes, I., Nathanson, J., Judge, T., & Fogelson-Turet, K. (1992). Rape callousness in college freshman: An empirical investigation of the sociocultural model of aggression towards women. *Journal of college student development, 33*, 454–461.
27. Attitudes toward feminism in this study were measured by assessing respondents' agreement with statements about gender roles such as, "A woman should be expected to change her name when she marries" and "It is all right for women to work but men will always be the basic breadwinners." These statements do not address feminists or the women's movement specifically. This is a common, but somewhat indirect, method of measuring feminism.
28. Haddock & Zanna, Preferring "housewives" to "feminists."
29. Alexander & Ryan, Social constructs of feminism.
30. Berryman-Fink, C., & Verderber, K.S. (1985). Attributions of the term *feminist*: A factor analytic development of a measuring instrument. *Psychology of women quarterly, 9*, 51–64.
31. Roy, R.E., Weibust, K.S., & Miller, C.T. (2007). Effects of stereotypes about feminists on feminist self-identification. *Psychology of women quarterly, 31*, 146–156.

32. McCabe, J. (2005). What's in a label? The relationship between feminist self-identification and "feminist" attitudes among US women and men. *Gender and society, 19*, 480–505.
33. Liss, M., O'Connor, C., Morosky, E., & Crawford, M. (2001). What makes a feminist? Predictors and correlates of feminist social identity in college women. *Psychology of women quarterly, 25*, 124–133.
34. *Ibid.*; White, A.M. (2006). Racial and gender attitudes as predictors of feminist activism among self-identified African American feminists. *Journal of black psychology, 32*, 455–478.
35. White, Racial and gender attitudes as predictors of feminist activism.
36. Halevi, S., & Blumen, O. (2005). "I carry out small wars": The impact of women's studies on Palestinian and Jewish students in Israel. *Journal of gender studies, 14*, 233–249.
37. Riley, S. (2001). Maintaining power: Male constructions of "feminists" and "feminist values." *Feminism and psychology, 11*, 55–78.
38. White, Racial and gender attitudes as predictors of feminist activism.
39. Myaskovsky & Wittig, Predictors of feminist social identity among college women.
40. Roberts, D. (1997). *Killing the black body: Race, reproduction, and the meaning of liberty.* New York: Vintage Books.
41. Simien, E.M. (2004). Gender differences in attitudes toward black feminism among African Americans. *Political science quarterly, 119*, 315–338.
42. Myaskovsky & Wittig, Predictors of feminist social identity among college women.
43. McCabe, What's in a label?
44. Zucker, A.N. (2004). Disavowing social identities: What it means when women say, "I'm not a feminist, but . . . " *Psychology of women quarterly, 28*, 423–435.
45. McCabe, What's in a label?
46. *Ibid.*; Liss *et al.* What makes a feminist?
47. Liss *et al.* What makes a feminist?
48. Toller, P.W., Suter, E.A., & Trautman, T.C. (2004). Gender role identity and attitudes toward feminism. *Sex roles, 51*, 85–90.
49. Kane, E.W. (2000). Racial and ethnic variations in gender-related attitudes. *Annual review of sociology, 26*, 419–439. Compare this to Myaskovsky and Wittig.
50. Smith, M.D., & Self, G.D. (1981). Feminists and traditionalists: An attitudinal comparison. *Sex roles, 7*, 183–188.
51. Yoder, J.D., Fischer, A.R., Kahn, A.S., & Groden, J. (2007). Changes in students' explanations for gender differences after taking a psychology of women class: More constructionist and less essentialist. *Psychology of women quarterly, 31*, 415–425.

52. Kane, Racial and ethnic variations in gender-related attitudes; McCabe, What's in a label?
53. Myaskovsky & Wittig, Predictors of feminist social identity among college women.
54. Saunders, K.J., & Kashubeck-West, S. (2006). The relations among feminist identity development, gender-role orientation, and psychological well-being in women. *Psychology of women quarterly*, *30*, 199–211.
55. Rudman, L.A., & Phelan, J.E. (2007). The interpersonal power of feminism: Is feminism good for romantic relationships? *Sex roles*, *57*, 787–799.
56. O'Beirne, *Women who make the world worse*, page xv.
57. Iazzo, A.N. (1983). The construction and validation of Attitudes Toward Men Scale. *The psychological record*, *33*, 371–378.
58. Maltby, J., & Day, L. (2001). Psychological correlates of attitudes toward men. *The journal of psychology*, *135*, 335–351.
59. Stephan, C.W., Stephan, W.G., Demitrakis, K.M., Yamada, A.M., & Clason, D.L. (2000). Women's attitudes toward men: An integrated threat theory approach. *Psychology of women quarterly*, *24*, 63–73.
60. Liss, M., Hoffner, C., Crawford, M. (2000). What do feminists believe? *Psychology of women quarterly*, *24*, 279–284; Liss et al. What makes a feminist?
61. Yoder et al. Changes in students' explanations for gender differences after taking a psychology of women class.
62. Glick, P., & Fiske, S.T. (1999). The Ambivalence toward Men Inventory: Differentiating hostile and benevolent beliefs about men. *Psychology of women quarterly*, *23*, 519–536.
63. Glick, P., Lameiras, M., Fiske, S.T., et al. (2004). Bad but bold: Ambivalent attitudes toward men predict gender inequality in 16 nations. *Journal of personality and social psychology*, *86*, 713–728.
64. Anderson, K.J., Kanner, M., & Elsayegh, N. (2009). Are feminists man-haters? Feminists' and nonfeminists' attitudes toward men. *Psychology of women quarterly*, *33*, 216–224.
65. Eagly, A.H., & Mladinic, A. (1994). Are people prejudiced against women? Some answers from research on attitudes, gender stereotypes and judgments of competence. In W. Stroebe & M. Hewstone (Eds.), *European review of social psychology* (Vol. 5, pp. 1–35). New York: Wiley.
66. Rudman, L.A., & Goodwin, S.A. (2004). Gender differences in automatic in-group bias: Why do women like women more than men like men? *Journal of personality and social psychology*, *87*, 494–509.
67. A thorough cataloging of gender discrimination is beyond the scope of this chapter but for excellent documentation of gender discrimination,

see: Valian, V. (1999). *Why so slow? The advancement of women.* Cambridge, MA: The MIT Press. See also: Faludi, S. (1991). *Backlash: The undeclared war against American women.* New York: Crown Publishers.

68. US Department of Labor, Bureau of Labor Statistics. (2007, September). *Women in the labor force: A databook.* Retrieved October 10, 2008 from www.bls.gov/cps/wlf-databook-2007.pdf

69. Bishaw, A., & Stern, S. (2006, June 15). *Evaluation of poverty estimates: A comparison of the American Community Survey and the Current Population Survey.* Poverty and Health Statistics Branch, Housing and Household Economic Statistics Division, US Census Bureau.

70. US Department of Labor, Bureau of Labor Statistics. (2005, May 13). *Women in the labor force: A databook.* Retrieved May 15, 2007, from www.bls.gov/cps/wlf-table17-2005.pdf

71. Screen Actors Guild. (2005). *TV performers again take hit from reality programming, 2004 casting data shows.* Retrieved May 12, 2007, from www.sag.org/?q=node/814. See also: Signorielli, N., & Bacue, A. (1999). Recognition and respect: A content analysis of prime-time television characters across three decades. *Sex roles, 40,* 527–544.

72. Ganahl, D.J., Prinsen, T.J., & Netzley, S.B. (2003). A content analysis of prime time commercials: A contextual framework of gender representation. *Sex roles, 49,* 545–551.

73. Lauzen, M.M., & Dozier, D.M. (2005). Maintaining the double standard: Portrayals of age and gender in popular films. *Sex roles, 52,* 437–446.

74. Seidman, S.A. (1999). Revisiting sex-role stereotyping in MTV videos. *International journal of instructional media, 26,* 11–22.

75. Leaper, C., Breed, L., Hoffman, L., and Perlman, C.A. (2002). Variations in the gender-stereotyped content of children's television cartoons across genres. *Journal of applied social psychology, 32,* 1653–1662.

76. Glascock, J., & Preston-Schreck, C. (2004). Gender and racial stereotypes in daily newspaper comics: A time-honored tradition? *Sex roles, 51,* 423–431.

77. Center for American Women and Politics. (2009). *Fact Sheet: Women in the US Congress 2009.* New Brunswick, NJ: Eagleton Institute of Politics.

78. Fiske, S.T., Cuddy, A.J.C., Glick, P., & Xu, J. (2002). A model of (often mixed) stereotype content: Competence and warmth respectively follow from perceived status and competition. *Journal of personality and social psychology, 82,* 878–902.

79. Haddock & Zanna, Preferring "housewives" to "feminists."

80. Glick, P., & Fiske, S.T. (1997). Hostile and benevolent sexism: Measuring ambivalent sexist attitudes toward women. *Psychology of women quarterly, 21*, 119–135.
81. Barreto, M., & Ellemers, N. (2005). The burden of benevolent sexism: How it contributes to the maintenance of gender inequalities. *European journal of social psychology, 35*, 633–642.
82. Glick, P., & Fiske, S.T. (2001). An ambivalent alliance: Hostile and benevolent sexism as complementary justifications for gender inequality. *American psychologist, 56*, 109–118.
83. *Ibid.*, pages 114–115.
84. Jost, J.T., & Kay, A.C. (2005). Exposure to benevolent sexism and complementary gender stereotypes: Consequences for specific and diffuse forms of system justification. *Journal of personality and social psychology, 88*, 498–509.
85. Glick *et al.* (2004). Bad but bold.
86. Christopher, A.N., & Mull, M.S. (2006). Conservative ideology and ambivalent sexism. *Psychology of women quarterly, 30*, 223–230.
87. *Ibid.*
88. Viki, G.T., Abrams, D., & Hutchison, P. (2003). The "true" romantic: Benevolent sexism and paternalistic chivalry. *Sex roles, 49*, 533–537.
89. Moya, M., Expósito, F., & Casado, P. (1999, July). Women's reactions to hostile and benevolent sexist situations. Paper presented at the 22nd General Meeting of the European Association of Experimental Social Psychology, Oxford, England; cited in: Glick & Fiske, An ambivalent alliance.
90. Glick, P., Sakalli-Ugurlu, N., Ferreira, M.C., & Aguiar de Souza, M. (2002). Ambivalent sexism and attitudes toward wife abuse in Turkey and Brazil. *Psychology of women quarterly, 26*, 292–297.
91. Viki, G.T., Abrams, D., & Masser, B. (2004). Evaluating stranger and acquaintance rape: The role of benevolent sexism in perpetrator blame and recommended sentence length. *Law and human behavior, 28*, 295–303.
92. Viki, G.T., Chiroro, P., & Abrams, D. (2006). Hostile sexism, type of rape, and self-reported rape proclivity within a sample of Zimbabwean males. *Violence Against women, 12*, 789–800.
93. Valian, *Why so slow?*
94. Heilman, M.E., Wallen, A.S., Fuchs, D., & Tamkins, M.M. (2004). Penalties for success: Reactions to women who succeed at male gender-typed tasks. *Journal of applied psychology, 89*, 416–427.
95. Study 3 from: Heilman *et al.* Penalties for success.
96. Anderson, K.J., & Smith, G. (2005). Students' preconceptions of professors: Benefits and barriers according to ethnicity and gender. *Hispanic journal of behavioral sciences, 27*, 184–201.

97. Thomas-Hunt, M.C., & Phillips, K.W. (2004). When what you know is not enough: Expertise and gender dynamics in task groups. *Personality and social psychology bulletin, 30,* 1585–1598.

98. Alexander & Ryan, Social constructs of feminism.

99. Grant, A. (2000). And still, the lesbian threat: or, how to keep a good woman a woman. *Journal of lesbian studies, 4,* 61–80. See also Elaine Donnelly's article for an example of women activists being called man-haters: Donnelly, Pentagon doesn't need an office of male-bashing.

100. See pages 67–68 in: Grant, And still, the lesbian threat.

101. *Ibid.,* page 66.

102. *Ibid.,* page 71.

103. Corbett, K.M. (1997, November). Lesbian-baiting: A threat to all military women. *Lesbian news, 23,* 16–18.

104. Liss *et al.* What makes a feminist?

105. See page 104 in: Markey, Male-bashing.

106. Lego, S. (1999). Monicagate and male bashing. *Perspectives in psychiatric care, 35,* 3–4.

107. Heckard, I.R. (1998, January/February). Male bashing: Is it trash talk or harmless humor? *Today's Christian woman, 20,* 46–48.

108. Heard, A. (1989, August). Stop blaming men for everything! *Mademoiselle, 95,* 183, 232, 234.

109. See page 72 in: Grant, And still, the lesbian threat.

110. Kane, Racial and ethnic variations in gender-related attitudes. McCabe, What's in a label?

111. See page 4 in: Mansfield, *Manliness.*

112. See, for instance: Heard, Stop blaming men for everything!

113. See page xi in: O'Beirne, *Women who make the world worse.*

114. Morrow, L. (1994, February 14). Men: Are they really that bad? *Time, 143,* 53–59.

115. *Ibid.,* page 54.

116. *Ibid.,* page 56.

117. *Ibid.,* page 59.

118. Markey, Male-bashing.

119. *Ibid.,* page 105.

120. *Ibid.,* page 105.

121. See, for instance: Heard, Stop blaming men for everything!

122. See page xv in: O'Beirne, *Women who make the world worse.*

123. Farrell, W. (1993). *The myth of male power.* New York: Berkley Books.

124. *Ibid.,* page 18.

125. Morrow, Men.

126. *Ibid.,* page 54.

127. For an examination of popular culture's perpetuation of women-as-teases, see: Anderson, K.J., & Accomando, C. (1999). Madcap misogyny and romanticized victim-blaming: Discourses of stalking in *There's Something About Mary*. *Women and language, 22*, 24–28.

128. See page 58 in: Morrow, Men.

129. See page xx in: O'Beirne, *Women who make the world worse*.

130. Saunders & Kashubeck-West, The relations among feminist identity development, gender-role orientation, and psychological well-being in women.

131. Pollitt, K. (2008, July 21). Who's afraid of Judy Maccabee? *The Nation, 287*, 12.

132. Gilligan, C. (1982). *In a different voice: Psychological theory and women's development*. Cambridge, MA: Harvard University Press.

133. Pipher, M. (1994). *Reviving Ophelia: Saving the selves of adolescent girls*. New York: Ballantine Books.

134. Sadker, M., & Sadker, D. (1994). *Failing at fairness: How America's schools cheat girls*. New York: Charles Scribner's Sons.

135. American Association of University Women. (1992). *The AAUW report: How schools shortchange girls*. Washington, DC: The American Association of University Women Educational Foundation.

136. For a review of these books see: Anderson, K.J., & Accomando, C. (2001). Boy books. *Antioch review, 59*, 108–111.

137. See page 241: Pollack, W. (1998). *Real boys: Rescuing our sons from the myths of boyhood*. New York: Random House.

138. *Ibid.*, page 232.

139. See page 23 in: Kindlon, D., & Thompson, M. (1999). *Raising Cain: Protecting the emotional life of boys*. New York: Ballantine Books.

140. Lewin, T. (2006, July 9). At colleges, women are leaving men in the dust. *The New York times*. Retrieved July 11, 2006 from www.nytimes.com/2006/07/09/education/09college.html

141. Stark, M., & Ebenkamp, B. (1999, October 25). The silence of the lads. *Brandweek, 40*, 22–23.

142. Lewin, T. (1998, December 13). How boys lost out to girl power. *New York times, 148*, p. 3.

143. Anderson, K.J., & Accomando, C. (2002). "Real" boys? Manufacturing masculinity and erasing privilege in popular books on raising boys. *Feminism and psychology, 12*, 491–516.

144. American Association of University Women. (2008, May 20). *AAUW report debunks so-called "boys' crisis" in education* [Press Release]. Retrieved October 9, 2008, from www.aauw.org/About/newsroom/press releases/whereGirlsAre_052 008.cfm

145. Mead, S. (2006, June). The truth about boys and girls. Retrieved February 12, 2008, from www.educationsector.org/research/research_show.htm?doc_id=378 705

146. Anderson & Accomando, "Real" boys?

147. Grillo, T., & Wildman, S.M. (1997). Obscuring the importance of race: The implication of making comparisons between racism and sexism (or other isms). In A.K. Wing (Ed.), *Critical race feminism: A reader* (pp. 44–50). New York: NYU Press.

148. Riley, Maintaining power.

149. Markey, Male-bashing.

150. Ibid., page 105.

151. See page 232 in: Heard, Stop blaming men for everything!

152. Cataldi, S.L. (1995). Reflections on "male bashing." *NWSA journal, 7*, 76–85.

153. Nicholas, S., Kershaw, C., & Walker, A. (Eds.) (2007, July). *Crime in England and Wales 2006/07*. Home Office, United Kingdom. Retrieved September 24, 2008, from www.homeoffice.gov.uk/rds/pdfs07/hosb1107.pdf

154. Finney, A. (2006, December). *Domestic violence, sexual assault and stalking: Findings from the 2004/05 British Crime Survey*. Home Office, United Kingdom. Retrieved September 24, 2008, from www.homeoffice.gov.uk/rds/pdfs06/rdsolr1206.pdf

155. Krebs, C.P., Lindquist, C.H., Warner, T.D., Fisher, B.S., & Martin, S.L. (2007, December). *The campus sexual assault (CSA) study: Final report*. Prepared for National Institute of Justice (NIJ Grant No. 2004-WG-BX-0010).

156. McFarlane, J., & Malecha, A. (2005). *Sexual assault among intimates: Frequency, consequences, and treatments*. Prepared for National Institute of Justice (Award No. 2002-WG-BX-0003). Retrieved September 24, 2008, from www.ncjrs.gov/pdffiles1/nij/grants/211678.pdf

157. US Department of Justice Office on Violence Against Women (2005–2006). *Report to Congress on stalking and domestic violence, 2005 through 2006*. Retrieved September 24, 2008, from www.ncjrs.gov/pdffiles1/ovw/220827.pdf

158. Cataldi, Reflections on "male bashing."

159. See page xviii in: O'Beirne, *Women who make the world worse*.

160. Mansfield, *Manliness*.

161. Anderson *et al*. Are feminists man-haters?

162. Glick, P., & Fiske, S.T. (2001). An ambivalent alliance: Hostile and benevolent sexism as complementary justifications for gender inequality. *American psychologist, 56*, 109–118; Glick & Fiske, The Ambivalence toward Men Inventory.

163. See page xv in: O'Beirne, *Women who make the world worse*.

164. Truman *et al*. Dimensions of masculinity.

165. Good, G.E., Hepper, M.J., Hillenbrand-Gunn, T., & Wang, L.-F. (1995). Sexual and psychological violence: An exploratory study of predictors in college men. *Journal of men's studies, 4*, 59–71; Jenkins, S.S., & Aubé, J. (2002). Gender differences and gender-related constructs in dating aggression. *Personality and social psychology bulletin, 28*, 1106–1118.

166. For a review, see: Moore, T.M., & Stuart, G.L. (2005). A review of the literature on masculinity and partner violence. *Psychology of men and masculinity, 6*, 46–61.

167. Kim, J.-Y., & Emery, C. (2003). Marital power, conflict, norm consensus, and marital violence in a nationally representative sample of Korean couples. *Journal of interpersonal violence, 18*, 197–219.

168. Truman *et al*. Dimensions of masculinity.

169. Leaper, C., & Anderson, K.J. (1997). Gender development and heterosexual romantic relationships during adolescence. In W. Damon (Series ed.) & S. Shulman & W.A. Collins (Issue eds.), *New directions for child development: Romantic relationships in adolescence* (pp. 85–103, No. 78, Winter). San Francisco: Jossey-Bass.

170. Valian, *Why so slow?*

171. For a review, see: Leaper & Anderson, Gender development and heterosexual romantic relationships during adolescence.

172. Yoder *et al*. Changes in students' explanations for gender differences after taking a psychology of women class.

173. Stake, J.E., & Hoffmann, F.L. (2001). Changes in student social attitudes, activism, and personal confidence in higher education: The role of women's studies. *American educational research journal, 38*, 411–436.

174. Case, K.A. (2007). Raising male privilege awareness and reducing sexism: An evaluation of diversity courses. *Psychology of women quarterly, 31*, 426–435.

175. Stake, J.E. (2007). Predictors of change in feminist activism through women's and gender studies. *Sex roles, 57*, 43–54.

176. Stake, J.E., & Malkin, C. (2003). Students' quality of experience and perceptions of intolerance and bias in the women's and gender studies classroom. *Psychology of women quarterly, 27*, 174–185.

177. Stake, J.E., & Rose, S. (1994). The long-term impact of women's studies on students' personal lives and political activism. *Psychology of women quarterly, 18*, 403–412.

178. Weisgram, E.S., & Bigler, R.S. (2007). Effects of learning about gender discrimination on adolescent girls' attitudes toward and interest in science. *Psychology of women quarterly, 31*, 262–269.

179. Aronson, E. (2004). Reducing hostility and building compassion: Lessons from the jigsaw classroom. In A.G. Miller (Ed.), *The social psychology of good and evil* (pp. 469–488). New York: The Guilford Press.

180. Petersen, R.P., Johnson, D.W., & Johnson, R.T. (1991). Effects of cooperative learning on perceived status of male and female pupils. *Journal of social psychology, 131,* 717–735.

181. Bigler, R.S. (1995). The role of classification skill in moderating environmental influences on children's gender stereotyping: A study of the functional use of gender in the classroom. *Child development, 66,* 1072–1087.

182. Valian, *Why so slow?*

FOUR

"Gays flaunt their sexuality": The myth of hypersexuality

I have no problems working with or being around homosexuals as long as they keep it private, as you would in a normal relationship. When they flaunt their homosexuality they deserve the harassment they get.[1]

Who is the better parent, a convicted killer or a lesbian? In 1996, Mary Ward found out the answer when she lost custody of her daughter Cassey to her ex-husband, John Ward, because she was a lesbian.[2] Cassey, 12, had lived with her mother all of her life. In his decision, the judge explained that he granted custody to the father because he believed Cassey "should be given the opportunity to live in a nonlesbian world." And that Cassey should have the "full opportunity to know that she can [l]ive another lifestyle if she wants and not be led into this lifestyle just by virtue of the fact of her living accommodations." John Ward's fourth marriage of two years was cited as evidence of stability. Never mind that John Ward had served eight years in prison for a second-degree murder conviction for shooting and killing his first wife. Mary Ward died of a heart attack in 1997 before she could appeal the decision.

This chapter explores the belief that lesbians and gay men are somehow conspicuous and provocative about sex and sexuality in ways that heterosexuals are not. This belief is expressed in a variety of forms and in a range of contexts, but it can be distilled to one issue: openness about one's (homosexual) orientation is equivalent to "flaunting it." The belief that gay men and lesbians advertise their sexuality is rooted in common errors in thinking and supported by a culture that tolerates and promotes homophobia and heterosexism. This chapter begins with an examination of two errors in thinking that are partly responsible for the belief that homosexuals flaunt their sexuality. Next, I examine other flaws in thinking that result from the larger context of hostility toward and discrimination against lesbians, gay men, and bisexuals – heterosexism and homophobia. Homophobia, and its link to the specific myth of gay flaunting, is discussed next. The chapter concludes with a discussion of strategies that can be employed in daily life to reduce the thinking that perpetuates this myth.

Gay associations: The illusory correlation

Illusory correlation is a term used by psychologists to describe a common error in thinking in which an apparent association mistakenly becomes locked in as a conclusion. Illusory correlation refers to an overestimation of the strength of a relationship between two variables. The variables in question may in fact not be related at all, or the relationship could be weaker than assumed. Central to the concept of illusory correlation is the idea that certain impressions and images are distinctive. This distinctiveness is significant – we tend to notice the unusual and atypical. In illusory correlation two elements become linked whether or not they have any real connection. Illusory correlation is particularly important in research on prejudice and discrimination. Through systematic research and controlled experiments, social psychologists have confirmed what members of minority groups have known all along: individual minority group members are required to stand in as representatives of their entire group. When an individual's behavior is regarded as unacceptable in whatever way, that behavior stands out as both less acceptable and more typical in the minds of non-minority observers. Illusory correlation is part of the explanation for this tendency.

An experiment by David Hamilton and Robert Gifford[3] demonstrates how illusory correlations develop. Participants in their study read a series of statements describing desirable and undesirable behaviors of members of two groups, Group A and Group B. The two groups were only distinguished by their group labels, not by more distinctive labels such as race or gender. There were twice as many statements about Group A (the majority group) as Group B (the minority group). Of each group's statements, two thirds described desirable behavior ("John, a member of Group A, visited a sick friend in the hospital"), and one third undesirable behavior ("Bob, a member of Group A, always talks about himself"). Even though there were more statements about Group A than about Group B, the ratio of desirable to undesirable behaviors was the same. Therefore an accurate evaluation of the two groups would be that they engage in the same amount of good and bad behavior. However, they found a bias: Group A (the majority) was perceived more favorably than Group B (the minority) because of the inclination to notice the distinctive behaviors in the statements – in this case the undesirable behaviors of Group B (there were fewer of these numerically). An illusory correlation is produced when the co-occurrence of the distinctive group and the undesirable behavior can lead to the perception that the group has a "natural" tendency towards the undesirable behavior. The more we notice this link the more accessible in memory it becomes and hence more likely to influence our subsequent judgments of the target group.

Let's examine how illusory correlation works in general and then explore the myth of gay flaunters. Take television news representations of minorities. In social environments in which whites in the US have little contact with African Americans the effects of illusory correlation on stereotypical thinking and, for example African Americans and crime, illustrates this. When we measure actual portrayals in media, African Americans are less likely to be portrayed as victims of crime than whites, when you take into account both groups' crime rates in the actual population.[4] Moreover, because African Americans are numerically a minority and are underrepresented on television programs, the vivid and negative portrayals of African Americans as criminals in network news and in prime time television programming stand out and shape perceptions that misrepresent real-life African Americans. Add this to the fact that African Americans are portrayed in less sympathetic ways than whites on the news[5] and the devastating effects of illusory correlation become clear. Jane Risen[6] and her colleagues found that, in some cases, the witnessing of just *one* uncommon event by a minority group member is enough to develop a stereotype about the particular event and the minority group. This is known as a *one-shot illusory correlation*.

Now consider representations of lesbians, gay men, and bisexuals in mass media. One argument might contend that heterosexuals are presented in both positive and negative ways in the media, and numerically there may be actually more negative portrayals of heterosexuals simply as a function of numerically more representations of heterosexuals overall. If this is the case, what is the complaint? What could be objectionable about negative representations of gay people if there actually are more negative representations of heterosexuals? Research on illusory correlation demonstrates the significant impact of the phenomenon of fewer representations of minorities overall. The complaint comes from the fact that negative portrayals of a less represented group are more vivid, more memorable, and have potentially more real-life impact than any negative representations of a majority group, in this case, heterosexuals. According to the predictions of illusory correlation, those negative and stereotypical portrayals will be more salient and memorable to the viewer than negative portrayals of heterosexuals. You can understand then why, for example, in post September 11 US, Muslim groups in the United States object to even a single negative portrayal of a Muslim terrorist in a popular film. There are so few portrayals of Muslims overall that this one negative representation could have a greater impact than hundreds of negative portrayals of non-Muslims.

The concept of illusory correlation has strong explanatory value for us in understanding stereotyped judgments of lesbians, gay men, and heterosexuals. J. Manuel Casas and his colleagues[7] measured the effect of stereotyping by mental health professionals on their memory and recall of information about people based on gender and sexual orientation. Mental health professionals (e.g. therapists and clinicians) were given cards that identified hypothetical persons with information about their gender and sexual orientation. Each card had additional information consistent with stereotypes of that group (e.g. gay man described as "promiscuous") as well as information inconsistent with stereotypes of that group (gay man described as "masculine"). After the participants studied the cards, their recall accuracy of the different kinds of information was measured. Casas found that more stereotype-consistent information was remembered than stereotype-inconsistent information. In other words, people better remember information that confirms their stereotypes than information that disconfirms their stereotypes. It is noteworthy that the participants in this study were mental health professionals – individuals who are trained experts in human behavior, are in positions to help people and are or should be unbiased, fair, and non-judgmental. These findings suggest that many of us, regardless of our training and background, are subject to errors in processing. It is very likely that one has contact with a lesbian or gay man every day (whether we realize it or not) but what people pay attention to and remember is the effeminate gay man and the masculine lesbian because the images are consistent with cultural stereotypes about lesbians and gay men.

Assumptions about gay people and gayness

Vividness: Gayness standing out

Social psychologists use the term *vividness effect* to describe the tendency to pay attention to only certain distinctive characteristics. In this case, certain examples of lesbians and gay men are more salient because they are more vivid and stand out. Many studies in social psychology and consumer behavior have been conducted on the nature and effectiveness of vivid appeals[8] – those messages that, while perhaps containing inaccurate information compared to more ordinary messages, create a striking and lasting if mistaken impression on the individual. Vivid appeals distort one's ability to fairly appraise the whole picture. Think about the most memorable television commercials: the Geico™ gecko who sells car insurance, or a famous athlete pitching Nike™ shoes. Neither of these commercials give you much information about the products they are selling but they do create vivid, memorable images. Vivid appeals work for several reasons. First, vivid images and events attract attention: a drag queen is more noticeable than a librarian. Second, vivid information appears to be more concrete and personal. If a co-worker wonders, *"Why do lesbians want to be men?"* hearing the question could just confirm the belief in your own similar stereotype. Third, vivid information acts to frame an issue, and it has the effect of focusing the audience's attention on issues and claims that the communicator feels are most important. For instance, if someone is preoccupied with how lesbians and gay men appear to violate gender roles and flaunt their sexuality, that is what becomes the focus of their concern – not for instance, how heterosexuals flaunt *their* sexuality. Finally, vivid images are memorable and come to mind easily.

So imagine watching your nightly television news. Your local network affiliate reports on your city's Gay Pride parade. What images does the news show? The "dykes-on-bikes" "butch" women in leather on motorcycles, drag queens in gigantic fuchsia-colored wigs, barely clothed young men in leather bikinis, men holding hands with other men, women with women and your reaction is, *"Why can't those people just act normal?"* or *"Why do I have to see this stuff on TV?"* The news report does not show the majority of lesbians and gay men who look quite ordinary and inconspicuous, suburban, corporate, academic, working class, or otherwise not remarkable. Such news reports do not show footage of families who come to the parade with diaper bags and strollers. In fact, if the news simply showed the spectators at the Pride parade viewers would see quite a range of people – families, grandparents, the usual variety of parade-goers. But you can imagine that this would not make for very interesting, *vivid*, news. Portraying lesbian, gay, and bisexual people as freaks, or at least as those out of the mainstream, is much more interesting news and therefore the stereotype that homosexuals are perverse and deviant is perpetuated. If the occasional glimpse of a Gay Pride parade is a person's only exposure to lesbians, gay men, and bisexuals, it is not surprising that this person attends to the most vivid images and makes the illusory correlation between mannishness and lesbianism, and flamboyancy and gay men. We begin to view lesbians and gay men (or those we *think* are lesbian and gay) through a lens that only sees masculine women and feminine men.

Once we have the information that a person is a lesbian or gay man that single characteristic assumes great significance and, we tend to see the person through a lens of stereotypes perpetuated by our culture. Several social psychology studies illustrate how people's assumptions guide their judgments of lesbians and gay men. A typical experiment works like this. Lee Jussim and colleagues[9] gave a writing sample claimed to be written by either a heterosexual man or a gay man. In reality, the writing sample was created by the researchers and the content was identical in the sample for both writers. Student participants were asked to rate the writing on whether they thought the writer was creative, intelligent, likeable, and mentally stable. Students reported liking the (supposed) heterosexual writer more than the (supposed) gay writer, and were more likely to think that the gay writer was mentally disturbed compared to the heterosexual writer. Again, the actual writing samples were the same for both types of writers. Jussim's study demonstrates how group labels bias people's perception of others. Although this study does not address the belief that lesbians and gay men flaunt their sexuality, it does demonstrate that people tend to have a set of (negative) expectations of lesbians and gay people and these expectations cloud and confuse their judgment making it more likely that lesbians and gay people are not judged as individuals but as members of groups about which there are specific negative stereotypes.

You can spot one

I have given up counting how many of my students believe they have "gaydar" and can tell whether a person is lesbian, gay, or straight. But there is a simple logical error revealed in this assumption. It's kind of like spotting a toupée – sure, we can spot toupées that look like toupées but we cannot spot the ones that do not look like toupées. As former US Secretary of State Donald Rumsfeld famously remarked, *we don't know what we don't know.*[10]

One aspect of sexuality that contributes to people's confidence in "spotting one" is that sexual orientation can be concealed from view to a greater extent than some other social statuses such as age, gender and race. It is uncommon for a person's gender to be unclear or ambiguous, and one's race is usually identifiable, although there are certainly instances of people of color identifying as multiracial rather than occupying a strictly bounded category. This fact encourages the tendency for people to see a masculine woman, who may or may not be a lesbian, and be convinced that their gaydar is working and they have indeed spotted a lesbian. Or to see a feminine man and believe, again accurately or not, that he is gay, and thus feel reinforced in the viewer's belief that lesbians are mannish and gay men are feminine. Never mind all the lesbians and gay men who do not fit the stereotype; such individuals never appear on the "gaydar" screen.

People tend to think lesbians and gay men are easy to spot because, as Mary E. Kite and Kay Deaux[11] found, heterosexuals' characterizations of lesbians and gay men, compared with heterosexuals, are based on visual markers rather than less obvious and concrete attributes. According to Kite and Deaux, gay men can supposedly be identified by their wearing of jewelry, their feminine mannerisms and walk, their feminine clothing, and high-pitched voices. Lesbians are apparently identifiable by their short hair, masculine appearance, and unattractiveness. Not insignificantly, heterosexuals, according to Kite and Deaux's study, can be identified because they are "normal." You can imagine with these stereotypes floating around in people's heads, how a whole world of lesbians, gay men, and bisexuals are totally missed because they do not conform to these stereotypes.

This combination of stereotyped images of lesbians and gay men and the fact that they are typically not distinguishable from heterosexuals has serious implications for the treatment of, not only lesbians and gay men, but also heterosexuals who might not conform to the heterosexual norm. The result is a tyranny of rigid gender and sexual orientation roles that hangs over all of us because anyone who does not conform to gender stereotypes could be

202 • Benign Bigotry

suspect. And lesbian/gay-baiting – the targeting of homosexuals, or suspected homosexuals for abuse – by heterosexuals would not be effective if there were a definitive way to identify someone's sexual orientation. And of course lesbian/gay-baiting would not be effective if there were no stigma attached to being lesbian or gay. But because there is no way of telling whether someone is gay or straight except if they tell you, and because there is a stigma associated with homosexuality, women are pressured to appear and behave adequately feminine and men are pressured to appear and behave adequately masculine. All of us, regardless of our sexual orientation, should desire to disrupt gender myths and the rigid rules that accompany gender roles. Negative views about homosexuality function to keep everyone in their place.

Anyone who is gay is too gay

But there is another level at which to examine the question about homosexuals flaunting their sexuality. What does the flaunting issue actually say about those who are concerned about it? I suspect that what people may really mean is that disclosing that one is gay is itself an act of flaunting. Just simply knowing that someone is gay is too distracting and distasteful for some people. To understand why people so readily believe that gay people flaunt their sexuality requires an examination of heterosexual privilege and heterosexism.

One of the ways powerful groups stay powerful is through privilege. As Allan Johnson[12] notes, privilege generally allows people to assume a certain level of acceptance, inclusion, and respect as they move through the world. Privilege grants cultural authority to make judgments about others. It allows certain people to define reality and to maintain prevailing definitions of reality that fit their experience. Privilege means being able to decide who gets taken seriously, who receives attention, and it confers a presumption of superiority and social permission to act on that presumption without having to worry about being challenged. To have privilege is to be able to move through life without being marked as an outsider, as deviant, as the *other*. One aspect of privilege is that the privileged are in the position of establishing and setting the basis of behavior by which conduct is appraised and "normal" is defined. Privileged groups are viewed as the norm, they are taken as the standard of comparison that represents the best that society has to offer, or at least the most normal. Those who are members of groups who are not the norm are compared, almost always unfavorably, to those seen as regular, normal people. For instance in the United States, a male-dominated patriarchal society, men are seen as the norm to which women are compared and viewed as different and deviant. For example, the normative nature of male privilege is represented in the language we use (e.g. *man's* best friend, the history of *mankind*), and in seemingly small but constant examples such as having a drawing of the (white) male body stand for all humans in anatomy classes. In my field, psychology, historically women were not used as research participants because they were considered to be too variable and it was assumed that data from women could not be generalized to all people, whereas data from men were thought to be generalizable to all. When mass media report on "gender issues," they usually mean issues related to women – in this case, men are seen as regular people, as normal, and women are marked and viewed as a special interest group. The same is true for race with whites seen as the norm and people of color as the *other*, as in "those people" – people who are different from you and me and other "regular" people.

Not surprisingly then, heterosexuality is considered to be the norm, while homosexuality is considered the *other*. Take a look at *The heterosexual questionnaire*. When these questions typically asked of lesbian and gay people by heterosexuals are framed in the reverse, you see how heterosexuality is the taken-for-granted norm. For instance, how often do heterosexuals have to explain why they are the way they are ("*Do you think you were born that way?*")? Heterosexuals are entitled to heterosexual privilege – the unearned and taken-for-granted advantages and benefits of being the norm. In his book, *Power, Privilege, and Difference*, Allan Johnson[13] lists some of the many advantages heterosexuals receive for being members of a group considered the norm. For instance, heterosexuals do not have to worry that if they get fired from a job, it may have been due to their sexual orientation; heterosexuals can live where they want without having to worry about neighbors who disapprove of their sexual orientation; and perhaps most relevant to our discussion here, heterosexuals do not run the risk of being reduced to a single aspect (sex) of their lives, as if being heterosexual summed up the kind of person they are. Instead, they can be viewed and treated as complex human beings who happen to be heterosexual.

Heterosexual questionnaire (excerpt)

(1977, Martin Rochlin)

1. What do you think caused your heterosexuality?
2. When and how did you first decide you were heterosexual?
3. Is it possible that your heterosexuality is just a phase you may grow out of?
4. Is it possible that your heterosexuality stems from a fear of others of the same sex?
5. If you have never slept with a member of your own sex, is it possible that you might be gay if you tried it?
6. If heterosexuality is normal, why are so many mental patients heterosexual?
7. Why do you heterosexual people try to seduce others into your lifestyle?
8. Why do you flaunt your heterosexuality? Can't you just be who you are and keep it quiet?

9. The great majority of child molesters are heterosexual. Do you consider it safe to expose your children to heterosexual teachers?

10. With all the societal support that marriage receives, the divorce rate is spiraling. Why are there so few stable relationships among heterosexual people?

11. Why are heterosexual people so promiscuous?

12. Would you want your children to be heterosexual, knowing the problems they would face, such as heartbreak, disease, and divorce?

The high stakes of parental rights and custody

One arena in which stereotypes about lesbians and gay men involve high stakes with dire consequences is in the area of parental rights. Lesbians and gay men may face a judge in child custody disputes or in adoption cases. Here you can see where merely *existing* as a lesbian or gay person is akin to flaunting your "lifestyle." Families can be and have been pulled apart and destroyed because a judge could not see past a parent's homosexuality and get past their stereotypes about homosexuals. It is not surprising then, in this cultural and political atmosphere that assumes merely being lesbian or gay constitutes "flaunting" one's sexuality, that judges in family law cases stereotypically and erroneously presume that gay and lesbian parents will perform, demonstrate and otherwise flaunt sexual behavior and that it is presumed heterosexual parents will not.[14] Just what an individual judge may understand as *flaunting* ranges from judge to judge but none of it is good. Sometimes, merely being in a relationship if a parent is lesbian or gay is grounds for losing custody of a child. Kimberly Richman[15] analyzed the language of all US appellate court decisions over the past 50 years in which there was a custody dispute involving a lesbian or gay parent, 235 cases in all. In 47% of the cases, the court criticized a lesbian or gay parent for associating with others who were openly lesbian or gay. For instance, sometimes in order for mothers to get custody of the children, they were barred from living with a woman partner. What underlies these decisions is judges' views that lesbian and gay relationships are bad for children. Judges have described lesbian and gay relationships as "unusual," "irregular," and "abnormal."[16] As Richman discovered, the implication here is that parents should be able to separate their behavior from their sexual identity and not "act on" their homosexuality. (Can you imagine a heterosexual parent being ordered to not *act on* their heterosexuality? To not become romantically involved with another person? To not affiliate with other heterosexuals?)

There is the sometimes tacit, sometimes explicit, expectation that it is a lesbian or gay parent's duty to shield children from the evidence of their sexuality. In one case a gay father was accused of "choosing his own sexual gratification" over his child merely because he openly affirmed his gay identity. In another analysis of child custody cases, Katherine Arnup[17] found judges making peculiar comparisons of parents' behavior. For instance, during one proceeding a judge stated, "Mrs. K's homosexuality is . . . no more of a bar to her obtaining custody than is the fact of Mr. K's drug use." Mrs. K was eventually granted custody of her child because the judge concluded: "[T]heir relationship will be discreet and will not be flaunted to the children or to the community at large."[18] In another case, the court criticized a lesbian mother and removed her child from her custody because the mother allegedly "felt her individual rights [to live with a companion] were as important as her child's."[19] Imagine a heterosexual parent being chastised in this way. On the other hand, a gay father was called untrustworthy by a judge for having *hidden* his homosexuality from family members. Lesbian and gay parents really are damned if they do and damned if they don't. The issue of "flaunting" is more serious than impressions, attitudes, and media images: It is a matter of life and death for millions of lesbians, gay men, and bisexuals.

The lesson from these cases, as well as the case of Mary Ward described at the beginning of this chapter, seems to be this: It's okay to be lesbian or gay as long as you're not *actually* lesbian or gay. It is relatively rare that heterosexuals have to prove that their relationships would not negatively affect their children – in fact, heterosexual relationships are perceived as a sign of *stability*, whereas lesbian and gay relationships are a sign of *flaunting*.

"What about the children?"

All this discussion regarding judicial concerns about lesbian and gay parents' flaunting (i.e. being open about) their sexuality brings up an important question. What impact does having a lesbian or gay parent have on a child? What is the impact of having a parent with a live-in partner? Charlotte Patterson[20] reviewed all available studies on the effects a lesbian or gay parent's sexuality has on a child. Not only are children not harmed in questions of, for example, psychological adjustment or self-esteem, but research shows that children raised by open lesbian and gay parents do just as well as children of heterosexuals. For example, the self-esteem among daughters of lesbian mothers whose partners lived with them was higher than the self-esteem of daughters whose lesbian mothers did not live with a partner (there were no comparable patterns with sons). The relationship between daughters' self-esteem and mothers with live-in partners is only correlational, meaning we cannot necessarily conclude that lesbians living with partners causes the daughters of lesbians to have high self-esteem. Perhaps mothers with high self-esteem themselves are more likely to be involved in a romantic relationship and to have daughters who also have high self-esteem. Regardless of how it is interpreted, there is no evidence to suggest that a live-in partner of a lesbian negatively impacts the children.[21] Other studies find that children raised by same-sex couples do not differ in their family and school relationships from children with heterosexual parents.[22] However, children of same-sex parents have reported less support from school administrators and teachers, compared to their peers with heterosexual parents.[23]

How does openness about parental sexuality actually affect lesbian and gay parents and their children? Patterson found that lesbian mothers' psychological well-being was related to the extent to which they were open about their sexual orientation with employers, ex-husbands, and children. A mother who felt comfortable disclosing her identity was also more likely to express a greater sense of well-being. In light of the child development research finding that children's adjustment in heterosexual families is often related to maternal mental health, we could expect factors that enhance mental health among lesbian mothers may also benefit their children. There is also some evidence that children whose fathers were rejecting of the mother's lesbianism tended to report lower self-esteem than those whose fathers were neutral or positive. Finally, the age at which children learn of a parent's lesbian or gay identity can impact how the child responds. Basically, the earlier a child learns of her parent's homosexuality, the better the child will feel about it and the more adjusted the child will be.

Now that same-sex marriage is legal in a few states in the US, it is possible to study the nature of those unions compared with heterosexual married couples. A study by Kimberly Balsam[24] and her colleagues compared same-sex couples in civil unions, same-sex couples not in civil unions, and heterosexual married couples on a variety of issues such as conflict, intimacy, and relationship quality. Balsam and her colleagues found that compared with heterosexual married participants, both types of same-sex couples reported greater relationship quality, compatibility, intimacy, and lower levels of conflict. Same-sex couples not in civil unions were more likely to have ended their relationships than same-sex civil union or heterosexual married couples. Finally, another study that compared the relationships between same-sex couples with three categories of heterosexual couples: dating, engaged, and married. Results indicated that individuals in committed same-sex relationships were generally not distinguishable from their committed heterosexual counterparts, with one exception: in laboratory observations, lesbian couples were more effective at working together than the other groups.[25]

In stark contrast to some judicial rulings, by all available accounts, it's best for children with a lesbian or gay parent to learn early of their parent's sexuality, have a parent who is open about their sexuality, to be in a stable romantic relationship, and to be in an environment where others are affirming or at least accepting of the parent's sexuality. You can imagine, with gay marriage being illegal in most states in the US, how this allows judges to use rather idiosyncratic discretion in custody matters. When there is no federal marriage protection, a judge feels no pressure whatsoever to recognize or validate lesbian and gay relationships.

Flaunting it at work?

The workplace is another domain where the line between flaunting one's sexuality and simply existing can be blurry. As with parenting issues, when lesbians and gay men find their sexuality a subject of focus and harassment at work, the ramifications can be devastating because of the impact on one's very livelihood (i.e. one's ability to make money). Estela Bensimon[26] analyzed faculty responses to a survey on the campus climate for lesbian and gay faculty at a university. Seventy-five percent of university professors who responded to the survey mentioned that being gay is private and shouldn't be "flaunted" in public. A typical response was, "*Why do they need everyone to know they are gay? I don't introduce myself as a heterosexual, why would I want to know their sexual orientation? It's nobody's business who you spend time with.*"[27] On the surface, this is a reasonable statement. We are talking about a professional environment, who wants to know whom others sleep with? But being gay or lesbian is not simply about who one sleeps with (although some heterosexuals seem to think so – see next section). As William Pugh[28] found, in a study of lesbian, gay, and bisexual professors: "The very fact of being gay, lesbian, or bisexual and of being open about it is often viewed by the intolerant as 'pushiness.'"

The logic underlying this reasoning according to Estela Bensimon hinges on an apparent private/public distinction of personal disclosure. This reasoning is as follows: lesbians and gay men have made a personal decision (i.e. a choice) to engage in homosexual behavior; therefore, to complain in public of inequalities derived from their individual and freely made choices undermines the protective intents in the separation between public and private. Therefore, as long as sexual orientation is viewed as a private matter, the workplace can deny responsibility to protect gay men and lesbians from unfair and unequal treatment. If lesbians and gay men would simply not make the choice to disclose their sexuality in the workplace, then no one would know, and therefore, no one would discriminate against them. A homophobic co-worker who is prejudiced may interpret the disclosure of a colleague's sexual orientation as an aggressive, flaunting act because they do not want to come into contact with "those" people whom their prejudices have taught them to distrust and fear. This perceived "pushiness" on the part of a gay man or lesbian disclosing their orientation can be punished by the denial of jobs and promotions. To some, honesty about one's identity can be construed as a political statement, rather than mere honesty. But being lesbian, gay, or bisexual, is part of a person's identity and cannot be separated from its political message. Coming out at work has been described by lesbian and gay employees as one of the most important points in their career.[29] As an example, look at the dilemma faced by a professor invited to a dinner party with colleagues:

The department has a party, and everyone's asked to bring their partners. So, the gay or lesbian person immediately faces a dilemma. Do they bring the partner and acknowledge the fact that this is who they are and their partner has an equal status with the spouses and other partners – the heterosexual partners – of other members of the department or do they just come to the party by themselves? Now, why would it be so bad just to bring the partner? Well, what it is, is that you're forcing people to acknowledge that you really are gay. It's not just something that's on paper or something that happens outside the university in your personal life, but you're bringing your personal life into your public life.[30]

If this person declines the invitation altogether because of the hassle it brings, then she risks appearing anti-social, and collegiality could be a factor in judging someone's tenure. Collegiality often includes joshing around and talking about family relationships, spouses, and other aspects of personal life. If your personal life is kept private, you seem unfriendly, but if you are open about your private life, you may be viewed as flaunting your sexuality. Subtle prejudice can manifest itself during hiring and promotion when a member of the search committee describes a lesbian or gay professor as *"someone who just doesn't fit in here."* The lesbian or gay professional's sexual orientation is a source of possible controversy in a manner that the heterosexual's is not. That one could face discrimination in the tenure or promotion process because of one's choice of a dinner-party date is a fear that heterosexuals rarely face.

There is a double standard used when judging the sexualized behavior of heterosexuals and lesbians and gay men. James Ward and Diana Winstanley[31] interviewed heterosexual and gay firefighters in the UK and found the common sentiment about the openness of gay firefighters about their sexuality: the sentiment is, being gay is okay, but talking about it is not. Fire stations, like police departments and the military, are highly masculinized environments where heterosexuality is surely flaunted in terms of men discussing sexual relations with women, pin-up calendars, etc. But for a gay or lesbian firefighter, merely disclosing one's sexuality amounts to too much information. Keeping one's sexuality a secret requires people not to talk about their partners, friends, family, or what they do on the weekend.

Equating homosexuality with sex

I've about decided if it wasn't for the sex I could be gay. Hell then you're just hanging out with your buddies.

Comedian Bill Engvall[32]

The fundamental notion that lesbians and gay men are believed to flaunt their sexuality is rooted in some heterosexuals' belief that the difference between homosexuality and heterosexuality can be reduced to the act of sex. It seems to be the case that heterosexuals sometimes equate homosexuality with sex. Let's look at the manifestations and consequences of this tendency to reduce sexual orientation, especially a homosexual orientation, to sexual behavior alone.

A common stereotype of gay men is that they are child molesters.[33] Think about it. Would you rather entrust your child to a baby sitter who is heterosexual or homosexual? When young boys are molested by men, this is often taken as evidence that the molester is a homosexual. However, many molesters are pedophiles, individuals who are sexually fixated on children. Sometimes the fixation is on male children, more often on female, and sometimes on both. Pedophiles do not develop mature sexual relationships with adults and some have never had an adult sexual relationship, either homosexual or heterosexual. Two studies are relevant here. Carole Jenny and her colleagues,[34] in a study on child abuse, examined 269 child molestation cases and found that 82% of the alleged offenders were heterosexual partners of a close relative of the child, such as a stepfather. In only two (0.7%) cases were the offenders identifiable as lesbian or gay. Jenny concludes, "In other words, in this sample, a child's risk of being molested by his or her relative's heterosexual partner is over 100 times greater than by someone who might be identifiable as being homosexual, lesbian, or bisexual."[35]

A. Nicholas Groth and H. Jean Birnbaum,[36] in a study of adult attraction to underaged individuals, studied the records of 175 men convicted of child sexual abuse. First of all, most victims were girls, a fact that is often lost in the face of anti-gay hysteria about child molestation. Second, in terms of the perpetrators, of the 175 men examined, none were gay men. In fact Groth and Birnbaum conclude their study by stating, "It appears, therefore, that the adult heterosexual male constitutes a greater sexual risk to under age children than does the adult homosexual male."[37]

Why, in view of available evidence, the myth of the link between gay men and child molestation persists can be explained by the simplistic and inaccurate belief that if a boy is molested by an adult man, the man must be a homosexual. Again, the man is probably a pedophile, not a gay man, but because it's a same-sex molestation, the myth persists. The myth that gay men are child molesters also contributes to the belief that homosexuals are sexual predators who set out and are able to "recruit" children and unsuspecting heterosexual adults into their "lifestyle."

In her analysis of court cases involving lesbian and gay parents described earlier Kimberly Richman found a consistent thread of concerns about "homosexual recruitment." Judges fear that a child will model himself after a gay role model or that a parent's "sexual disorientation"[38] will rub off on a child or the child will catch it as if it's a gay cooty.

If this were true, why couldn't the heterosexual parents of lesbians and gay children convert *them* to heterosexuality? If sexual orientation developed in a role-model fashion, there would be few lesbians and gay men in our society because of the clear social sanctions against it. And why would lesbians and gay men want to recruit children? Lesbians and gay adults are interested in relationships with other lesbian and gay adults, not heterosexuals and not children.

Is there any truth to support the belief that children of lesbians or gay men become gay? A number of studies have examined whether children of lesbians and gay men are more likely to become lesbian or gay themselves compared to children raised in heterosexual households. Research says no. Also, children of lesbian or gay parents are no different than children raised by heterosexuals in terms of their gender identity (a person's self-identification as female or male) and gender-role behavior (the extent to which a person's activities are gender stereotyped). The only exception found is a slight tendency for daughters of lesbian mothers to be more interested in rough-and-tumble play and masculine-stereotyped toys such as trucks (there were no comparable differences for sons).[39] As Charlotte Patterson concluded in her summary of these studies, "In all these studies, the behavior and preferences of children in unconventional families were seen as falling within conventional limits."[40] Personally, I am disappointed that children of lesbian and gay parents are as gender stereotyped as their counterparts with heterosexual parents. Subverting rigid gender stereotypes can have benefits for girls and boys especially when they grow up and interact in adult romantic relationships.[41]

In addition to the implications discussed above, heterosexuals' equating lesbian or gay identity or "lifestyle" with only sexual behavior has implications for programs aimed at prejudice and discrimination reduction in schools. Many schools in the United States have programs, sometimes related to bullying and conflict resolution, aimed at reducing racial and gender prejudice and discrimination. These programs would obviously lend themselves to working against anti-lesbian and gay prejudice. However, many of these programs do not include the topic of sexual orientation because some teachers and school administrators believe the discussion would automatically be part of "sex education" and so they fear parents and politicians will complain, or children will need signed permission slips in order to participate in such a curriculum.

Heterosexual obsession with gay sex

STEPHEN COLBERT: *Lesbian, um I was imagining that you wanted to tell us about your first lesbian experience. Did you wanna do that?*
LESBIAN: *No. Thanks. But no.*
STEPHEN COLBERT: *Okay. Maybe later?*
LESBIAN: *No. I'm good. Thanks.*

Daily Show correspondent Stephen Colbert interviewing a lesbian at the 2004 Democratic National Convention.[42]

Everywhere one turns it seems there are jokes and references to gay and lesbian sex. Jokes about male prison rape, or references to heterosexual men's desire to witness lesbian sex, are common in popular culture. There seems to be an odd fascination, bordering on obsession, in popular culture and among some heterosexuals about homosexual sex, whereas there seems to be no parallel on the part of lesbians and gay men about heterosexual sex. Social science data support this fascination of lesbians and gay men and the sex they engage in.

Sue Sharpe[43] interviewed middle- and high schoolers about their attitudes about homosexuality. Among some other features of homosexuality, the physical aspects of lesbian and gay relationships bothered the young people. A concern that lesbians and gay peers will try to seduce them was also expressed. In Katherine Arnup's analysis of child custody cases involving lesbian mothers, she found that some judges have a prurient interest in the subject of lesbianism. Judges' attempts to determine what precisely constitutes "homosexual acts" when the mother explicitly identifies herself as a lesbian, seem to go beyond legitimate fact-finding. In Kimberly Richman's analysis of court documents from lesbian and gay parent custody cases, she reported that in one case, the judge questioned extensively the mother and her partner about their sexual activities. After, the judge stated that he was "struck by the primacy that . . . the two lesbians . . . give to multiple organisms [*sic*]. They mean more to them apparently than the children."[44] Perhaps they meant more to the judge than the children.

Some social scientists, particularly those influenced by psycho-analytic theory, argue that some actively homophobic people are protecting their egos from their own homosexual tendencies. While this theory is thought of as a cheap shot by some, to automatically assume those uncomfortable with homosexuality are indeed gay themselves, a study by Henry Adams and his colleagues[45] is an intriguing examination of the psychoanalytic hypothesis about homophobia. They divided a group of heterosexual men into *homo-phobes*, defined as those with an irrational fear, hatred, and intole-rance of lesbians and gay men, and *non-homophobes*, based on their responses on a survey about attitudes towards homosexuals. Each man viewed three segments of video: sex between two women, sex between two men, and sex between a woman and a man. During viewing, each man's penis was attached to a penile plethysmograph, an instrument that measures penile circumference (erections). After viewing the clips, each man was asked to report his degree of arousal to each clip. Thus, Adams and his colleagues had two measures of arousal: physiological as measured by the plethysmo-graph, and the men's own self-report. The results revealed a start-ling disconnect between physiological and stated arousal among the homophobic men. Both groups of men reported feeling more aroused watching the lesbian sex and the heterosexual sex videos than the gay sex. However, when it came to the men's *physiological* arousal, the homophobic men showed significantly more arousal while watching the gay men having sex than the non-homophobic men did. Paradoxically, the men who hate homosexuals were aroused by the gay video while the men who are comfortable with homosexuals were not aroused. The easiest explanation for these paradoxical findings comes from psychoanalytic psychology: the homophobic man doth protest too much. Gay men's sex threatens their own homosexual impulses. This explanation suggests that men who actively dislike gay men may have homosexual tendencies themselves that they are acting against – maybe they are in fact gay. While the men who do not have anything to prove, who are not aroused by other men, do not feel the need to express negativity toward gay men. The argument that homophobes-are-latent-homosexuals is intriguing to be sure (maybe when homophobes hear about this study, they'll shut up about gay men for fear of being suspected of being closeted). However, sexual desire isn't the only explanation for men's erections. Erections can indicate other arousal states such as fear and embarrassment. Also, we must be cautious and not assume that every homophobe is a closeted homosexual – not everyone who is homophobic is gay just as not every closeted lesbian or gay man is homophobic. But this research does suggest that perhaps a segment of those men who are fearful and hateful towards gay men might in fact have same-sex desires themselves.

Who really flaunts their sexuality?

So do homosexuals flaunt their sexuality? Probably not nearly to the extent people think. Do heterosexuals flaunt *their* sexuality? Absolutely. Consider this. We are bombarded with conspicuous and extravagant heterosexual display: wedding rings, holding hands and kissing in public, and heterosexual co-workers seem compelled to show off pictures of their wives and husbands and girlfriends and boyfriends on their walls and desks.

The thing to notice here is the intricate and ubiquitous displays of heterosexual normativity and the exhibitions of heterosexual sex and romance that are placed front-and-center, with bright spotlights even when romance, sex, and heterosexuality are not at issue and the venue is sexuality-neutral (as opposed to its centered place in, say, a wedding ceremony). The ways in which for example heterosexuals on television talk shows talk about their other-sex partners incessantly; friends, relatives, and co-workers inviting you to an engagement or bridal shower; bridal magazines and bridal expos, nearly every television show and film; MTV *Spring Break* reporting; St. Patrick's Day parades; Valentine's Day. What is significant here is the lack of positive images of gay romance paired with claims of gay flaunting in the middle of constant virtual heterosexual orgies.

Imagine if a claim were being made that the young women we see exposing their breasts in *Girls Gone Wild* videos represented all, or even typical, 20-year-old white heterosexual women. But this claim would be resisted because most people believe that they know "normal" white heterosexual 20-year olds and know they do not behave like that (or at least do not typically behave that way).

Homophobia, not homosexuals, is the problem

There are consequences of reducing and equating lesbian, gay or bisexual orientations to merely sex with implications for our original question about why homosexuals supposedly flaunt their sexuality. First, if sexual orientation is just about *behavior*, then people say that homosexuals should be able to control their behavior – just choose to have sex with other-gender people. But why would lesbians or gay people want to change their behavior any more than would heterosexual people? Second, as Suzanne Pharr argues,[46] in her landmark analysis of homophobia, by making sexual orientation a bedroom issue people feel free to argue that sex should be kept private, behind closed doors. Therefore, by a woman merely disclosing she is a lesbian, for example, she appears to be flaunting it.

Heterosexuals are not required to disclose their sexual orientation because heterosexuality is assumed.

Perhaps instead of focusing on stereotypes of lesbians, gay men, and bisexuals, and monitoring lesbians, gay men, and bisexuals' behavior for apparent oddities, we should focus on *homophobia* and *heterosexism*. In the United States, lesbians and gay men do not enjoy the same civil rights as heterosexuals. They can be fired or not hired because of their sexual orientation, and cannot marry in most states therefore they are not granted the nearly 1,000 rights married couples have, from tax breaks, to hospital visitation rights. Sixty-nine percent of lesbian and gay youth have been physically threatened and assaulted because of their sexual orientation.[47] So perhaps our focus should be on the system of heterosexism and those individuals who are homophobic. Before outlining some strategies to reduce homophobia, heterosexism and stereotypes about lesbians, gay men, and bisexuals, let's turn to some features of homophobia relevant to the myth presented at the beginning of this chapter.

One important characteristic of homophobia, and this is the case for any kind of bigotry, is that the homophobe, or bigot, flourishes in a climate of ignorance. While many homophobes have met lesbians, gay men, or bisexual people personally, few have gotten to know one well, so their ideas about homosexuality rarely come from experience with actual lesbians, gay men, and bisexuals. Their ideas come from secondary sources such as mass media and other homophobes. Therefore, their ideas about homosexuality are based on stereotypes and myth. Homophobes are not interested in the truth about homosexuality because that would require them to modify their beliefs and to make adjustments for all the variety in individuals. Indeed being bigoted virtually requires avoiding the objects of one's bigotry, so that eventually there is no first-hand knowledge of the subject anywhere to be found. While there are myths and stereotypes about heterosexuals – for example the hypersexual construction worker or the hyposexual nerdy intellectual – at least some of what most straight people know about other straight people is based on direct observation.

The characteristics of homophobia I describe above come from psychiatrist Martin Kantor.[48] In his discussion of his clinical patients, Kantor outlines characteristics of homophobes, some of which are relevant to our discussion here regarding the myth about gay people flaunting their sexuality. As a psychiatrist in a clinical setting, Kantor's discussion of homophobia emphasizes the pathological nature of any phobia. Thus, in Kantor's analysis, homophobia is treated like any other phobic response – it is irrational and it interferes with ordinary daily functioning. It is not simply a logical or social or personal preference, nor is it necessarily an expression of values. At the same time, Kantor's discussion is most useful in the ways it suggests that homophobia is irrational, like the pathological fear of flying or the paranoid's feelings of persecution.

In Kantor's analysis, one relevant characteristic of homophobes is that they can be *histrionic* and *prone to excessiveness*. They get overexcited about homosexuality and have a reaction to it as someone who is afraid of flying who can only recall stories of plane crashes and cannot think about the fact that flying is one of the safest modes of transportation. Homophobes' anxiety feeds on itself and spreads until panic takes over. Histrionic homophobes see lesbians and gay men as part of a "homosexual problem" that could take over the world. This histrionic reasoning is central in anti-gay marriage rhetoric. Politicians have been successful at conveying anti-gay hysteria in the form of having to defend heterosexual marriage against lesbians and gay men who could take it over. Anti-gay marriage legislation has been called the *Defense of Marriage*. Of course, how could two men who want to legally marry have anything to do with a woman and man who marry? Against whom are heterosexuals defending marriage? To use Kantor's language, in the mind of histrionic homophobes, they are defending heterosexual marriage against homosexuals who want to steal it away from heterosexuals and convert them. Emotional and ideological factors overwhelm logic in this position.

According to Kantor, understanding homophobia as a clinical phenomenon with clear social implications, homophobia can be understood in its similarities to paranoia. Paranoids feel that enemies are singling them out and persecuting them; homophobes tend to feel that lesbians and gay men are out to seduce them. And also like paranoids, homophobes may appear perfectly normal and rational until their fixation comes up – homosexuality – at which point they become agitated and irrational and obsessed with their enemy. This should partly explain why many homophobes appear overly fascinated with homosexuality, obsessed with homosexuality and gay sex in particular.

Putting it all together

This chapter explored the myth that homosexuals are conspicuous and provocative about sex and sexuality in ways that heterosexuals are not. Research on illusory correlation finds that those negative and stereotypical portrayals of lesbians and gay men will be more memorable and meaningful to the viewer than negative portrayals of the heterosexual majority. People are also more likely to remember schema-consistent information than schema-inconsistent information. In other words, we are more likely to remember things in line with our stereotypes and disregard what we consider exceptions to our schematic rules. In addition, many heterosexuals tend to believe that they can identify lesbians and gay men by the way they look. They don't realize that lesbians and gay men who do not conform to stereotypes are missed from the perceiver's radar. The (inaccurate) belief that lesbians and gay men can be spotted by how they look has important implications for homosexuals and heterosexuals. This belief produces a tyranny of gender-role rigidity whereby anyone who does not conform to gender roles – a man who acts or looks a bit too feminine, a woman who acts or looks a bit too masculine – regardless of their actual sexual orientation, can be a target of gay-baiting or gay-bashing. Therefore, there is pressure for women and men to conform to gender stereotypes both in the way they look and the way they act. Homophobia keeps everyone, regardless of their sexuality, in their place.

Declaring that homosexuals flaunt their sexuality is a declaration of heterosexual privilege. The implication is that heterosexuals are normal, that their romantic and sexual behavior is normal and natural. As Allan Johnson notes, part of heterosexual privilege is that heterosexual people do not have their entire humanity reduced to a single aspect of their lives: who they are intimate with. In contrast, lesbians, gay men, and bisexuals' openness about their sexuality, and by openness, I don't mean shouting it from the rooftops, is akin to flaunting it. From a heterosexual perspective, as evidenced by judges who view acknowledging one's sexuality as a gay person as dangerous to children, or the firefighters in the UK who are accepting of gay firefighters as long as the topic never comes up in a conversation, openness equals *flaunting*. Imagine what it would be like to ask heterosexuals in the workplace, whether in an office or a fire station, to never mention any aspect of their sexuality – no discussion of dating, weddings, bachelor parties, vacations, sexual intercourse, what they did over the weekend, nothing. Many heterosexuals believe that homosexuals are obsessed with sex.[49] I argue here that it is heterosexuals who are obsessed with homosexual sex: from the judges in Kimberly Richman's and Katherine Arnup's analyses of judicial behavior, to comedians making prison rape jokes, to homophobes described by Martin Kantor as obsessed with homosexuals and homosexuality.

Strategies for change

The harmful and destructive effects of homophobia and heterosexism go beyond prejudice and discrimination against individual
lesbians, gay men, and bisexuals. Homophobia and heterosexism
harms everyone in the society in which they operate. From fear of
being seen as homosexual, homophobia prevents people from creating meaningful relationships with same-sex individuals. Homophobia creates and maintains divisions among family members, it
breaks up families, and excludes people from the benefit of familial
relationships and childrearing. It is everyone's responsibility, regardless of sexual orientation, to deal with homophobia and heterosexism.

Preventing prejudice and decreasing discrimination
toward lesbians and gay men

Normalizing non-prejudice

Perhaps one of the most effective strategies to reduce prejudice
toward lesbians and gay men in the political climate of the early
twenty-first century is to legislate against it. That is, pass legislation
making homosexuality a protected category like gender, religion,
and race, which would make discrimination against lesbians and
gay men illegal and achieve the eventual goal of creating norms
making prejudice against lesbians and gay men unethical and
immoral. The lessons learned from racial desegregation can be useful
in understanding how this works. In his writing on racial desegregation of US schools in the 1950s and 1960s, Elliot Aronson[50]
discusses the conditions under which integration of black and white
students in schools was successful. What were the factors associated
with whether or not integration was a success? (1) The degree of
commitment of politicians, local policymakers, and community
leaders to the cause; and (2) the inevitability of integration.

Specifically, in those communities where their members realized that integration was inevitable because it would be enforced by law, integration occurred more quickly and smoothly than in those communities where their citizens believed they could avoid integration and where their community leaders were not committed to full integration. A similar phenomenon occurred regarding racial integration in the US military, according to Aronson. As southern men entered the army and came into contact with a relatively less discriminatory set of social norms, they became less prejudiced against African American soldiers.[51] What's responsible here is the existence of new norms to which to conform – there's no use fighting against integration if it's inevitable, and military supervision takes a this-is-just-how-its-done-around-here position. In this case, pressure to conform compels people to behave the right way.

Notice that this logic of changing people's behavior first, then changes in their attitudes will follow, is counter-intuitive; most people believe that in order to get someone to change their behavior, they have to be convinced to buy into the cause first by changing their attitude. This is how many thought school desegregation should occur – slowly and gradually, wait for whites' attitudes to change then integrate slowly. However, studies in social psychology find otherwise – get people to change their behavior, then their attitudes, which become inconsistent with how they are behaving, no longer make sense, therefore their attitudes change to be consistent with their new, less discriminatory behavior.

Unfortunately, our most powerful politicians and legislators are doing precisely the opposite with regard to civil rights for lesbians and gay men. Former president Clinton further institutionalized homophobia and heterosexism in the military when he helped institute the Don't-Ask-Don't-Tell policy regarding lesbians and gay men who serve. Prior to Don't-Ask, women and men who were suspected of being homosexual were expelled from the military with a dishonorable discharge. With the instituting of the supposedly more tolerant and gay-friendlier policy of Don't-Ask-Don't-Tell, lesbians and gay men could serve as long as they are not public about their homosexuality (this policy obviously reflects and reinforces the cultural myth that homosexuals have a tendency to flaunt their homosexuality). Ironically, since the passage of Don't-Ask, lesbians and gay men are being thrown out of the military at a higher rate than before Don't-Ask.[52] To add insult to injury for the millions of lesbians and gay men who voted for President Clinton's re-election in 1996, he signed the Defense of Marriage Act (DOMA), a federal law stating that any state in the US was not required to recognize another state's recognition of same-sex marriage. While Canada, Spain, and several other European countries are passing marriage equality rights bills, former US President George W. Bush attempted to take the institutionalization of heterosexism to a new, previously inconceivable, extreme. Bush's goal was to add an amendment to the United States Constitution defining marriage between a man and a woman, preventing lesbians and gay men from marrying. Imagine what our country would look like if Presidents Clinton and Bush had institutionalized protections for lesbians and gay men and not the opposite. Norms of acceptance and tolerance, and more importantly, legislation giving lesbians and gay men an equal footing with heterosexuals, would be evolving. Of course, anti-discrimination legislation would not make homophobia swiftly disappear any more than civil rights legislation in the 1960s made discrimination against people of color swiftly disappear. However, gay rights legislation would have made overt and obvious discrimination inappropriate and illegal and the US would be moving in the direction of normalizing lesbian and gay people and their relationships. If legal acceptance of lesbians and gay men were inevitable, enforced starting with our president on down, our country would be in a better position in terms of creating norms in this regard.

Contact complicates conceptions

One study[53] compared Israeli students who had taken a course on homosexuality and homophobia and those who did not. Before the course, all students were given a survey that measured both their levels of homophobia and their responses to free associations with the concept of homosexuality. As part of the course, the students met with a gay man and his mother who shared their personal stories with the class. After the course, students who were exposed to the course content showed decreased levels of homophobia and significant transformations of their free associations, from their production of associations such as "AIDS," "deviance," and "social rejection," to "out of the closet," "homophobia," and "love." The students reported that the most powerful aspect of their experience was meeting the gay man and his mother and hearing their stories, as well as gaining empirically based information about homosexuality. Another study[54] found similar patterns, although the reduction of homophobic and anti-gay attitudes occurred only with those students who had moderately anti-gay attitudes, whose attitudes were less fully formed, not those with weak or strong attitudes.

Therefore, in addition to the specific institutionalization of non-prejudice norms regarding homosexuality, research suggests interaction between heterosexuals and lesbians and gay men tends to decrease heterosexuals' homophobia. Social psychologists who study intergroup relations refer to this phenomenon as the *contact hypothesis*. The contact hypothesis is the notion that contact between members of different groups will improve relations between them. You can probably think of instances where contact between members of two different groups would not result in prejudice reduction, for instance white households who employ black or Latina maids do not necessarily have household members who are less prejudiced than households that do not have a woman of color as a maid. There are four conditions under which contact between members of different groups can reduce prejudice.[55] First, groups that are required to cooperate with each other can result in reduced prejudice. If members of a high school's Gay–Straight Alliance are required to work with the Campus Christians toward some overarching goal that benefits both groups, a reduction in prejudice may result. Related to this point, studies have found that if members of a group are *required* to work with each other (e.g. project at work) rather than given a choice, a decrease in prejudice is more likely to result.[56]

Second, people who are coming into contact have to be on an equal footing. Picture a lesbian and straight man who are co-workers and they have to produce a project together towards some specific goal. This interaction could result in prejudice reduction. Third, *acquaintance potential*, or contact over an extended period of time, is much more effective than a brief encounter between group members. Extended contact has the potential of getting to know someone personally; reducing some of the apparent significance of traits and characteristics that distinguish us from someone else and, in the process, discovering that we really aren't very different from each other. For instance, if a close relative becomes involved with someone of the same sex, your acceptance of that particular person and your acceptance of homosexuality in general may increase more than if you have occasional contact with an acquaintance. Barry Goldwater, conservative senator from Arizona and 1964 US presidential candidate, held attitudes about gay rights that might surprise some when compared with conservative Republicans presently. Prior to his death in 1998 he actively worked on behalf of lesbian and gay rights making gay rights part of his larger libertarian beliefs in the constitution. His progressive views regarding lesbian and gay rights may have been due, in part, to his having a gay grandson, as well as other relatives who are gay.[57]

Indeed research shows the more contact heterosexuals have with lesbian, gay, and bisexual people the more positive one's attitudes are about homosexuality.[58] One study looked at college students' attitudes before and after one of their professors disclosed his homosexuality in class. They compared these students' attitudes with students taking the same kind of course with an instructor who did not come out. Indeed students in the gay instructor's class showed more positive attitudes many weeks after the disclosure than did students in the presumably heterosexual professor's class.[59]

Fourth, the reduction and eventual elimination of prejudice requires consistent institutional support, whatever the larger context happens to be. Intergroup contact works best as a prejudice-reduction tool when it occurs in a setting in which existing norms explicitly favor group equality. Those in authority – school officials, politicians, and others – must unambiguously endorse egalitarian norms. You can imagine the impact when, for instance, the president of the United States declares that a major policy priority is to pass a constitutional amendment that would deny lesbians and gay men the right to marry. This declaration has a chilling effect not only on those millions of lesbians and gay men who want to marry but also on heterosexuals' attitudes about lesbians and gay men.

Capitalizing on cognitive consistency: cognitive dissonance and prejudice reduction

A major way the contact hypothesis works to reduce prejudice is that once people from different groups get to know each other, they often find that they have more in common than not – many people have similar values, needs, and morals, even if they have different sexual orientations. For heterosexuals, once they find that lesbians, gay men, and bisexuals are not so different from them, they have little reason to dislike them. This is where the fascinating and powerful social psychological theory of cognitive dissonance comes in. The theory of cognitive dissonance says that people work to achieve internal consistency – people attempt to keep their behavior and their attitudes consistent with each other. When their behavior and beliefs become internally inconsistent, people become uncomfortable and therefore highly motivated to reduce the dissonance this inconsistency creates. In order to reduce dissonance, either one's behavior must change in order to be consistent with one's attitude, or one's attitude must change in order to be consistent with one's behavior. In many cases, it's easier to change one's attitudes than behavior, because sometimes behavior, behavior which has already been completed, cannot be undone.

Let's take the example of a homophobic person and link this back to the contact hypothesis. Say a homophobic person shares the workplace with a lesbian. If the four conditions of contact are met, there's a good chance the homophobe will, over time, view the lesbian as an individual more so than a member of the gay community, the homophobe will discover that the lesbian shares some goals, values, hopes and desires, etc. Pretty soon, homophobic prejudice (i.e. attitudes) becomes inconsistent with working together (i.e. behavior). If lesbians are so bad, why does the homophobe continue to work with one and why does the homophobe view her as fairly similar to him? In this way the *attitude* of homophobia has become inconsistent with the *behavior* and actual experience of working with the lesbian – the homophobe's attitudes and behavior are inconsistent. Because it's usually easier to modify one's attitude than find a new job, one way of resolving the dissonance is to adjust one's beliefs about homosexuals. Similarly, if you have a family member who is gay, who you regularly see during holidays and other family functions, is it really useful to see that person as abnormal and pathological? It may be for some highly homophobic people, but for others, seeing the humanity of a gay person makes disliking them too difficult.

In addition to workplace and family applications cognitive dissonance has implications for reducing homophobia and hetero-sexism at the coming out stage of a friendship or professional relationship. If a gay man comes out to a person who does not hold homophobic attitudes, the person might think, "*I have always liked you*" and "*I feel OK about homosexuality*" – two thoughts that are consonant with each other. However, if the gay man comes out to a homophobe, she might think "I have always liked you" and "I dislike homosexuals" – two inconsistent attitudes – the homophobe will probably feel dissonance. Because dissonance is an uncomfort-able state, the homophobe might be motivated to adjust her attitudes. One way the discloser might facilitate attitude change (i.e. dissonance reduction) in the listener is to remind the person, "I'm the same person I was before I told you this about myself" or "Even your old fashioned parents support gay rights" or "Does a person's sexual orientation really matter when there are all of the things you admire about me?"[60]

Controlling your cognitions

Stereotype reduction can also be worked on at the individual cog-nition level through a strategy called *stereotype suppression*. This mental strategy, which has been used for a range of goals from managing food cravings to controlling depressing thoughts, entails avoiding thinking of negative thoughts and replacing them with distractor thoughts. In the case of stereotyped thinking, when you find yourself applying stereotypes to a member of a certain group, you can replace them with non-stereotypical thoughts. Research on the efficacy of stereotype suppression is mixed.[61] In some cases, deliberately trying to avoid thinking about a topic makes you think about it even more, especially people with strong prejudices. Margo Monteith[62] and her colleagues tested this strategy in a study where people were given a photo of two gay men who were a couple and were asked to write a passage about a typical day in their life. Some of the participants were instructed to avoid stereotypical preconceptions in their description, while others were not given such instructions. For participants low in prejudice, suppressing stereotypes was effective, while for those with strong prejudice suppressing the stereotypic thoughts actually increased the accessibility of the stereotypes.

Some individuals can avoid prejudicial responses, if they have the motivation and ability to do so. As a result of living in a prejudiced society, stereotypes are often highly accessible and easily used. However, for those individuals who strongly endorse egalitarian values that conflict with initial stereotypical thinking, this discrepancy in thinking can induce guilt and this guilt can be a motivator to suppress prejudicial thinking. According to Patricia Devine[63] and her colleagues, many people want to do and say the right thing, and the discrepancy between their spontaneous stereotypical thinking and their non-prejudiced standards leads to feelings of compunction. As a result, these individuals will be motivated to avoid subsequent stereotyping. Also, it is possible that people can just get into a habit of monitoring their prejudicial thoughts and then controlling their behavior.[64]

Analyzing your assumptions at work, school, and in your community

Homophobia must be addressed on an individual basis; however one must remember that individual acts of anti-gay bias do not happen in isolation, independent of a larger system that supports heterosexism. So dealing with specific homophobic acts must be considered in a larger context of heterosexism, just as dealing with racial discrimination must be considered not as one mean individual against a victim but as part of a larger system of inequality. With this in mind, we must respond to homophobia immediately and directly. Whenever you hear an anti-gay joke, just as when you hear a sexist or racist joke if you laugh along with others or merely remain silent, you are supporting bigotry. It's not good enough to remain silent as a way to show your disapproval. Silence in these cases means support because when heterosexism is institu-tionalized (e.g. supported and enforced by laws and policies), all that is required to perpetuate it is for people to remain silent about it, for people to not object. Therefore, while you may not be that person who makes a gay joke in the break room, you support the gay-joke-tellers with your silence by not disrupting the heterosexist status quo.

What follows are some specific strategies for dealing with homo-phobia and heterosexism in your community, at work, and in schools.

If you are a heterosexual, do not leave it to lesbians and gay men to do the work of undoing homophobia for you. Homophobia and het-erosexism are everyone's problem. If for no other reason, heterosexuals should worry about it because if they step out of the rigid gender roles our society has in place, they risk being gay-baited themselves. If your son goes to pre-school with polish on his fingernails, he can be a target of anti-gay discrimination. Homophobia and heterosexism keep everyone in their narrowly defined place.

Don't make assumptions about others' sexuality. If someone doesn't use a gender-specific pronoun when discussing a relation-ship, don't assume one for them. Use non-gender-specific language when referring to others' spouses or romantic partners. It never hurts to not assume, but it can hurt to assume. Also, don't assume that elderly people are heterosexuals. Respect an older person's loss of a same-sex partner as you would a heterosexual's.

In your workplace, ask your human resources officer about same-sex partner benefits and policies that protect from anti-gay discrimination. You don't have to be a lesbian, gay man, or bisexual to care about this! If nothing else, asking these questions raises the consciousness of the human resources department. And it might make you think twice about whether you want to invest yourself in an organization that actively discriminates.

Have something related to the lesbian, gay, bisexual, or transgender community in your office or cubicle in a prominent place. A book, a sticker, a poster, or a flyer will make a lesbian or gay person feel comfortable and safe. And stop worrying people will think you are lesbian or gay yourself if you have such paraphernalia! Only through such alliances and the actions of non-gay people can homophobia be undone at the individual and institutional levels.

If you are a teacher or professor, use role models and examples of lesbian and gay people casually but consistently when talking about relationships and families. And if you are a psychology or social science professor, stop using homosexuality as an example of psychopathology or social deviance. The American Psychiatric Association does not recognize homosexuality as a mental illness, the American Sociological Association does not regard it as a form of deviance, and neither should you.

If you are a school teacher or parent, respond to slurs that kids use such as "gay" and "fag." Don't dismiss or treat these words as general bad names such as "stupid," they are more than that. They are a message about gender rules and are hurtful especially to children who are or will become lesbian or gay, and even for children who are not and will not be gay. The unchecked use of these words leads to reinforcing and approving of discrimination and bigotry.

If you are a parent, ask the school administrators of your child's school about anti-bullying policies that specifically address homophobia. All parents should do this, not just lesbian and gay parents or parents of a lesbian or gay child. You do not want your child raised and educated in a school environment that systematically encourages or tolerates prejudice and discrimination. No one is safe in environments that disregard the social significance of these forms of bullying and disparagement.

If you are a teacher, school counselor, or administrator, learn about and refer to community organizations. Familiarize yourself with resources and call them before encouraging a student to seek out these resources. Make sure they are ongoing and make sure they actually offer what you are after in making the referral. Also, become aware of gay-themed bibliographies and refer to gay-positive books. In your curriculum, make sure that you include and normalize the presence of and achievements of gay men and lesbians. Avoid the tendency to "set the record straight," meaning to refrain from (or to avoid) mentioning the contributions of lesbians and gay men.

If you are an active member of a religious community, take a leadership role at your place of worship for promoting acceptance of homosexuality that includes making a congregation a comfortable place of worship for all people, one that values and respects all kinds of people, and one that practices the precepts of inclusion and equality in its own hiring and theological decisions. Ask religious leaders about their position and attitudes toward lesbian and gay people and make clear to them your position. Reducing prejudice and the many forms of discrimination that result from it is in all our hands, and it is our responsibility to make the specific efforts that will raise awareness and transform attitudes.

NOTES

1. See page 98 in: Bensimon, E.M. (1992). Lesbian existence and the challenge to normative constructions of the academy. *Journal of education, 174*, 98–113.
2. Scout, D. (1996, October). Murderer gets custody of child over lesbian mom. *Lesbian news, 22*, 28.
3. Hamilton, D.L., & Gifford, R.K. (1976). Illusory correlation in interpersonal perception: A cognitive basis of stereotypic judgments. *Journal of experimental social psychology, 12*, 392–407.
4. Dixon, T.L., Azocar, C.L., & Casas, M. (2003). The portrayal of race and crime on television network news. *Journal of broadcasting and electronic media, 47*, 498–523.

5. *Ibid.*
6. Risen, J.L., Gilovich, T., & Dunning, D. (2007). One-shot illusory correlations and stereotype formation. *Personality and social psychology bulletin*, 33, 1492–1502.
7. Casas, J.M., Brady, S., & Ponterotto, J.G. (1983). Sexual preference biases in counseling: An information processing approach. *Journal of counseling psychology*, 30, 139–145.
8. See, for instance: Pratkanis, A., & Aronson, E. (2001). *Age of propaganda: The everyday use and abuse of persuasion.* New York: W.H. Freeman and Company.
9. Jussim, L., Nelson, T.E., Manis, M., & Soffin, S. (1995). Prejudice, stereotypes, and labeling effects: Sources of bias in person perception. *Journal of personality and social psychology*, 68, 228–246.
10. Secretary Rumsfeld media availability. (2002, May 22). Retrieved September 26, 2004, from www.globalsecurity.org/military/library/news/2002/05/mil-020522-dod01.htm
11. Kite, M.E., & Deaux, K. (1987). Gender belief systems: Homosexuality and the implicit inversion theory. *Psychology of women quarterly*, 11, 83–96.
12. Johnson, A.G. (2006). *Privilege, power, and difference*, (2nd edition). New York: McGraw-Hill.
13. *Ibid.*
14. Brophy, J. (1991). New families, judicial decision-making, and children's welfare. *Canadian journal of women and the law*, 5, 484–497.
15. Richman, K. (2002). Lovers, legal strangers, and parents: Negotiating parental and sexual identity in family law. *Law and society review*, 36, 285–324.
16. Arnup, K. (1989). "Mothers just like others": Lesbians, divorce, and child custody in Canada. *Canadian journal of women and the law*, 3, 18–32.
17. *Ibid.*, page 27.
18. *Ibid.*, page 27.
19. Richman, Lovers, legal strangers, and parents, page 313.
20. Patterson, C.J. (2003). Children of lesbian and gay parents. In L.D. Garnets and D.C. Kimmel (Eds.) *Psychological perspectives on lesbian, gay, and bisexual experiences* (pp. 497–548). New York: Columbia University Press.
21. For a review, see: Patterson, C.J. (2006). Children of lesbian and gay parents. *Current directions in psychological science*, 15, 241–244.
22. Rivers, I., Poteat, V.P., & Noret, N. (2008). Victimization, social support, and psychosocial functioning among children of same-sex and opposite-sex couples in the United Kingdom. *Developmental psychology*, 44, 127–134.
23. *Ibid.*; Wainright, J.L., & Patterson, C.J. (2008). Peer relations among adolescents with female same-sex parents. *Developmental psychology*, 44, 117–126.

24. Balsam, K.F., Beauchaine, T.P., Rothblum, E.D., & Solomon, S.E. (2008). Three-year follow-up of same-sex couples who had civil unions in Vermont, same-sex couples not in civil unions, and heterosexual married couples. *Developmental psychology, 44*, 102–116.

25. Roisman, G.I., Clausell, E., Holland, A., Fortuna, K., & Elieff, C. (2008). Adult romantic relationships as contexts of human development: A multimethod comparison of same-sex couples with opposite-sex dating, engaged, and married dyads. *Developmental psychology, 44*, 91–101.

26. Bensimon, Lesbian existence and the challenge to normative constructions of the academy.

27. *Ibid.*, page 98.

28. See page 101 in: Pugh, W.W.T. (1998). "It's just my job to be 'out'": Tenure stories of lesbian, gay, and bisexual academics. *Journal of gay, lesbian, and bisexual identity, 3*, 93–112.

29. Ward, J., & Winstanley, D. (2006). Watching the watch: The UK Fire Service and its impact on sexual minorities in the workplace. *Gender, work and organization, 13*, 193–219.

30. Pugh, "It's just my job to be 'out'" page 105.

31. Ward & Winstanley, Watching the watch.

32. Promotion for Engvall's standup routine, Here's Your Sign. (Air date July 31, 2004). In *Comedy central network*.

33. Herek, G.M. (2002). Gender gaps in public opinion about lesbians and gay men. *Public opinion quarterly, 66*, 40–66.

34. Jenny, C., Roesler, T.A., & Poyer, K.L. (1994). Are children at risk for sexual abuse by homosexuals? *Pediatrics, 94*, 41–44.

35. *Ibid.*, page 44.

36. Groth, A.N., & Birnbaum, H.J. (1978). Adult sexual orientation and attraction to underage persons. *Archives of sexual behavior, 7*, 175–181.

37. *Ibid.*, page 181.

38. See page 302 in: Richman, Lovers, legal strangers, and parents.

39. For a summary of these studies, see: Patterson, (2003). Children of lesbian and gay parents.

40. *Ibid.*, page 506.

41. Leaper, C., & Anderson, K.J. (1997). Gender development and heterosexual romantic relationships during adolescence. In W. Damon (Series ed.) & S. Shulman, & W.A. Collins (Issue eds.) *New directions for child development: Romantic relationships in adolescence* (pp. 85–103, No. 78, Winter). San Francisco: Jossey-Bass.

42. Colbert, S. (2004) The daily show [Television series episode] (Air date August 9, 2004). In *Comedy central network*.

43. Sharpe, S. (2002). 'It's just really hard to come to terms with': Young people's views on homosexuality. *Sex education, 2*, 263–277.

44. See page 314 in: Richman, Lovers, legal strangers, and parents.
45. Adams, H.E., Wright, L.W., Jr., & Lohr, B.A. (1996). Is homophobia associated with homosexual arousal? *Journal of abnormal psychology, 105,* 440–445.
46. Pharr, S. (1997). *Homophobia: A weapon of sexism.* Berkeley, CA: Chardon Press.
47. Lesbian, gay, bisexual, and transgendered youth issues. (2001, April/ May). *SIECUS report supplement, 29,* 1–5.
48. Kantor, M. (1998). *Homophobia: Description, development, and dynamics of gay bashing.* Westport, CT: Praeger.
49. Mohr, R.D. (2007). Anti-gay stereotypes. In P.S. Rothenberg (Ed.) *Race, class, and gender in the United States* (7th edition, pp. 603–609). New York: Worth.
50. Aronson, E. (2008). *The social animal* (10th edition). New York: Worth.
51. *Ibid.,* cited on page 336.
52. Servicemembers Legal Defense Network. (2004). *Conduct unbecoming: The tenth annual report on "Don't Ask, Don't Tell, Don't Pursue, Don't Harass."* Retrieved January 17, 2008, from http://sldn.3cdn.net/ 77d5825b8eof3454f2_1cm6bgace.pdf
53. Ben-Ari, A.T. (1998). An experiential attitude change: Social work students and homosexuality. *Journal of homosexuality, 36,* 59–71.
54. Bassett, J.D., & Day, K.J. (2003). A test of the infusion method: Emphatic inclusion of material on gay men in a core course. *Journal of teaching in social work, 23,* 29–41.
55. For a longer discussion of these four factors, see: Jones, M. (2002). *Social psychology of prejudice.* Upper Saddle River, NJ: Prentice Hall.
56. Pettigrew, T.F., & Tropp, L.R. (2006). A meta-analytic test of intergroup contact theory. *Journal of personality and social psychology, 90,* 751–783.
57. Grove, L. (1994, July 28). Barry Goldwater's left turn. *Washington post.* Retrieved December 14, 2004, from www.washingtonpost.com/wp-srv/ politics/daily/may98/goldwatero72894.htm
58. See, for instance: Finlay, B., & Walther, C.S. (2003). The relation of religious affiliation, service attendance, and other factors to homophobic attitudes among university students. *Review of religious research, 44,* 370–393.
59. Waldo, C.R., & Kemp, J.L. (1997). Should I come out to my students? An empirical investigation. *Journal of homosexuality, 34,* 79–93.
60. These examples come from: Yep, G.A. (1997). Changing homophobic and heterosexist attitudes: An overview of persuasive communication approaches. In J.T. Sears & W.L. Williams (Eds.), *Overcoming heterosexism and homophobia: Strategies that work* (pp. 49–64). New York: Columbia University Press.

238 • Benign Bigotry

61. For a review of the work in the area of stereotype suppression, see Chapter 12 in: Whitley, B.E., Jr., & Kite, M.E. (2010). *The psychology of prejudice and discrimination*. Belmont, CA: Wadsworth.
62. Monteith, M.J., Spicer, C.V., & Tooman, G.D. (1998). Consequences of stereotype suppression: Stereotypes on AND not on the rebound. *Journal of experimental social psychology, 34,* 355–377.
63. Devine, P.G., Monteith, M.J., Zuwerink, J.R., & Elliot, A.J. (1991). Prejudice with and without compunction. *Journal of personality and social psychology, 60,* 817–830.
64. Whitley & Kite, *The psychology of prejudice and discrimination*.

FIVE

"I'm not a racist, I'm colorblind": The myth of neutrality

Now, I don't see color. People tell me I'm white and I believe them because police officers call me "sir."

Stephen Colbert, host of The Colbert Report[1]

The notion of colorblindness has been idealized popularly since the late 1960s as a frame of mind that could combat racism.[2] Perhaps the most well-known reference to a colorblind ideal is from Dr. Martin Luther King, Jr.,'s famous "I have a dream" speech in which he imagined an America where his children would be judged "not by the color of their skin but by the content of their charac- ter." But what is entailed in colorblind beliefs and in the policies and practices that would accompany such a position? Is colorblind- ness good for people of color? Is it good for society overall? And what about racial colorblindness at the individual level, in terms of people's attitudes about race and ethnicity? In a multiracial, multi- ethnic society such as the US, what does it mean for a person to desire not to see race? Is it possible for people to be colorblind, to ignore someone's race or ethnicity in their interactions, to judge people only by the content of their character? If color matters in society, as part of one's self-concept, in social identity, in social policy, and in everyday life, what does it mean to not see it?

The appeal of racial colorblindness

Some individuals, who are genuinely invested in ending discrimination based on race, believe that a colorblind approach is the best way to end discrimination. The principle behind racial colorblindness is that people ought to be judged according to their character, talents, and contributions, and that their membership in racial groups should not factor into how they are treated. It suggests, for example, that employers or college admissions boards should not solicit information about gender, race, or other group membership data as part of their evaluation of whether an applicant should be hired or admitted. Thus, in a colorblind society, people presumably would be assessed on only their merits and qualifications. In this way, prejudice and stereotyping and their effects should decline greatly because race would no longer be considered by institutions and individuals in evaluations of members from stereotyped groups.[3] According to this view, taking race into account in hiring and in education, and even noticing it in interpersonal interactions, is "racist" – either against those who have traditionally been the target of racism, or against whites, as in the case of affirmative action.

Do people see color? Can people be colorblind?

How readily do people perceive color and sort others into racial categories? Can individuals successfully avoid noticing the color of someone's skin? As we have seen in the "They must be guilty of something" chapter, perception studies find that individuals spontaneously and unconsciously categorize people by race (as well as by gender, and to a lesser extent, by age). Snap decisions made in the *police officer's dilemma* demonstrate the speed with which perceivers may spontaneously judge the innocence or guilt of a suspect based on race. Advances in research using functional magnetic resonance imaging, or fMRI (i.e. brain scans), help illustrate that people spontaneously process the race and gender of faces presented to them, and that they do so extremely quickly, automatically, and non-consciously.[4]

For better or worse, people quickly and accurately sort people into culturally established categories according to race and gender, although as indicated in results from a study conducted by Michael Norton[5] and his colleagues, this sorting ability is a reluctant skill for some white people. In a series of studies, Norton found that because of pressure to appear colorblind, whites attempt to *appear* to not notice race, while they actually do. The researchers showed white American university students a set of photographs, each of which could be judged on seven dimensions: race (black/white), gender, age (over 30/under 25), color of the background in the photo (blue/red), hair color (light/dark), facial expression (smiling/not smiling), and facial hair (present/absent). On a computer, participants categorized each photo on only one of the dimensions. For instance, if a photo was to be categorized by facial hair, the participant would click "present" or "absent." Next, the participants read a questionnaire that included some of the photos from the previous task. The questionnaire asked them to *imagine* themselves performing the computer-based sorting task. Participants ranked the seven dimensions in terms of how quickly they believed they would be able to categorize the photos on the basis of that dimension. Results revealed a discrepancy between how accurate the participants were when they actually sorted the photos on the computer, compared to when they were asked to guess at their accuracy in the hypothetical questionnaire. In the computer-based task, participants were 99.1% accurate on race categorization. Race was the dimension that participants sorted third most quickly, with background color and gender being first and second. But in the hypothetical task, participants estimated that race would be the dimension they would complete second slowest (with age being the very slowest). Whites thus underestimated the speed with which they would be able to categorize by race. And because whites didn't underestimate their ability to categorize background color, it's not just their inability to estimate color specifically, it is the meaning of color as it is associated with ethnicity. Interestingly, they overestimated their speed at categorizing gender (compared to how they actually categorized it). The researchers suspected that participants substituted a less controversial dimension – gender – for a more controversial one – race. When the same study was done with African American respondents, they found little discrepancy between actual computer-based sorting and hypothetical sorting. African Americans apparently do not feel the same pressure to appear "colorblind" as do whites.

In a second study, Norton[6] and his colleagues examined the consequences of whites' reluctance to admit the extent to which they use race to differentiate people. White students were paired with other "students" who were actually accomplices working with the experimenters. Two conditions were set up whereby the accomplice was either African American or white, and the pair was to play a game in which one member of the pair was randomly assigned the "questioner" role and the other the "answerer" role. In fact, the game was rigged so the white participant was always the "questioner" and the accomplice was always the "answerer." The answerer was given 32 photos that varied along the dimensions of gender, race, and background color. Questioners were told that on each trial their goal was to identify the photo the answerer was looking at by asking as few yes/no questions as possible. Once a photo was identified, the answerer flipped to the next page, and a new trial started. The researchers suspected that, in order to appear colorblind, the white participants would go to great lengths to avoid asking about race, particularly when their partners were African American. Indeed, white participants were more likely to ask about race when interacting with a white partner (93% of the trials with whites) than when interacting with an African American (64% of the trials with African Americans). In other words, white participants were more hesitant to bring up race with an African American than with a white person. The race of the partner also affected how participants talked about race. Participants working with white partners mentioned "black" or "African American" in 57% of the trials; while participants working with black partners used the terms in only 21% of the trials. Because race is a basic social category, avoidance of using race affected the questioners' performance. Asking about the race of the person in the photo cut in half the number of possible photos to have to identify. Thus, participants paired with an African American partner were less efficient and needed more questions to get the correct answer, and therefore performed less well than participants paired with a white partner. Whites' awkward avoidance of talk about race has been found by other researchers who have interviewed whites about their colorblind attitudes.[7] Other studies have found that when some whites attempt to appear unbiased toward African Americans, they tend to have more awkward interactions than both less prejudiced whites and more overtly prejudiced whites.[8]

In the same study, independent assistants, who had nothing to do with the study, were asked to judge the videotaped interactions (minus the sound) between participant/questioner and partner/answerer, on the basis of perceived friendliness and eye contact. Those participants who were rated as less friendly and having less eye contact were the participants who were less likely to ask about race. Thus, when whites attempt to be colorblind, there are accompanying costs: they appear to be less friendly and make less eye contact. It may be that the cognitive and emotional burden when whites are attempting to avoid race-related issues hinders the normal subtle social graces. The irony of this is that the whites who tried hardest to appear colorblind appeared to be the least friendly when interacting with African Americans. They may well have had no idea that they came across as being less friendly. Finally, the researchers conducted a follow-up survey and found that those participants who had tended to avoid questions about race during the photo game were apt to report colorblind ideology when given a paper–pencil test measuring colorblindness (e.g. they agreed with statements such as, *"When I interact with other people, I try not to even notice the color of their skin"* and *"If everyone paid less attention to race and skin color, we would all get along much better"*). The measurement of colorblind attitudes is discussed at length in the next section.

Several conclusions can be drawn from these studies. First, whites do quickly and accurately sort people based on race. Second, whites either do not realize that they do this, or would prefer to appear that they do not. Third, whites who espouse a colorblind belief system avoid discussing race with African Americans more than do whites who are not colorblind. And, finally, when whites attempt to "act" colorblind, their interactions with African Americans may be less efficient and they appear to be less friendly. This last point may help illuminate why some whites and people of color have frustrating interactions in which the person of color believes the white person behaved in a prejudiced manner, while the white person believes she behaved in an unbiased manner. Is this motivation to appear unprejudiced necessarily maladaptive? It would seem so, based on Norton and colleagues' data. However, the authors speculate that concerns about appearing unbiased reflect a desire among whites to be more egalitarian, this behavior could be a step in the right direction, and could perhaps be an intermediate step toward eventually less awkward interactions. Taken together, these studies offer strong support for the salience of race and ethnicity in interpersonal interactions. As hard as one might try, and as politically expedient as it may be, it is close to impossible to ignore color. Colorblindness on a perceptual level is not a realistic goal.

Colorblind, or blind to discrimination?[9]: Measuring colorblind attitudes

The Norton and colleagues studies contrasted people's automatic, spontaneous ability to categorize based on race, with their efforts to manage their own behavior and appear colorblind. What about those who espouse colorblind *attitudes*? Are people who hold colorblind attitudes less likely to be bigots than those who do not?

What does colorblindness mean in terms of individuals' beliefs and attitudes? Once again the experimental and empirical nature of social psychology provides techniques for measuring behavior. Through the replication of real-life situations in the laboratory, we are able to examine behavior rather than rely on declarations, and to assess what people actually do, rather than what they say they do. When referring to attitudes, rather than perceptions, social psychologists describe colorblindness as the belief that race should not and does not matter in the judgment of others.[10] Just as Dr. Martin Luther King, Jr., had envisioned, many people would agree that race *should* not matter in terms of how others are perceived and judged. But the latter part of the definition, that race *does* not matter, is the more controversial component of the definition because it suggests that racial and ethnic membership can be, or are, irrelevant to the ways individuals are treated. To those who espouse colorblindness, taking account of racial and ethnic membership is illegitimate and could lead to discrimination against minorities and, especially, "reverse discrimination" against whites. Helen Neville and her colleagues[11] developed a scale to assess colorblind beliefs using statements such as, "*Everyone who works hard, no matter what race they are, has an equal chance to become rich*" and "*It is important that people begin to think of themselves as American and not African American, Mexican American, or Italian American.*" Men and whites are more likely to hold colorblind attitudes than are women, Latina/os, and African Americans. Neville and colleagues found that colorblind racial attitudes, as they were measured in their study, were correlated with *modern* racism. Modern racism is a form of subtle prejudice that entails the belief that, while discrimination existed in the past, racism is no longer a problem in the US and that African Americans just need to work harder to be successful. Colorblind attitudes, as measured by Neville, are also associated with a *belief in a just world*,[12] an idea, also discussed in Chapter 2, that people deserve what they get, and that good things happen to good people and bad things happen to bad people. Colorblind attitudes also coincide with the denial, minimization, and distortion of the existence of structural racism in the US.[13]

How do those who espouse colorblind attitudes actually relate to people of color? Colorblind attitudes are correlated with a range of other attitudes. For instance, psychotherapists who espouse colorblindness report feeling less empathy towards clients, regardless of either the therapists' or the clients' ethnic background. Those psychotherapists are also more likely to hold African American clients, in particular, responsible for solving their own problems than are therapists who do not espouse colorblind attitudes.[14] Research has demonstrated that the stronger the colorblind attitudes people have the less likely they will be to support affirmative action.[15] Also, a strong belief in colorblindness has been related to increased anxiety and fear of racial and ethnic minorities among white college students.[16] The studies I have described were conducted mostly on white people's colorblind attitudes. One study with African American participants found that African Americans who hold colorblind attitudes tend to internalize racist stereotypes of African Americans and blame African Americans for economic and social disparities between African Americans and whites.[17]

Colorblindness or multiculturalism?

Colorblind and multicultural ideologies are often contrasted as two different paths to increased tolerance and prejudice reduction. The multicultural approach is based on a set of beliefs that recognize and accentuate ethnic group differences, while the colorblind approach has the goal of minimizing differences. Does one perspective lead to less prejudice and conflict than the other? Two studies have compared these two perspectives. Christopher Wolsko and his colleagues[18] asked white US college students to read an essay espousing either a colorblind or a multicultural approach to improving ethnic relations. The colorblind essay argued that *"intergroup harmony can be achieved if we recognize that at our core we are all the same, that all men and women are created equal, and that we are first and foremost a nation of individuals."* The multicultural essay emphasized that *"intergroup harmony can be achieved if we better appreciate our diversity and recognize and accept each group's positive and negative qualities."* Students were then asked to write down five reasons why adopting either a colorblind or a multicultural perspective (depending upon the version of the essay they read) would strengthen the US. They then completed a questionnaire that measured ethnocentrism, warmth towards others, and stereotypes of various social groups, including African Americans and Latina/os. How did the earlier exposure to a colorblind or multicultural message affect respondents' later stereotypes and feelings about ethnic minorities? Exposure to the multicultural message increased both positive and negative stereotyping, but also increased positive regard for African Americans and Latina/os. Those exposed to both the multicultural and colorblind message showed less ingroup favoritism, meaning they endorsed fewer pro-white stereotypes. This suggests that motivating people to think about the importance of improving interethnic relations (using either strategy) can have an effect (at least temporarily) of producing less prejudiced attitudes. The group exposed to the multicultural message also perceived the values of whites and African Americans as more different than did those exposed to the colorblind message. This last finding could be interpreted as indicating that a multicultural approach produces fewer perceived similarities between groups and thus fewer bridges between whites and African Americans. However, the authors interpreted the finding to mean that those exposed to the multicultural message showed a greater appreciation of the different social realities experienced by ethnic minorities and white Americans.

A second study used similar procedures and found results that favored the multicultural approach. Jennifer Richeson and Richard Nussbaum[19] asked white US college students to read statements endorsing either a multicultural or a colorblind perspective. Then, to reinforce what they had read, they were asked to generate a list of reasons why the approach they read about was good. Next, they read statements supposedly made by other participants, endorsing the same perspective. The participants then completed a race Implicit Association Test. You will recall from earlier discussions in this book that the IAT measures implicit attitudes (or associations) via reaction times when sorting items on the basis of blackness/whiteness and goodness/badness. In the final stage of the study, participants completed an explicit survey measure of warmth toward African Americans, Asian Americans, Latina/os, and whites. The participants who were exposed to the colorblind argument showed more pro-white bias on the IAT, and provided more pro-white attitudes on the explicit rating of warmth than did the students exposed to the multicultural argument.

A remarkable point regarding the two studies is that the ideological prompts, in the form of colorblind or multicultural messages, worked: they influenced the subsequent attitudes of respondents in important ways. So which approach – colorblind or multicultural – is more closely linked to prejudice reduction? Results from the Wolsko and colleagues and the Richeson and Nussbaum studies are somewhat mixed but point in the direction favoring a multicultural approach to reducing prejudice. One thing we don't know, however, is how long exposure to a message continues to affect the participants in these studies. But even a short-lived effect would suggest meaningful impact on a person say, in a workplace in which a co-worker or supervisor espouses a particular ideology repeatedly over time, or the effect on a person of exposure to a television news outlet with a certain ideological bent. The results from these two studies, and even the Norton and colleagues study described earlier, have implications for the intergroup contact approach to prejudice reduction. Many current approaches to bettering intergroup relations involve contact with members of different groups. To the extent that proponents of the colorblind approach also advocate intergroup contact, the actual behavior displayed by colorblind individuals during those contact situations may hinder intergroup relations and attitudes.

Is a colorblind approach ever useful? Sheri Levy[20] and her colleagues reviewed the psychological literature on colorblind attitudes and found that these attitudes function somewhat differently for children and adults, and for whites and African Americans. To some extent, the colorblind approach can be used to facilitate tolerance between groups by diverting people's attention away from race and ethnicity and toward commonalities across people, or people's uniqueness as individuals. This approach seems to work for children and for African Americans. Colorblindness seems to have more of an egalitarian meaning for children and for African Americans than for white adults. This is not to suggest that African Americans think like children. The problem seems to be with white people's approach to colorblindness, an approach that appears to stem from a position of minimizing past mistreatment of people of color and disregarding present racism. In contrast, for children, who tend to overcategorize people as they learn about group differences, a colorblind approach helps divert attention from race categorization to a more nuanced understanding of people. African American adults are more likely than white adults to attach an egalitarian meaning to colorblindness. In the context of racism, the colorblind perspective can be used to justify inaction through denial, thereby maintaining the current power structure and preserving the privileges of the dominant group.

Colorblindness really means white = normal

A colorblind racial framework is a set of beliefs that minimizes and ignores race as an important issue in American society. Why does such a framework lead to negative behavior among whites toward African Americans (as was the case in the Norton and colleagues study) or pro-white sentiments among whites (found in Wolsko's and Richeson & Nussbaum's studies)? Why doesn't colorblindness lead to equal treatment for all, as some politicians and scholars promise?

Who gets to be "American"?

Equality in the treatment of all citizens is articulated as a core value in American society. Such a value is likely to be reflected in consciously expressed attitudes and in beliefs of inclusivity of all ethnic groups. People would be expected to be especially motivated to appear egalitarian. Detecting unconscious or automatic associations in this domain may reveal mechanisms that undermine or depart from the intended endorsement of equality that color-blindness sanctions. In a series of six studies, Thierry Devos and Mahzarin Banaji[21] examined what it means to be American and who qualifies as American. Their research is a good example of work that assesses the split between *explicit* attitudes, measured by self-report survey questions, and *implicit* attitudes, assessed by the speed with which people make associations. In other words, by measuring both explicit and implicit attitudes, one can examine the gap between what people apparently *really* think and what they *say* they think. Because so many studies comprised Devos and Banaji's research, I will not detail each of their procedures, but will instead outline the critical features of their most relevant studies and then focus on their results and on how those findings relate to colorblindness.

Devos and Banaji measured the extent to which individuals associate African Americans, Asian Americans, and white Americans with being "American," and compared explicit and implicit responses. An explicit measure would ask a question such as, *"How strong are the ties between Asian Americans and the American culture?"* Implicit measures were assessed using the Implicit Association Test that measured the ease or speed with which respondents paired American symbols (e.g. an American flag, Mt. Rushmore) with faces from each of the three ethnic groups.

On explicit measures, white respondents tended to see Asian Americans as less American than African Americans and white Americans; and they considered African Americans just as American or somewhat less American than white Americans. But when the same attitudes were measured implicitly, when respondents did not have time to control and mask their responses, both African Americans and Asian Americans were seen as less American than white Americans. For white Americans, whites were viewed, implicitly at least, as the *true* Americans, and everyone else seemed to be considered interlopers.

In order to see if they could shake loose the grip of the whiteness = American association, Devos and Banaji created an explicit and implicit measure of associations of American Olympic athletes. They selected African Americans representing athletic events such as track and field. If African Americans are well-known American athletes, wouldn't they be seen as "true" Americans? For the implicit measure, they used photos of white and black Olympic athletes and paired them with American and foreign (flags or uniforms from other countries) symbols. On explicit measures, black athletes were judged to be more strongly associated with being American than white athletes – not very surprising because of the prevalence of African Americans in certain Olympic sports. However, on implicit measures, white athletes were much more strongly associated with American symbols, and African American athletes with foreign symbols. Even in an arena in which African Americans dominate, and even when people know that explicitly, their automatic and unconscious beliefs indicate that they believe that African Americans are less American than whites. Even the fact that African Americans are not recent arrivals to the US, and are strongly associated with America in the domain of sports *explicitly*, did not offer protection against them being thought of as foreign at the level of automatic associations regarding who are "true" Americans.

Next, Devos and Banaji again attempted to disrupt the American = white association by comparing famous Asian Americans with famous white Europeans. Certainly famous Asian American celebrities who are unmistakably American would be seen as more American than would white European celebrities who are unmistakably *not* American, right? American symbols were paired with famous Asian Americans (Connie Chung, Lucy Liu), famous white Americans (Ben Stiller, Robert Duvall), and famous white Europeans (Elizabeth Hurley, Gérard Depardieu). If people's notions of "American" include all actual Americans, regardless of race or ethnicity, then the famous Asian Americans would be readily paired with American symbols. However, if people's notion of "American" included only whites, then any white person would be seen as more American than an Asian American. Who was seen as most "American?" Not surprisingly, it was easier to pair American symbols with famous white Americans than with famous Asian Americans. But, it was also easier to pair American symbols with names of famous white *Europeans* than with famous Asian Americans! In other words, even fame and success in America were not enough for Asian Americans to be perceived as American. Whiteness trumps actually being from America when it comes to perceptions of "true" Americans.

Devos and Banaji's consistent finding, that American = white, does not occur for white respondents only. For both Asian American and white respondents, it was easier to pair "white" with "American" than "black" with "American." Even Asian Americans viewed their own groups as less American than they viewed whites. But this was not the case for African American respondents – they just as easily paired "black" with "American" as they did "white" with "American," on implicit measures. Although viewed by whites and Asian Americans as less American than whites, African Americans viewed themselves as just as American as whites and more American than Asians. If asymmetries in terms of power and status are critical factors in determining who are true Americans, one would expect African Americans to be more strongly excluded from the American national identity than Asian Americans, an ethnic group positioned more favorably on the social ladder. But this was not the case. To summarize, white Americans are construed as prototypical exemplars of the category "American." The cultural "default" value for "American" is "white." Devos and Banaji summarized their findings by saying, "The propensity to equate American with White cannot easily be overridden and is sometimes completely dissociated from conscious beliefs or knowledge about ethnic–national associations."[21]

Interviews and anecdotal data support what Devos and Banaji established experimentally. In his interviews with white Americans, Derald Sue[22] found that whiteness is seen as a universal identity, again, the cultural default. When white people are asked about their ethnic identity they are much more likely than are people of color to describe themselves as a "human being" or "just a person." When Sue asks, "What does it mean to be White?" white respondents say things like, "*It doesn't affect my life*," or "*It's not important to me*." Respondents would rather not think about their whiteness; they deny that it is important, or that it affects them. "*People are people*," "*We are all Americans*." These are whites' *explicit* answers, but we know from Devos and Banaji's work on *implicit* associations that people tend to think that whites are the only *real* Americans. Student comments in my classes are consistent with what Devos and Banaji found experimentally and what Sue found in interviews. When I teach *Psychology of Prejudice*, occasionally a white student will say, "*Why do we have to talk about people's ethnicity all the time, can't we just be Americans?*" These students espouse a colorblind perspective and feel exasperated at ethnic minority groups that emphasize their ethnicity. In fact, some of my white students do not believe they even have an ethnicity. They think that ethnicities are for people of color, just as when someone describes an "ethnic" restaurant, they mean something that people of color make and eat, not "white" food. Whiteness represents institutional normalcy and whites are taught to think of their lives as morally neutral, average, and ideal.[24]

The problem with the colorblind perspective is that it is not neutral; it means whites are the "normal" cultural default, non-whites are the *other*. This belief is not always reflected in explicit attitude measures, but it is consistently detected in implicit attitude measures. The research from Devos and Banaji's study suggests that ethnic and racial groups differ in the ease with which they would be included in an American identity. The propensity to equate "American" with "white" may facilitate the integration of white ethnic groups (e.g. Irish, Italian) into the "American" category but it also means that there are groups excluded from the national identity. The term *exclusionary patriotism*[25] refers to the idea that the strength of American identity comes from antagonism toward ethnic minorities. Instead of promoting unity and solidarity, expressions of patriotism or national identity could go hand in hand with an exclusion of ethnic minorities from the national identity.[26] You can begin to see then, that when politicians and activists argue for racial colorblindness and make the argument "*Can't we all just be American?*" that may be a worthy goal, but that is not how most people, and by most people I mean whites as well as, to some extent, people of color, think. For most people, being "American" is exclusionary. True Americans, to most people, are white.

Another study looked at this issue of exclusivity. Qiong Li and Marilynn Brewer[27] looked at how *framing of unity* affects the relationship between patriotism and nationalism. In the United States, after the attacks of September 11, 2001, there were many discussions about national unity. Many Americans' loyalty to the US was questioned. Former President George W. Bush led the charge with statements such as, "Either you are with us, or you are with the terrorists,"[28] suggesting that there was only one way to be a patriot – support the president's policies. Li and Brewer studied the factors that affect the relationship between two separate but related concepts: *patriotism* as distinct from exclusionary patriotism, and *nationalism*. Patriotism refers to pride and love for country, and, in social psychology terminology, involves secure ingroup identification without outgroup derogation (Chapter 1 discusses outgroup derogation at length). Patriotism, then, is having a love and pride for one's country without viewing other countries as inferior to one's own. Nationalism also refers to positive ingroup identification, but, unlike patriotism, it also involves insecure ingroup identification, and intergroup differentiation that includes the view that one's country is superior to others and should be dominant. Nationalism involves chauvinistic arrogance and the desire for dominance in international relations. Because they share the feature of positive ingroup evaluation, nationalist and patriotic attitudes are correlated. But they differ in their intergroup attitudes – patriotism tends to entail positive international cooperation while nationalism is negatively correlated with international cooperation and positively correlated with militarism.

Li and Brewer asked white American college students to complete a survey with statements meant to tap into patriotism: *"I am proud to be American; although at times I may not agree with the government, my commitment to the US is strong;"* and nationalism: *"The first duty of every young American is to honor the national American history and heritage,"* and *"People should support their country even if the country is in the wrong."* Statements about tolerance, multicultural values, attitudes about various groups, and inclusiveness and national identity were also included in the survey. Attached to the beginning of the survey was an introductory paragraph designed to prompt national unity. The paragraph emphasized either a *"core essence"* of national identity, mentioning 9/11 and stating that we have come to understand what we have in common as Americans and that, as a nation, our focus is on the core essence of what it means to be American; or a *"common goal"* version that also brought up 9/11 and then stated that we have a common purpose to fight terrorism and work together to help 9/11 victims. Li and Brewer thus experimentally manipulated national unity to see if the two different primes affected how similarly participants would respond to the patriotism and nationalism statements.

Having participants think of a *core-essence-based* notion of national unity resulted in increased nationalism in association with heightened patriotism more than it did when a *common-goal-based* notion was presented. This means that when participants read the core-essence introduction, their responses to the statements about nationalism and patriotism were more strongly correlated than when they read the common-goal introduction. In contrast, when they read the common-goal condition, patriotism and nationalism were relatively independent in the readers' minds, meaning that patriotism did not carry with it negative aspects of nationalism such as intolerance, and the denigration of other countries. Also when the core essence of national unity was primed in Li and Brewer's study, respondents' strong patriotism was associated with cultural intolerance, whereas when the common-goal version of unity was primed, patriotism did not correlate with intolerance. Nationalism was associated with intolerance in both conditions. The kind of national unity promoted by patriotism with nationalism and reflected by the core-essence idea is similar to the "exclusionary patriotism."[29] Overall, Li and Brewer found that how national unity is framed can affect whether someone is more patriotic and/or nationalistic. Under conditions of threat and uncertainty, such as a post-September 11 world, patriotic zeal may activate nationalistic values. Patriotism may reinforce a sense of unity and solidarity in the face of adversity if there is an emphasis on common interests and common fate, rather than on homogeneity of culture. How does the Li and Brewer study on frames of national unity relate to colorblind racial attitudes? Like the studies described earlier, comparing multicultural and colorblind approaches to improving intergroup relations, Li and Brewer's study demonstrates the implications of emphasizing uniformity in what it is to be American, this being consistent with a colorblind point of view, versus emphasizing that there are different ways one can be American, a view compatible with multiculturalism.

Colorblindness and assimilation

Advocates of the colorblind perspective presume that reducing the salience of others' race or ethnicity will reduce the degree to which judgments are clouded by negative beliefs about the group. As we have seen, this approach to reducing racial prejudice is not viable because people *do* notice race and *do* treat people differently based on race, even if they do not want to and think they shouldn't.

Also, the fact that white people are viewed as the cultural norm, and are seen as the only "true" Americans, puts people of color in the disadvantaged position of having to try to assimilate into a white norm. The studies described above have a common theme running through their results: the lure of *assimilation*. Assimilation, in the context of colorblindness, is the process whereby minority groups blend into the dominant group's values, behaviors, language, and culture.

Bernardo Ferdman[30] conducted an experiment that examined whether paying attention to a person's social category would increase social distance, or dislike, etc. Ferdman created a videotape of a Latino man in different management situations. For each of the situations, there were two different versions: a "normative" version during which he handled the situation as an Anglo would, and a version in which he handled the situation as a Latino would. Unfortunately, Ferdman did not describe how the Anglo versus Latino management styles differed, although he did conduct focus groups with Latina/os who evaluated the versions to provide validation of the cultural differences in the two versions. White managers who worked in business viewed the videotape of the Latino man in one of the situations. But before they saw the video, participants read a fact sheet that included excerpts from an interview with the man. For one third of the participants, individuating features, such as hobbies, were highlighted. For another third, the man highlighted his ethnicity, how he was part of Latina/o organizations and how his ethnicity was important to him. The final third read information with both ethnic group and individuating information. So there were two key variables manipulated in the study: (1) the management situation in which the man behaved in a way consistent with Anglo or Latina/o norms; and (2) information provided regarding the man's self-described individuating information, his ethnicity, or both. After reading the fact sheet and viewing the videotape, each manager completed a questionnaire that rated the man on social distance, success in handling the situation presented in the video, and how similar the respondents felt to the man in the video.

White managers reacted more negatively to the version of the man who acted "Latino" than the man who acted "Anglo." The white managers felt more social distance from the man, felt he was less similar to them, felt that he handled the management situation less well, and acted less like typical managers, when the man acted "Latino." What about when the man in the video presented individuating information versus information about his ethnic background? The colorblind perspective predicts that the white managers would rate the Latino man most positively when he presented individuating information (not about his ethnicity) and saw the man acting Anglo. The white managers actually evaluated the Latino man most positively when he was presented with both individuating (e.g. hobbies) *and* ethnic information, and least positively when he was presented with individuating information alone. This effect was the same regardless of whether, in the video, the man acted "Latino" or "Anglo." Proponents of the colorblind perspective would suggest that ethnicity being made salient as a person enters a workplace could lead to discrimination or to the person not "blending into" (i.e. assimilating) the workplace. But these findings contradict this concern. Taken together, the results of Ferdman's study suggests that: (1) when initially hired, people of color should "act like," that is, take on the mannerisms and behavioral style of, the dominant group; and (2) people of color should not minimize their ethnicity. These two points are somewhat contradictory and result in a person of color having to walk a fine line in the workplace between not ignoring his ethnic minority status, but also behaving in a way that is palatable to the dominant group. Ferdman's study has implications for affirmative action, the topic of the next chapter. Affirmative action might be successful in increasing the number of women and minorities gaining entry, yet is less successful in improving retention and promotion. Colorblindness might make the majority feel better and less threatened, but it is not necessarily better for minorities. So while diversity is good for the workplace, outsiders need to assimilate once they are in the organization.

One problem with racial colorblindness is that it functions to erase differences among people and it forces those who differ from the white norm to assimilate into or to imitate whiteness. This minimization of race can take ridiculous forms. Janet Schofield[31] examined colorblindness at a desegregated middle school. She interviewed teachers and students and observed day-to-day goings-on at the school. She concluded that while colorblind approaches in schools may minimize awkward interactions involving racial issues, possible discrimination against African American students is ignored or is not recognized. Schofield observes that a white norm is maintained and that if African American students are not assimilated into the white norm, they are viewed as deviants. Their lack of fit is attributed to other factors than race. For instance, a teacher intentionally miscounted votes on a student government election to pick a "responsible child" (white) instead of the "unstable child" (black) who actually won. The colorblind approach's erasure of race was also evidenced in the fact that some students did not know that Martin Luther King, Jr., was African American. Instead of issues and conflicts being negotiated on an intergroup dimension in which race and ethnicity are relevant issues; the school, teachers, and administrators attempted to minimize any intergroup dimensions and replace them with an individualist approach.

Colorblindness is a powerful means of justifying racial inequality because it "unraces" race. It takes racism out of the picture and replaces it with an apparently liberal discourse of fairness and equal opportunity. It is difficult to know whether or not the teachers and administrators of the school Schofield observed deliberately took a colorblind approach in order to advantage white students and disadvantage African American students. One thing that is clear about benign bigotry is that the perpetrator of prejudice and discrimination does not need to be deliberate, motivated, or aware of her biases, in order to discriminate.

Assimilation is probably an effective strategy for a new person to blend into an existing group. If you join a sorority or fraternity in college, you would expect to assimilate to the norms and "culture" of that particular group. When you get a new job, you seek to observe and understand the norms and organizational culture. Blending into the existing culture would be a good strategy for success. Thus when we consider assimilation in the context of racial colorblindness, a person of color who is a recent immigrant to a country will feel particular pressure to assimilate. But colorblind politics, at least in the US, is relevant mainly to groups that have lived in the US for decades and even centuries. Many African Americans, for instance, have American ancestors dating back to the 1700s – their ancestors have been Americans for as long as most white Europeans of today. Yet, it is the less powerful group, without regard for the longevity of their national heritage, that is viewed as less "American" and who must assimilate. Assimilation means a person of color must conform to white values and culture, not vice versa. So people of color, not whites, do the work of assimilation.

The momentum of colorblindness in politics and law

In 1996, the state of California passed a ballot initiative that outlawed affirmative action in hiring and college admissions in the state. Capitalizing on the myth that affirmative action is "reverse discrimination," the initiative was called the "California Civil Rights Initiative." The name of the proposition was viewed by many as a cynical attempt to co-opt language of the civil rights movement. "Civil rights" was invoked to protect those who had benefited from a system that discriminates against minorities. A proponent of the proposition, former governor of California Pete Wilson,[32] invoked the words of Martin Luther King Jr., Thomas Jefferson, and Abraham Lincoln in his argument against affirmative action and in favor of racial colorblindness. The sentiments of King, Jefferson, and Lincoln represented ideology meant to protect those oppressed and less privileged, although Wilson used their words to argue that whites and men are disadvantaged and that it is minorities who obtain "*special privileges*" from "*color coded preferences.*"[33] Six years later, Californians voted on another ballot proposition, this one provocatively called the "Racial Privacy Initiative". This was an initiative to ban any classifications based on race or ethnicity in the state (except in law enforcement and in some medical research). For example, the state would be prevented from tracking hate crimes, discrimination in hiring or admissions, and even some medical conditions that disproportionately affect particular racial or ethnic groups.[34] It apparently would not even allow university researchers (like me!) to consider race/ethnicity as a factor in research.[35] As with the name of the "California Civil Rights Initiative", the title "Racial Privacy Initiative" appeared intentionally misleading designed to imply that one's race or ethnicity could be made private – that skin color could be ignored and that racial colorblindness could be codified.

In 2007, the US Supreme Court ruled that race and ethnicity could not be considered in determining placement of students in public schools. Many school districts in the US use race and ethnicity, along with other factors, in determining the particular school that children will attend. The school districts argued that if race and ethnicity are not taken into account, schools will re-segregate and will begin to reassume the characteristics they had until the 1960s. This would result in "black" schools that would be under-resourced and "white" schools that would have superior resources. In his majority opinion, Chief Justice John Roberts wrote, "The way to stop discrimination on the basis of race is to stop discriminating on the basis of race."[36] Roberts' statement epitomizes the racial colorblindness position. *If you're against race discrimination, don't notice race. Colorblindness is the key to ending discrimination.*

Like Roberts, many argue that we should simply declare ourselves to be a colorblind society in which neither whites nor minorities receive benefit or burden due to their race. But colorblind laws are not the only way to be "colorblind." In fact, in order for color-blindness to "work" at the legal and societal level, it must work at the individual level. For individuals, colorblindness is an attractive strategy for avoiding racism or the appearance of racism. For whites who strive for colorblindness, the strategy is, *If I do not see race, how can I be a racist?* This individual strategy is understandable, given the pressure and desire to avoid appearing racist. And certainly, seeing race is a prerequisite for racism. But is it possible, in practical and meaningful ways, to live in a multiethnic society and not see race or color? What does it mean for an individual to take a color-blind position? Are those individuals who claim colorblindness less biased than those who acknowledge color? And what would it mean to have ballot initiatives mandating that society ignore race, if individuals cannot ignore race?

Putting it all together

As we've seen again in this chapter, race and ethnicity play a significant role in how people interact with others. In today's society, there is certainly pressure to appear unprejudiced. Many whites want to not notice race, or at least, not to appear to notice race.[37] Color-blindness, therefore, may be an attractive ideal: if a person does not see race, how can she be a racist? Whites who think that they do not see color may believe their interactions with people of color are seamless, when, in fact, they may be awkward.[38] Thus, one problem with colorblindness at the individual level is that people are in fact *not* colorblind, they do notice race and they treat people differently depending on race. A self-perception of colorblindness is linked to a variety of attitudes centered on a lack of empathy. Posed as a goal for racial equality, the idea of colorblindness reflects and creates a complex and problematic view of racial equality. Belief in color-blindness protects whites from realizing that they benefit from racism. Today, most writers and politicians who invoke the Martin Luther King, Jr., quote mentioned at the beginning of the chapter are political conservatives[39] who argue in favor of racial colorblind-ness as part of the anti-affirmative action position. By 1980, the colorblind position had become part of the US Republican party platform.[40] A major problem with the colorblind position, particu-larly in politics and mass media, is as long as race is hidden from consciousness, the dominant racial and ethnic group can maintain the illusion that they are not responsible for the state of race relations because they do not knowingly engage in racist behavior, and even consider talking about race off limits. Derald Sue[41] argues that, for whites, colorblindness is a denial of the unfair power imbalance, allowing whites to deny their privilege while still receiving its bene-fits. The benefits that accrue to whites serve to keep them satisfied and enlist their unwitting complicity in maintaining unjust social arrangements. On the other hand, colorblindness and assimilation take a toll on those subordinate groups pressured to assimilate. They are forced to subordinate their characteristics, traditions, and cul-ture, in order to blend in with the dominant group. As Ferdman found in the case of Latinos, ethnic minorities are expected to assimilate, but, at the same time, the dominant group expects them to represent their minority status. This is a delicate and costly balance. Assimilation is a task that takes a lot of energy.

Colorblindness is problematic on a societal and political level as well. When the colorblind approach has been compared to a multicultural approach to improving ethnic relations, the multicul-tural approach proves to be more effective.[42] Because of power differences between groups, colorblindness in society, as in individuals, uses "whiteness" as the imagined norm by "whiting" out differences and perpetuating the belief of sameness. The denial of power imbalance, unearned privilege and racist domination are couched in the rhetoric of equal treatment and equal opportunity.[43] Whites may have no awareness of their privileged status *even as they protect their interests*. While white individuals will acknowledge that disparities in education or other realms exist, they are more likely to attribute inequality to a lack of ambition and effort on the part of minorities than to structural favoritism toward whites that has been built into US institutions for generations.[44] Colorblind racism forms an invisible yet impregnable ideological wall that shields whites from America's racial reality.[45]

More cynical uses of colorblindness have included shutting down any discussion of the idea that race and ethnicity are relevant dimensions. In the current colorblind political era, those in the public arena who write about the realities of race and racism are the ones accused of fostering racial divisions.[46] By regarding race-related matters as *non*-racial, natural, or being rooted in people's choices, whites deem proposals to remedy racial inequality as illogical, undemocratic, and "racist," in reverse.[47]

Strategies for change

Creating complicated categories

In Chapter 1 (*"They all look alike"*), and Chapter 4 (*"Gays flaunt their sexuality"*), I discussed the use of the contact hypothesis as a strategy for prejudice reduction. The contact hypothesis asserts that, when certain conditions are met, increased contact between groups should result in decreased prejudice. The contact hypothesis assumes that prejudice is the result of categorizing people according to their group membership and not recognizing individual charac-teristics that make them distinct from group stereotypes. The four necessary conditions for contact to successfully reduce prejudice are: (1) the contact must be on an equal footing; (2) the contact should involve cooperation in achieving a common goal; (3) there must be contact over an extended period in order for acquaintance potential, and (4) there must be institutional support for such contact.

Three processes for changes in thinking relevant to the myth of colorblindness can be tied into the contact hypothesis in interesting ways. The first strategy is called *decategorization* (also called *personalization*).[48] During initial contact between groups, based on the conditions necessary for successful intergroup contact outlined above, people can be expected to view members of outgroups in terms of stereotypes. As contact is maintained, a process of decategorization will occur, whereby people begin to see others in terms of their individual personalities and characteristics rather than as simply members of the outgroup. Decategorization allows for the discovery that members of outgroups are just as unique and as variable as are members of the ingroup. The outgroup category (e.g. "blacks" or "Jews") begins to lose its effectiveness in helping ingroup members understand who the outgroup person is and what she is like. The category that the other person was originally lumped into is no longer useful once one gets to know the person as an individual – you see all the ways in which the person does not fit the stereotype and therefore the stereotype stops being useful. Ingroup members also begin to see the outgroup person in terms of multiple social identities – such as *father, union activist, Christian,* rather than only as a member of the salient outgroup category, such as "African American." Awareness that people have complex social identities lessens the importance of group boundaries by making the lines between groups more fuzzy and permeable and less distinct and impenetrable.

The process of decategorization may appear to resemble racial (or other categories of) colorblindness – not seeing people in terms of group membership and ignoring group differences. But as we have seen in the research described in this chapter, colorblindness is not possible and is therefore not a realistic goal for reducing prejudice. The change in thinking that I am describing here does not stop simply because color has been ignored. In other words, decategorization along one dimension alone is not very effective in prejudice reduction. Change results primarily from the development of a multifaceted, multilevel categorization that diminishes the influence of any one dimension. Such decategorization has some demonstrated success in the reduction of prejudice when the four conditions of successful intergroup contact have been met.[49]

After prolonged contact with members of the outgroup, a second process may occur, that of *salient categorization*. Salient categorization occurs when one begins to view outgroup members as representatives of the outgroup in general, but, informed by what one knows about individual members of the outgroup as being unique and variable, one begins to change negative views of the entire outgroup. Ideally, what happens with both decategorization, and then with more contact, salient categorization, is that the outgroup member is seen as typical of her group while still disconfirming negative aspects of the group stereotype. If only the first process, decategorization, occurs, and the outgroup member's characteristics become more complicated in the eyes of the observer, the outgroup member may run the risk of being pegged merely as an *exception* to the outgroup stereotype. For positive attitudes to generalize from the particular group member to the group as a whole, the stereotype-disconfirming member must be seen as otherwise typical of her group. For this to be effective, the two competing processes must work in concert.

Finally, *re-categorization* resulting in a *common ingroup identity* might be achieved. Re-categorization occurs when ingroup and outgroup members are induced to re-categorize themselves as members of a *superordinate* identity. The context within which two or more groups interact may discourage "us" versus "them" thinking, and facilitate a broader "we" category. Both groups understand that they have many characteristics, desires, values, hobbies, and jobs in common, all of which outweigh any differences in broad group membership. For instance, in the US, after the September 11, 2001 attacks, many people who were previously in separate and antagonized groups re-conceptualized themselves as members of the larger, common ingroup, "Americans." Temporarily, there was a sense of a common "us," which cut across racial, ethnic, and class boundaries.

Unfortunately, because of the structured nature of inequality, most intergroup contact situations never reach the stage of recategorization, or do so only temporarily and at another group's expense. For instance, while many Americans became united shortly after the attacks on September 11, 2001, other Americans, Arab and Muslim Americans particularly, were not included in this newly formed superordinate identity and were instead excluded and marginalized for their suspected links to terrorists. Nonetheless, you can see the potential of breaking down group stereotypes with increased contact with members of outgroups.

One additional caveat regarding the contact hypothesis of reducing prejudice has to do with the type of interactions members of different groups have with each other. As the studies I have reviewed in this chapter show, those who advocate the colorblind approach or who believe themselves to be colorblind when they interact with outgroups, may display awkward or even offensive behavior that may not yield positive intergroup relations. Therefore, the first order of prejudice reduction business is for us to give up our belief that we are colorblind.

Controlling your cognitions and values confrontation

Another strategy for prejudice reduction is a practice described in Chapter 1. *Stereotype suppression* is practiced at the level of individual cognition. This mental strategy, which has been used for a range of goals from managing food cravings to controlling depressing thoughts, entails avoiding thinking negative thoughts and replacing them with distractor thoughts. In the case of stereo-typed thinking, when you find yourself applying stereotypes to a member of a certain group, you replace those thoughts with non-stereotypical thoughts. As I said in Chapter 1, research on the efficacy of stereotype suppression is mixed.[50] In some cases, delib-erately trying to avoid thinking about a topic makes you think about it even more, especially if you are a person with strong prejudices. Margo Monteith[51] and her colleagues tested this strat-egy in a study in which people were given a photo of two gay men who were a couple and were asked to write a passage about a typical day in their life. Some of the participants were instructed to avoid stereotypical preconceptions in their description, while others were not given such instructions. For participants low in prejudice, suppressing stereotypes was effective, while for those with strong prejudice toward gay men, suppressing the stereotypic thoughts actually increased the accessibility of the stereotype.

Some individuals can avoid prejudicial responses if they have the motivation and ability to do so. For those who wish they could see past racial and ethnic categories but have given up on the fiction of racial colorblindness, stereotype suppression may be a good alterna-tive strategy to failed attempts at colorblindness. Stereotype suppres-sion may work for those individuals who strongly endorse egalitarian values but continue to have bigoted reflexes (those who fit the description of someone with subtle prejudice). This discrepancy in thinking can induce guilt and this guilt can be a motivator to suppress prejudicial thinking. According to Patricia Devine[52] and her colleagues, many people want to do and say the right thing, and the discrepancy between their spontaneous stereotypical thin-king and their non-prejudiced standards leads to feelings of com-punction. As a result, these individuals will be motivated to avoid subsequent stereotyping and to actively suppress such thoughts.

Several researchers have found that when low-prejudice people have been made aware that they have behaved in a way inconsistent with their egalitarian values, they feel guilty and are motivated to change their future behavior. This line of research is one of the few that has examined the reduction of subtle forms of Prejudice. For example Leanne Son Hing[53] and her colleagues examined the role of *hypocrisy induction* as a successful prejudice reduction technique. White Canadian college students who were *aversive* racists (those with low levels of explicit prejudice and high levels of implicit prejudice) were compared with non-racists (those with low levels of both implicit and explicit prejudice) on a hypocrisy induction task. Both groups were asked to write an essay on the importance of treating people equally regardless of their race, gender, etc. This was an easy task for all participants because they all espoused nonprejudiced beliefs (at least explicitly). Next, half of the participants in each group experienced the hypocrisy induction condition: They were asked to write about situations in which they acted negatively toward an Asian person. Later, all participants were asked to respond to an initiative to make financial cuts in various student clubs, including the Asian Students Association's budget. They were told that the budget cuts were inevitable but that they should give their opinions on which groups should be given reduced budgets. Son Hing and her colleagues found that the hypocrisy induction had a different effect on the participants' behavior based on whether or not the participant was truly nonprejudiced versus only explicitly non-prejudiced (i.e. an aversive racist). Aversive racists who were confronted with the discrepancy between publicly advocating for equal rights in their essays, but then having to admit to discriminating against Asians in the past, were less likely to cut funds from the Asian Students Association compared to aversive racists who were not asked to complete the hypocrisy induction task. Being confronted with their own hypocrisy forced aversive racists to become aware of the negative aspects of the attitudes that they usually suppressed. In contrast, the truly low-prejudiced participants who completed the hypocrisy induction task did not cut funds to the Asian Students Association less, compared to those in the control condition (who did not experience hypocritical feelings). To summarize, aversive racists in the non-hypocrisy inducing control condition tended to discriminate against Asians by cutting their funding. However, in the hypocrisy condition, aversive racists treated Asians positively when their negative attitudes were made salient. The researchers suggest that aversive racists need to experience consciousness-raising to avoid behaving in a discriminatory manner. As I stated above, when people are made aware of the discrepancy between their ideal attitudes and the actual attitudes reflected in their behavior, negative feelings act as a sort of self-punishment and motivate people to engage in non-discriminatory behavior. The results of Son Hing's study found that these processes work for benign bigots (in this instance, aversive racists) but not for truly low-prejudiced people who do not need to experience hypocrisy to do the right thing.

Inducing empathy

Another strategy discussed in Chapter 1 is inducing empathy. Getting people to feel empathy toward a stigmatized group can play a powerful role in prejudice reduction. The work of Daniel Batson and his colleagues demonstrated that attitudes toward people with AIDS, homeless people, drug addicts, and even murderers, in addition to whites' attitudes toward people of color, can become more positive with empathy. Much of this research happens in a laboratory setting where participants are induced to feel empathy toward members of a target group and then are asked about their attitudes toward the target group later. One of Batson's studies[54] found that, in addition to attitude change, empathy can lead to behavior change, in a positive direction, toward a target group. American college students

272 • Benign Bigotry

(ethnicity unknown) listened to a taped interview of a drug addict in which he discusses his addiction and incarceration. In the control condition, participants were asked to remain "objective" while listening to the interview, but in the "empathy" condition, participants were asked to imagine the feelings of the person being interviewed. This simple difference in instruction had a significant impact on how participants viewed drug addicts in general, not only this particular addict. Participants in the empathy condition were later found to feel more positive toward drug addicts and were more likely to recommend increasing student funds for an agency to help drug addicts, even though it meant taking money away from other agencies, and even though it would not help the particular addict they heard in the interview. So not only did participants who were primed to think empathically feel different about drug addicts than those told to remain "objective," they also supported taking action to help addicts to a greater degree than those told to remain "objective." The participants' responses were not simply a reflection of sympathy expressed to help relieve an individual's need – they made choices about helping that stigmatized group, even though the help did not benefit the particular person who evoked the sympathy. In other words, care evoked by empathy felt for a member of a stigmatized group can generalize to the group and can create motivation for action on behalf of the entire group.

Teaching children about prejudice?

Should children learn about discrimination? There is some intriguing research on the effects of children learning about gender and racial discrimination. This area of research is still new and underdeveloped, perhaps because of concerns that children learning about discrimination as part of curricula might cause them distress. Or, just as some fear that sex education research might make children think about sex, will talking to children about prejudice poison them or make them feel bad? In Chapter 3, "Feminists are man-haters," I talked about an experiment by Erica Weisgram and Rebecca Bigler[55] in which they taught girls who were interested in science about gender discrimination in science fields. Compared to the girls who did not attend a session on gender discrimination, those who did showed increases in self-efficacy within science and were more likely to believe that science is a worthwhile subject of study. Most girls who participated in the gender discrimination lesson believed that discrimination can be overcome by having more women scientists and many girls indicated that learning about gender discrimination made them feel that they should enter the field to fight discrimination. Now I would like to describe a study on the effects of learning about racism by Julie Hughes and her colleagues.[55] They presented twenty-minute lessons, over six school days, to African American and white 6–11-year-olds. The lessons were biographies of famous Americans, some white, some black. Half of the children listened to lessons that included explicit information about some of the discriminatory experiences endured by the famous African Americans from whites. The other half of the children listened to the same lessons without reference to discrimination. For white children, those who participated in the racism condition had more favorable views of African Americans when their attitudes were assessed one or two days after the last session. Specifically, the white children who learned about racism expressed stronger values of racial fairness, showed higher levels of defensiveness, showed higher levels of guilt (for children over age 7 only), and endorsed more counter-stereotypical views of African Americans. So for the white children in the study, learning about racism is likely to promote prejudice reduction. In contrast to the effects on white children, African American children's attitudes were no different depending on the discrimination condition versus the non-discrimination condition. Hughes and her colleagues suppose that African American children may not have been influenced by the lessons about discrimination due to the possibility that they had already learned about discrimination from their parents or other adults.

NOTES

1. Colbert, S. (2007). The Colbert report [Television series episode] (Air date March 13, 2007). In *Comedy Central Network*.
2. Bonilla-Silva, E. (2003). *Racism without racists: Color-blind racism and the persistence of racial inequality in the United States*. Lanham, MD: Rowman & Littlefield Publishers, Inc.
3. For a discussion, see: Nelson, T.D. (2006). *The psychology of prejudice*. Boston: Pearson.
4. Ito, T.A., & Urland, G.R. (2003). Race and gender on the brain: Electrocortical measures of attention to the race and gender of multiply categorizable individuals. *Journal of personality and social psychology, 85,* 616–626.
5. Norton, M.I., Sommers, S.R., Apfelbaum, E.P., Pura, N., & Ariely, D. (2006). Color blindness and interracial interaction: Playing the political correctness game. *Psychological science, 17,* 949–953.
6. *Ibid.*
7. Bonilla-Silva, *Racism without racists*.
8. Dovidio, J.F. (in press). On the nature of contemporary prejudice: Outcomes and process. In *Proceedings of the third biennial EO/EEO research symposium*. Cocoa Beach, FL: Defense Equal Opportunity Management Institute. Cited in: Dovidio, J.F., Gaertner, S.L., Kawakami, K., & Hodson, G. (2002). Why can't we just get along? Interpersonal biases and interracial distrust. *Cultural diversity and ethnic minority psychology, 8,* 88–102.
9. Accomando, C. (September 30, 1993). Colorblind, or blind to discrimination? *Arcata eye*.
10. Neville, H.A., Lilly, R.L., Duran, G., Lee, R.M., & Browne, L.V. (2000). Construction and initial validation of the Color-Blind Racial Attitudes Scale (CoBRAS). *Journal of counseling psychology, 47,* 59–70.
11. *Ibid.*
12. Lerner, M.J. (1980). *The belief in a just world: A fundamental delusion.* New York: Springer.
13. Neville, H., Spanierman, L., Doan, B.-T. (2006). Exploring the association between color-blind racial ideology and multicultural counseling competencies. *Cultural diversity and ethnic minority psychology, 12,* 275–290.

14. Burkard, A.W., & Knox, S. (2004). Effect of therapist color-blindness on empathy and attributions in cross-cultural counseling. *Journal of counseling psychology, 51,* 387–397.
15. Awad, G.H., Cokley, K., & Ravitch, J. (2005). Attitudes toward affirmative action: A comparison of color-blind versus modern racist attitudes. *Journal of applied social psychology, 35,* 1384–1399.
16. Spanierman, L.B., & Heppner, M.J. (2004). Psychosocial costs of racism to whites scale (PCRW): Construction and initial validation. *Journal of counseling psychology, 51,* 249–262.
17. Neville, H.A., Coleman, M.N., Falconer, J.W., & Holmes, D. (2005). Color-blind racial ideology and psychological false consciousness among African Americans. *Journal of black psychology, 31,* 27–45.
18. Wolsko, C., Park, B., Judd, C.M., & Wittenbrink, B. (2000). Framing interethnic ideology: Effects of multicultural and color-blind perspectives on judgments of groups and individuals. *Journal of personality and social psychology, 78,* 635–654.
19. Richeson, J.A., & Nussbaum, R.J. (2003). The impact of multiculturalism versus color-blindness on racial bias. *Journal of experimental social psychology, 40,* 417–423.
20. Levy, S.R., West, T.L., & Ramirez, L. (2005). Lay theories and intergroup relations: A social-developmental perspective. *European review of social psychology, 16,* 189–220.
21. Devos, T., & Banaji, M.R. (2005). American = white? *Journal of personality and social psychology, 88,* 447–466.
22. *Ibid.*, page 463.
23. Sue, D.W. (2004). Whiteness and ethnocentric monoculturalism: Making the "invisible" visible. *American psychologist, 59,* 761–769.
24. *Ibid.*
25. Sidanius, J., & Petrocik, J.R. (2001). Communal and national identity in a multiethnic state: A comparison of three perspectives. In R.D. Ashmore, L. Jussim, & D. Wilder (Eds.), *Social identity, intergroup conflict, and conflict reduction* (pp. 101–129). Cary, NC: Oxford University Press.
26. Li, Q., & Brewer, M.B. (2004). What does it mean to be an American? Patriotism, nationalism, and American identity after 9/11. *Political psychology, 25,* 727–739.
27. *Ibid.*
28. Address to a Joint Session of Congress and the American People (2001, September 20). The White House: Office of the Press Secretary. Retrieved October 15, 2007, from www.dhs.gov/xnews/speeches/speech_0016.shtm
29. Sidanius & Petrocik, Communal and national identity in a multiethnic state.

30. Ferdman, B.M. (1989). Affirmative action and the challenge of the color-blind perspective. In F.A. Blanchard & F.J. Crosby (Eds.), *Affirmative action in perspective* (pp. 169–176). New York: Springer-Verlag.
31. Schofield, J.W. (1986). Causes and consequences of the colorblind perspective. In J.F. Dovidio & S.L. Gaertner (Eds.), *Prejudice, discrimination, and racism* (pp. 231–253). Orlando, FL: Academic Press, Inc.
32. Wilson, P. (1996). The minority–majority society. In G.E. Curry (Ed.), *The affirmative action debate* (pp. 167–174). Reading, MA: Addison-Wesley.
33. Reynolds, W.B. (1996). An experiment gone awry. In G.E. Curry (Ed.), *The affirmative action debate* (pp. 130–136). Reading, MA: Addison-Wesley.
34. Sue, Whiteness and ethnocentric monoculturalism.
35. Chemerinsky, E. (2003, August 22). Why California's racial privacy initiative is unconstitutional. Retrieved May 5, 2008, from www.cnn.com/2003/LAW/08/22/ findlaw.analysis.chemerinsky.race/
36. Mears, B. (2007, June 28). Divided court rejects school diversity plans. CNN.com. Retrieved November 26, 2007, from www.cnn.com/2007/LAW/06/28/scotus.race/index.html
37. Norton *et al.* Color blindness and interracial interaction.
38. *Ibid.*
39. Including former California governor Pete Wilson in: Wilson, The minority–majority society. See also, Terry Eastland in: Eastland, T. (1996). *Ending affirmative action: The case for colorblind justice.* New York: BasicBooks. See also, William Bradford Reynolds in: Reynolds, An experiment gone awry.
40. Carr, L.G. (1997). *"Color-blind" racism.* Thousand Oaks, CA: Sage Publications, Inc.
41. Sue, Whiteness and ethnocentric monoculturalism.
42. Richeson & Nussbaum, The impact of multiculturalism versus color-blindness on racial bias. See also: Wolsko *et al.* Framing interethnic ideology.
43. Sue, D.W. (2003). Dismantling the myth of a color-blind society. *Black issues in higher education, 20,* 106.
44. For example, Brodkin's study of the impact and legacies of the 1944 GI Bill shows that white American men disproportionately received its housing, educational, and employment benefits, while people of color and women were systematically excluded. Brodkin describes the program as one of the biggest and best affirmative action programs in the history of our nation for white men. See: Brodkin, K. (2007). How Jews became white folks and what that says about race in America. In P.S. Rothenberg (Ed.), *Race, class, and gender in the United States* (7th edition, pp. 38–53). New York: Worth.
45. Bonilla-Silva, *Racism without racists.*

46. *Ibid.*
47. *Ibid.*
48. For an extensive discussion of these processes, see: Whitley, B.E., Jr., & Kite, M.E. (2010). *The psychology of prejudice and discrimination.* Belmont, CA: Wadsworth.
49. For a review of the literature on decategorization and prejudice reduction, see: Whitley & Kite, *The psychology of prejudice and discrimination.*
50. For a review of the work in the area of stereotype suppression, see: Jones, M. (2002). *Social psychology of prejudice.* Upper Saddle River, NJ: Prentice Hall.
51. Monteith, M.J., Spicer, C.V., & Tooman, G.D. (1998). Consequences of stereotype suppression: Stereotypes on AND not on the rebound. *Journal of experimental social psychology, 34,* 355–377.
52. Devine, P.G., Monteith, M.J., Zuwerink, J.R., & Elliot, A.J. (1991). Prejudice with and without compunction. *Journal of personality and social psychology, 60,* 817–830.
53. Son Hing, L.S., Li, W., & Zanna, M.P. (2002). Inducing hypocrisy to reduce prejudicial responses among aversive racists. *Journal of experimental social psychology, 38,* 71–78.
54. Batson, C.D., Chang, J., Orr, R., & Rowland, J. (2002). Empathy, attitudes, and action: Can feeling for a member of a stigmatized group motivate one to help the group? *Personality and social psychology bulletin, 28,* 1656–1666.
55. Weisgram, E.S., & Bigler, R.S. (2007). Effects of learning about gender discrimination on adolescent girls' attitudes toward and interest in science. *Psychology of women quarterly, 31,* 262–269.
56. Hughes, J.M., Bigler, R.S., & Levy, S.R. (2007). Consequences of learning about historical racism among European American and African American children. *Child development, 78,* 1689–1705.

SIX

"Affirmative action is reverse racism": The myth of merit

But Americans of all races and creeds, men and women, are disgusted with the system of reverse discrimination.

Former Governor of California, Pete Wilson[1]

At the core of our shared belief in the American Dream is the assumption that basic qualities, valued widely in American society, will allow any individual to prevail. *Pull yourself up by your own bootstraps.* Hard work, determination, persistence, and dedication render any playing field level, goes the familiar narrative. It stands to reason, then, that those who do not succeed have only themselves to blame. The industrious rise through force of their own effort while the lazy founder on the rocks of failure because they lack the fundamental characteristics required for success. This is a dominant narrative in America.

How, then, does the controversial, often misunderstood principle of affirmative action fit into this narrative? Cherished narratives of this sort are tricky and full of baggage that encumbers our ability to think through social realities and policies. We often respond with a kind of reflex when something challenges our assumptions, and often we do not examine all the premises that underlie either our assumptions or the new challenge. Affirmative action is such a challenge, and it goes to the heart of some basic, if mythic, narratives that explain and govern our lives. A number of dangerous myths we live by and half-truths tend to obscure the real meanings of affirmative action and its potential to make the American dream an actuality.

A major stumbling block to our genuine understanding of the motivations and meanings behind affirmative action is the belief that, contrary to the very central principle of meritocracy, affirmative action would actually confer an unfair advantage on some person or some group and that an affirmative action program would *prefer* one category of persons over another thereby violating one of the major ground assumptions we live by. According to the dominant narrative in the United States, affirmative action can only be seen as the introduction of *preferences* in an otherwise fair system. Affirmative action, the reasoning goes, is simply wrong, perhaps even un-American, because it confers unfair preferences for, and advantages onto, women and people of color, while men and whites are still forced to play by the rules.

As we come to the final topic of this book, it should be clear to the reader that despite the hopes and myths that help support our society and encourage us to participate fully, the playing field is unfair. There is subtle but systematic discrimination against marginalized groups and unearned privilege for others. This chapter examines the necessity of affirmative action. I often hear from well-meaning people that there is no need for affirmative action. If civil rights legislation already exists, the reasoning goes, if laws exist to protect all people from illegal discrimination, affirmative action programs are then both unnecessary and unfair. Commitment to the ideals of American equality sometimes distorts our ability to see clearly the actual inequalities in the daily lives of women and people of color.

Benign bigotry, as a concept and as a set of beliefs and practices, is at the heart of understanding exactly why affirmative programs are necessary. Specifically the subtle, often unconscious and inconspicuous, forms of bias are at the very center of the affirmative action debate because these forms of discrimination are common in daily life – in the classroom, in the workplace, and in ordinary daily encounters and decisions. Because the detection of bias is so difficult, the only way to ensure fairness is to take a proactive approach to ensuring that discrimination does not take place. In order to understand affirmative action and the sentiments that run counter to it, let us look carefully at portrayals of affirmative action in the mass media, myths and common misunderstandings of what affirmative action is, and how it functions to perpetuate the myth that affirmative action amounts to reverse discrimination.

Affirmative action: Separating myths from reality

Affirmative action traces its history to 1965 when President Johnson signed Executive Order 11246 requiring all federal contractors to take "affirmative action" to ensure equality of employment. EO 11246, combined with amendments added later, constitutes what is now affirmative action in the US. In spirit and in original design, affirmative action was intended, through specific guidelines and requirements, to reduce and eliminate discriminatory practices in workplace hiring and promotion (and later, in college admissions), and was meant to ensure equality of opportunity for women and people of color. Federal contractors that receive money from the federal government are required to develop written affirmative action programs. Public schools, colleges, and universities, and approximately 22% of the businesses that employ the US labor force, are, according to the provisions of the act, required to engage in self-analysis for the purpose of discovering any barriers to equal opportunity. Organizations that receive federal funding should attempt to engage the services of minority contractors in proportion to the number of minority contractors available to perform the work. Affirmative action is meant to educate institutions and regulate ordinary practices that have for too many generations been ruled by habits of mind and business that are products of benign bigotry.

President Johnson's Executive Order 11246 specified two requirements. First, organizations are required to monitor their workforce statistics, paying attention to the representation of women and people of color with requisite skills relevant to the profession or occupation in their organization as compared to the availability of such people for employment. Second, if a dramatic difference exists between available qualified people and the composition of the organization, it is incumbent upon the organization to develop proactive efforts, such as recruitment and advertising, to ensure consistent development of hiring pools which are in compliance with the affirmative action guidelines. In addition, organizations are responsible for developing other activities, programs, and training courses designed to generate genuinely equal conditions. External outreach attempts to broaden awareness of hiring opportunities, and internal training programs designed to maximize opportunities for promotion, need to be incorporated as regular and routine aspects of conducting business. Numerical goals and timetables should be established based on the availability of qualified applicants in the job market.

Numerical goals are not quotas (quotas and quota-setting are illegal), nor are they "set-asides" for specific groups. Affirmative action was facilitated, in part, through "set-aside" programs in which a specified number of government contracts were dedicated to minority and women-owned businesses. President Clinton, however, did away with this practice. Rather, the goal-setting process in affirmative action planning is used to focus on and to assess the effectiveness of affirmative action efforts designed to eradicate and prevent discrimination. Quotas are used only in cases in which a specific and formal finding of discrimination has been made, and, in these cases, quotas are meant to remedy any disadvantages created by discriminatory practices. When discrimination is discovered, the Office of Federal Contract Compliance Programs (OFCCP) works with the organization to develop reasonable goals that can lead to decreased discrimination. If the organization does not comply with the OFCCP suggestions, it faces the possibility of losing its federal funding eligibility for a period of days or months. Every organization that falls under affirmative action guidelines is required to engage in this self-monitoring process and every year a certain number of organizations are audited by the OFCCP. If an organization fails to meet its goals, it needs to demonstrate a good-faith effort toward reaching the goals. The OFCCP employs only a few hundred people and doesn't have the resources necessary for an abundance of regulatory investigations.[2]

The fundamental goals and practices of affirmative action are shared across programs, although the specific design and implementation of programs vary along a dimension of prescriptiveness. On the low end of prescriptiveness there are opportunity enhancement programs such as focused recruitment (e.g. advertising a job opening in a publication that caters to people of color), or special training (with no weight given to the demographics of an applicant in decision making) that can influence hiring or selection decisions. There are also *tie-break* methods whereby members of the target group are given preference over others if their qualifications are equivalent. Finally, there is a perception by many that there is a practice of preferential treatment given to members of targeted groups even when group members' qualifications are inferior to those of the non-target groups. Those programs would include quotas, and such quotas are illegal. The latter category, highly prescriptive affirmative action programs, are opposed most vigorously by the public because they violate people's sense of merit-based justice.[3]

Also, sadly, although not a part of the real landscape of affirmative action implementation, perceived quota-based programs have become the basis for most of the misconceptions, prejudices, and bad will in the public mind toward affirmative action.

Opinion polls and portrayals in media

Again, the general public in the US tends to think of strong preferential treatment when they think about affirmative action. When people believe (falsely) that affirmative action equals quotas, they believe it amounts to *reverse discrimination* – and this, chiefly, entails the belief that affirmative action results in discrimination against men and white people. The inaccurate belief that affirmative action consists of strong preferential treatment and quotas is fueled by the mass media, in large measure by opponents of affirmative action. For instance, former California governor, Pete Wilson, who spear-headed the campaign to repeal affirmative action in his state in the 1990s, describes affirmative action as "preferential treatment" and those who benefit from it as members of "protected" and "preferred groups" who are only "so-called underrepresented" minorities.[4] It should be clear by this point in the book that women and people of color are hardly "protected" and "preferred."

That affirmative action is misunderstood as a policy and is regarded as a procedure that gives women and people of color preference over white men is fueled by at least three sets of beliefs. First, as discussed in Chapter 2, people tend to believe in a *just world*.[5] According to the just world theory, if people fail (fail to be hired, fail to be admitted to a college) their failures are reflections of their own lack of ability or tenacity. People who do succeed are the individuals best qualified to move ahead. Second, objections to affirmative action practices emerge from a belief that the system is a natural phenomenon that, if left alone, will operate in a fair manner. People tend to believe that the "normal" hiring and college admissions process is meritocratic – that the application process is fair and that the system itself, is self-correcting and that, the most qualified person will be hired or admitted. In actuality, the system is a product of human action and social forces and might require human intervention to make it work. Third, even though most people are committed to equality, as we have discovered throughout this book, many individuals hold unconscious beliefs that people of color and women tend to be less qualified than white men, which makes it difficult for people to accurately perceive situations of unfairness.[6]

But are people's positions on affirmative action always based on arguments about merit? There can be an element of racism in the rejection of affirmative action, at least among the white Midwestern American university students that Stephen Johnson[7] studied. Johnson engaged participants in a problem-solving task. Participants were told that they would be competing with someone in a different room for the best solution to a problem. Participants were led to believe that their competitor was either African American or white. After the task, all participants were told that they had lost the competition, but some for different reasons than others. Half were told they lost because of their competitor's superior problem-solving abilities. The other half, however, were told that although both participant and competitor performed similarly, the competitor was deemed the winner because she or he was from a poor background, was economically disadvantaged, and had probably faced injustice in her or his life. Obviously, this second condition was set up to appear as though the competitor was a beneficiary of preferential treatment. The participants' reactions would be analogous to people's misunderstanding and misconceptions of what affirmative action does. After the participants were informed they had lost, the experimenter presented an opportunity for retaliation by telling each participant that their judgment of the other person was an important factor in the final decision to award points and that if the participant had anything negative to say about the other person, the experimenter would take that into account when awarding points to the competitor. The participant would not receive extra points, but could prevent the other person from receiving the extra points. Using the analogy of affirmative action, if the participants were against affirmative action solely on the basis of merit – i.e., that people should not gain what they haven't earned – the participants would penalize the competitors who won due to previous disadvantage, regardless of the competitor's race. If racial prejudice was a factor in the participants' decisions, they would penalize an African American competitor more than a white competitor.

Did it matter whether the competitor was white or African American when it came to the participant retaliating? It did not matter if the participants thought they lost due to the others' superiority. In fact, when the participant's loss was believed to be because of the other person's superior performance, the participants were less aggressive toward the African American competitor than toward the white competitor. However, when the participant's loss in the competition resulted from the other person having been given the advantage due to their deprived background, the participants retaliated against the African American competitors more than they did against the white competitors. Discrimination against blacks occurred even though the participants gained nothing for themselves by retaliating. It appears that Johnson's participants disliked preferential treatment, but *really* disliked African Americans receiving it at their expense. So, while many claim that their opposition to affirmative action is about fairness, and not about racism, for some people, racism does play a role in their opposition.

Affirmative action and equal opportunity: What's the difference?

One common belief about affirmative action is that it is unnecessary. If a person is discriminated against in employment based on gender or ethnic background, there are anti-discrimination laws in place protecting people from such treatment. If someone is discriminated against in the US, they can file a complaint with the Equal Employment Opportunity Commission. So is affirmative action necessary? Faye Crosby and her colleagues[8] outline the difference between equal opportunity and affirmative action. Equal opportunity seeks to achieve a system in which all individuals are given the same treatment. Laws are in place to prevent intentional or blatant discrimination based on age, race, gender, religion, disability or nationality (there are no US federal laws protecting lesbians and gay men against discrimination – one can legally discriminate against homosexuals). Equal opportunity assumes that when there is no overt discrimination, equal opportunity exists for all members of all groups. But the research on subtle prejudice finds that even when equality of opportunity appears to exist, people's subtle, covert, and often unconscious behavior undermines the reality of equal opportunity. The various stages at which subtle prejudice affected the selection process are discussed later in this chapter.

Affirmative action is proactive and calls for actions to ensure that equal opportunity actually exists. Crosby describes affirmative action as a *monitoring system*.[9] She argues that even policies that appear to be neutral with regard to ethnicity and gender can operate in ways that advantage some and disadvantage others. A monitoring system like affirmative action is necessary because imbalances can be difficult to detect. Affirmative action examines whether equal opportunity exists, and if it does not, a plan can be implemented for taking concrete measures to eliminate barriers and establish true equality of opportunity. Organizations covered by affirmative action law (those receiving money from the federal government), must determine the availability of qualified workers in target categories. Target categories include women and four ethnic groups – African Americans, Asian Americans, Latina/os, and Native Americans. The organization determines the number of women and people of color in their work place and compares their numbers (incumbency) to that of what would reasonably be expected to be available in the relevant geographic recruiting area. If the number of women and people of color in the organization is significantly less than those available, the company is required to develop a plan using proactive measures to attempt to eliminate the discrepancies between the availability and incumbency. The organization must set goals and demonstrate a good-faith effort to bolster the numbers of those they are lacking. Goals outlined in an affirmative action program are not quotas. The organization is not required to change the demographic makeup of the organization dramatically, or even at all, as long as it shows a good-faith effort at attempting to expand opportunities for members of target groups.

Faye Crosby notes that the legal system assumes that individuals can always detect when they are victims of discrimination and that they will protest the discrimination they have received. However, this assumption does not take into account that bias today is subtle, covert, and may be unconscious and unintentional. Subtle bias is, by definition, difficult to detect and difficult to prove, and the targets of subtle discrimination may not even be aware it is happening.[10] And often, those who have been discriminated against are hesitant to report discrimination. There is a tendency to see complainants as trouble-making whiners who lack a sense of humor. I have seen complainants be treated as tattle-tales who are seen as victimizing the perpetrators of discrimination. Many people who are victims of discrimination see how other victims are treated after they have made an official report of discrimination or sexual harassment and do not want to risk the ostracism that often accompanies the exposure of mistreatment. To summarize, *equal opportunity* is not sufficient to protect against discrimination because it assumes: (1) that any and all discrimination is overt and obvious; (2) that targets will detect discrimination against them; and (3) that targets will always report discrimination.

The role of subtle prejudice in the affirmative action debate

The belief that overt and conspicuous bigotry has decreased is supported by research.[11] As I discussed in the Introduction to this book, white Americans' attitudes toward African Americans in the early part of the twenty-first century are ambivalent, consisting of both positive and negative elements. Pro-black attitudes tend to come from recognition of the obstacles African Americans face in America. Whites' pro-black feelings aren't so much "pro"-black as they are feelings of sympathy or pity. In this analysis, whites' anti-black feelings tend to include blaming blacks themselves for their disadvantages in education, employment, and economics.[12] Inequities in achievement are understood as a consequence of some defect in performance or some deficiency in values and ethics. In this way, white ambivalence toward African Americans is rooted in two competing core values in American society: *individualism*, as embodied in the Protestant work ethic of pulling oneself up by the bootstraps, and *humanitarianism–egalitarianism*, embodied in values emphasizing equality and fairness. Those who subscribe to an egalitarian value system sympathize with groups whose members they view as victims of injustice, including African Americans and others from historically marginalized groups. A strong adherence to egalitarianism enables many whites to regard themselves as unprejudiced and nondiscriminatory and these individuals might support affirmative action programs. In spite of appearances, though, this positive component of the ambivalence toward African Americans is *not* assumed to include genuinely pro-black attitudes or even sentiments of true friendship between whites and African Americans. Some whites feel discomfort, uneasiness, and perhaps even fear of African Americans, while, at the same time, they maintain their egalitarian self-image.[13] How does the ambivalence that underpins benign bigotry relate to affirmative action? First of all, the targets of the prejudice may not realize they are being discriminated against, outside observers may not notice it, and the perpetrators may not be fully aware of their discriminatory behavior. The subtle form of discrimination is immediately relevant to the debate regarding whether passive "equal opportunity" approaches to employment and admissions are adequate or whether active affirmative action programs are necessary. Also, fairness is an important component of people's support or opposition to affirmative action. For many whites, support for the *principle* of affirmative action represents the egalitarian value; the opposition to the *implementation* of affirmative action programs reflects the individualism value.[14] Affirmative action threatens an economic order that is believed to be just in principle and to work well in fact.

Of course racism isn't the only type of prejudice relevant to the affirmative action debate. Prejudice and discrimination against women is often covert and subtle. Sexism, like other forms of bias, can be divided into "old-fashioned" sexist ideas about women and more contemporary and subtle forms of prejudicial treatment. To at least some degree, the values that underlie subtle racism also underlie subtle forms of sexism.[15] Modern or subtle sexists believe that sexism is a thing of the past, and that women as a group are given preferential treatment in hiring decisions. Subtle sexism reflects an underlying resentment toward the subordinated group (women) by the dominant group (men) – although women may also hold these attitudes. As I have discussed extensively in the "Feminists are man-haters" chapter, a major component of these new forms of sexism is the rewarding of women who hold traditional roles (e.g. stay-at-home mothers) and the penalizing of women who are non-traditional (e.g. working women). Thus, prejudice against women is not merely antipathy toward a given group. The content of many people's prejudice comprises negative and positive attributes, and the positive attributes perpetuate subordination because the target is viewed as incompetent or in need of protection. As we saw in the

"Feminists are man-haters" chapter, a patronizing yet positive orientation towards women that serves to reinforce gender inequality is, itself, a form of prejudice.

Where things can go wrong in employment and education

Institutions often claim that they do not discriminate because they use the same standards to hire, retain, and promote all of their employees. In the Introduction to this book, I described a study by John Dovidio and Samuel Gaertner[16] that compared people's tendency to express overt racism and subtle racism at two different times in order to see if people's attitudes change over time and if they become more tolerant. In the rating of white and black job candidates, there were no race-based differences in the recommendations for candidates with either strong or weak qualifications. However, African American candidates with ambiguous qualifications were recommended less often than whites with the same ambiguous qualifications. When a white candidate's qualifications were ambiguous, students rated them as if their qualifications were strong; but a black candidate with the same qualifications was rated as weak. Thus, whites seem to be given the benefit of the doubt by other whites, a benefit not extended to African Americans. The fact that bias often occurs when one's qualifications are ambiguous is an important point. As I stated in the Introduction, most people are not brilliant nor are they stupid, most fall somewhere in the middle. Comedian Chris Rock's routine is relevant here when he says:

> Now when you go to a class there are 30 kids in the class: 5 smart, 5 dumb and the rest they're in the middle. And that's just all America is: a nation in the middle, a nation of B and C students . . . [A] black C student can't even be the manager at Burger King. Meanwhile the white C student just happens to be the President of the United States of America![17]

This is the nature of benign bigotry. Subtle, yet significant, discrimination can occur in any and in many aspects of the workplace and university life.

As we have seen in previous chapters, whites tend to discriminate against people of color when their discrimination can be justified on nonprejudicial grounds. For instance, whites will provide aid to both a black and a white person when the individual is in need of help because of no fault of their own. However, when a person requests help but appears "lazy," whites will more often aid another white person than a black person. When the deservingness of the recipient is more questionable, making the failure to help more justifiable, blacks are disadvantaged relative to whites.[18] Whites gain undeserved advantages and blacks are subjected to undeserved *dis*advantages. Thus, racial prejudice among whites is likely to be expressed in subtle, indirect, and rationalizable ways, whereas more direct and obvious expressions of prejudice are avoided.

In this section, I describe the various stages of the employment and admissions process in which subtle discrimination can occur. But first, there is one caveat to the discussion that follows. I do not discuss *test bias*, an important part of an affirmative action discussion. Biases in standardized tests that are used in university admission and hiring procedures have historically disadvantaged women and people of color by making them appear to be less qualified candidates. For excellent discussions regarding test bias, I recommend books by Barbara Bergmann, Faye Crosby, Daniel Golden, and Tim Wise.[19]

Before we look at the way benign bigotry operates in the application process, let's examine the idea of meritocracy. The belief in *meritocracy*, the notion that those who are hired for jobs and accepted into prestigious universities are hired and accepted as a result of individual effort and talent, and that the most competent person is hired and accepted, is, in practical terms, a myth. The idea of meritocracy assumes a level playing field, a system that is fair, and an even starting place. What you have seen throughout this book, and what will be reinforced and tied directly to the employment and admissions process, is that because of past and present discrimination against women and people of color, as well as past and present unearned privilege awarded to whites and men, the playing field is not level. Deconstructing the myth of meritocracy is crucial to the understanding of how subtle discrimination operates and this plays a vital role in deconstructing the myth that affirmative action is reverse discrimination.

Recruitment: It's who you know

Bias occurs in the earliest stages of college admissions and hiring – in recruitment. Before affirmative action, and even currently, the way potential job candidates often hear about a job opening is through word-of-mouth. So-and-so knows so-and-so and he has a son who is a recent college graduate who is looking for a job. Friends contact friends over lunch, or on the tennis court, and say, "*Hey, we're looking for a new [fill in the blank], know anyone?*" While word-of-mouth recruitment may appear innocent and not necessarily rife with bias, it is exclusionary. Because white men still dominate high level positions, they are most likely to be in contact with other white men who have sons or sons-in-laws or nephews who are white men and thus white men are most likely to hear about a position opening and are more likely to be interviewed. They are thus more likely to be hired than a woman or a person of color. Word-of-mouth recruitment is especially hurtful to people of color because, in the US, while legal segregation is largely in the past, informal segregation is still the norm. Few people have cross-ethnic friendships. Think about your last holiday celebration. Who sat around the table with you? How many of those people were of a different ethnicity than you? If you are like most people, you spend time with people of your own ethnic background.

So word-of-mouth recruitment for jobs puts people of color at a distinct disadvantage.

More formally, in college admissions, *legacy admissions* also put ethnic minorities and poor whites at a clear disadvantage. Three recent books offer a scathing look at the "preferences of privilege"[20] that operate in American colleges and universities: Jerome Karabel's *The Chosen*; Daniel Golden's *The Price of Admission*; and David Schmidt's *Color and Money*. At Ivy League colleges, an intergenerational tradition exists that is known as "legacies" whereby members of families apply to, are accepted for admission, and attend, the schools where their parents are alumni. Children and other relatives of alumni of Ivy League colleges are approximately three times as likely to be admitted as applicants who are not "legacies."[21] Because rich whites have nearly entirely comprised the student populations of such institutions historically, this particular invisible form of the thwarting of equal opportunity is woven into the very fabric of Ivy League tradition.

Then there are *development cases*. At most top colleges in the US, the fundraising office supplies admissions with a list of applicants of wealthy donors, known as "development cases," applicants who are often accepted even if they rank near the bottom of their high school classes or have SAT scores 300–400 points below rejected applicants.[22] Legacy admits and development cases constitute an invisible kind of "affirmative action" for rich white people based on unearned and invisible privilege. These two practices violate the core principle narrative of merit and equality of opportunity that are the cornerstone principles of the myth of meritocracy. These practices, and the lifetime benefits that accrue to beneficiaries and in their effects over generations, in actuality produce substantially greater advantage for rich white people than actual affirmative action does for people of color.[23] In actual practice, it is the students admitted as legacies and development cases who violate the notion of meritocracy and who are admitted for reasons expressly other than merit and individual achievement. Jerome Karabel writes, "findings [from the Office of Civil Rights] about legacy applicants were, if anything, even more embarrassing. For unlike athletic skill, which is arguably a form of merit, being the child of an alumnus was nothing more than an accident of birth. Nevertheless, Harvard gave strong preference to legacies, admitting them between 1981–1988 at a rate of 36 percent – more than double the rate for all applicants."[24] And, according to an Office of Civil Rights investigation, legacies ranked lower than non-legacy admits on every important rating: personal, extracurricular, academic, teacher, and counselor.[25] Both legacies and athletes performed below average at the colleges that Karabel investigated.[26] Even at the height of affirmative action, legacies and athletes were admitted at a rate higher than were African Americans. Legacies and athletes carry clear "plus factors" and are members of "tagged categories." You might think that if athleticism is a plus factor, that should help some applicants of color, such as African Americans. However, Daniel Golden notes that there is a specific social class dimension to those athletes admitted to elite schools – admittance and scholarships tend to go to upper-class sports dominated by whites such as crew, horseback riding, golf, and sailing.

One might think that Asian Americans, often referred to as the "model minority," might have a clear advantage in academic pursuits relative to other people of color. However, Asian Americans have been described as the "new Jews"[27] of college admissions. Despite their higher-than-average academic qualifications, they face hidden quotas designed to keep them out of elite colleges, as Jewish Americans had nearly a hundred years earlier. To summarize the findings in Karabel's, Golden's, and Schmidt's investigations, the number of well-to-do whites given preference to highly selective colleges overwhelms any real or imagined advantage conferred on people of color through affirmative action.

Subtle prejudice during the application process

When I teach about discrimination in my classes, inevitably someone raises a hand with a personal anecdote of discrimination. And after a student tells a story of a personal discrimination experience, often another student will say, "*How do you know it was discrimination? Maybe that interviewer is mean to everyone, not just black people.*" That is a good point. While the stories that students share with the class are vivid and often make intuitive sense, anecdotes are easily dismissible as only one person's experience and one that might be subject to the faulty recall of imperfect memory or paranoia. Decades ago, discrimination was more blatant and less subject to interpretation. A woman would inquire about a position and the employer would say, "*We don't hire ladies. This is man's work.*" Today, discrimination manifests in subtle ways, sometimes without the discriminator realizing she is discriminating and sometimes not noticeable by the target of that discrimination. Fortunately, we have social psychology experiments to put personal anecdotes to the test. We can systematically study discrimination in carefully controlled environments.

In this section I present some research on bias that occurs at the level of application screening. One experiment that received a lot of media attention is a study by Marianne Bertrand and Sendhil Mullainathan.[28] They responded with fictitious resumes to 1,300 help-wanted ads printed in Chicago and Boston newspapers. They sent out 5,000 resumes that varied by race of applicant (either African American or white), applicant name (based on census data regarding most often used names for each group), and quality of the resume (some were low caliber and some high). Overall, regardless of the quality of the resume, resumes with white names received 50 percent more callbacks for interviews than resumes with black names. In other words, a white applicant should expect a call back for every 10 applications while an African American would need to submit 15 applications to receive the same number of call backs.

Also, the quality of the resume affected the callback rate for white applicants, but not for black applicants. In other words, blacks did not benefit from having high caliber qualifications. This finding suggests that there is a *ceiling effect* for African American applicants – meaning there are limits to how talented an African American applicant is perceived to be.

In another experiment,[29] white American university students were asked to judge college admissions applicants based on transcripts and SAT scores. Applicants were described as either white or black and were either strongly, moderately, or weakly qualified. When the student evaluators reviewed weak applications, there were no differences in their evaluations of white or black candidates. When applicants had moderate qualifications, whites were evaluated slightly, but not significantly, better than were African Americans. However, when the candidate was highly qualified African Americans were evaluated less positively than were whites. Furthermore, when the materials used for judging were analyzed according to how directly they related to the information presented in the applicant's transcript, the less directly related the item was to the transcript information, the greater was the racist bias. In other words, the more vague, subjective, and irrelevant judgment criteria are, the more bias there is in judges' ratings. This study corroborates work that finds that whites tend to evaluate African Americans less favorably than whites on subjective dimensions of work performance.[30] Results from this study suggest that keeping performance criteria clear and specific and making sure it pertains to actual performance may decrease discrimination.

Applicant gender plays a role in hiring as well. In one experiment,[31] fictitious resumes of ten psychologists with PhDs were sent to heads of psychology departments across the US. The department heads were asked to rank the psychologists according to the professorial rank at which they should be hired. The summaries contained information about productivity, teaching, administrative work, and sociability. The names were rotated in such a way that the same resume sometimes carried a man's name and sometimes a woman's, although there was no way for the department heads to know that the experiment was testing for gender bias. As predicted, whether a woman's or a man's name was at the top of the resume mattered. The resumes with men's names were assigned the advanced rank of Associate Professor. When the same resumes carried women's names, however, they were assigned the entry-level rank of Assistant Professor. In other words, identical qualifications bought a man a higher rank than a woman. This occurred even though the women and men were rated as equally desirable appointments. So gender discrimination did not occur in terms of *hiring* – both women and men were equally desirable appointments. The discrimination was more subtle in that it appeared that resume reviewers believed that women were not ready to be advanced-level professors, while men with the exact same qualifications were. It is as though they thought, "*Some day, she'll be a great professor.*" For men, they might have thought, "*He's ready to hit the ground running.*" This kind of benign bigotry is subtle yet significant. Assistant professors do not have tenure, so the women in this study would not have the protections and privileges of tenure, while associate professor positions do have tenure, with all the protection and privilege that entails. There are also pay differences. Not only do professors who are men make more than women with the *same rank*, but also, there is a significant pay difference between someone who is hired as an assistant professor and someone who is hired at the higher rank of associate professor.[32] These two studies show that before a woman or person of color even gets in the door, even on paper alone, bias exists. Employers' beliefs, or *schemas*, of minorities set up expectations even before meeting an applicant.

Subtle sexism is evidenced in the content of letters of recommendation for job candidates. Frances Trix and Carolyn Psenka[33] examined letters of recommendation of successful applicants for medical faculty positions in the US over a three-year period. They found significant differences between recommendations written for women and men who are medical doctors. First, letters of recommendation written for men were longer than were letters for women. Longer letters suggest, in subtle ways, that there is more to say about men than women, that men have accomplished more, and perhaps, even that the letter writer is more invested and more impressed with the applicant because the author has taken the time to write a thorough letter. Second, letter-writers employ gendered terms, such as *gratuitous modifiers* used to describe women candidates. For instance, "lady physician" was used for women. It is hard to imagine the parallel description of men (e.g. "gentleman physician"). The use of gendered modifiers suggests that male physicians are the norm, while woman physicians are the marked exception – the term "physician" gets modified by "lady." In addition, letters written for women were more likely to use gendered descriptive adjectives such as "compassionate" while letters for men used terms such as "accomplishment" or "achievement." Trix and Psenka used the term *letters of minimal assurance* to describe one pattern of difference in which women were described as pleasant and easy to get along with, rather than as competent and accomplished. *Doubt raisers* were more often part of letters for women than for men, including such items as hedges, irrelevant content, and faint praise (e.g. "She is quite close to my wife"; "It appears that her health and personal life are stable"). Finally, more *grindstone adjectives* (working hard, dependable, thorough) were used in letters on behalf of men ("She worked hard on the projects that she accepted"), suggesting that when women succeed it is because they work hard, not because they are able or talented in a fundamental way. The differences in letters of recommendation written for women and men were not overtly negative – the letter writers probably did not even realize they wrote differently for women and men. Nonetheless these differences are important because they demonstrate how the accumulation of relatively small subtle differences can add up to a different picture of women and men doctors: There is more to say about men's accomplishments based on the assumption that men belong in the position of doctor, while women doctors are still a novelty ("lady doctor"), their position is tentative and tenuous. Women are represented as pleasant and hard working but men get the job done because of their inherent capability.

Bias during interviews

If people from a stigmatized group manage to get past initial screening, their interview experience can be a challenge. Carl Word and his colleagues[34] trained white American university students to interview applicants for a job. These trained interviewers interviewed either an African American or white applicant for a job. Even though the interviewers were trained on how to conduct an appropriate interview, subtle but significant differences were found in the ways they conducted themselves with African Americans and whites. When the applicant was black, the interviewer unwittingly sat farther away, made more speech errors – that is spoke less proper English – and terminated the interview 25% sooner than when the applicant was white. Does this differential treatment have an effect on the performance of the applicant? In a second experiment, Word and his colleagues trained their interviewers to treat white students in the same manner that the interviewers had treated either the white or black applicants in the previous experiment. The experimenters videotaped the students being interviewed. Independent judges unfamiliar with the hypotheses of the study rated those who had been treated like the black applicants as being more nervous and less effective than those treated like the white applicants. The results of this study lead us to conclude that when people of color are interviewed by a white person, their performance may suffer, not because there is anything wrong with them but because the interviewer is likely to behave (unwittingly) in a way that makes the interviewees uncomfortable.

Interviewer behavior can negatively affect women interviewees as well. Julie Woodzicka and Marianne LaFrance[35] had women who were being interviewed for a job receive sexually harassing questions (vs. questions that were not sexual in nature). Those women who received the harassment during the interview exhibited more diluted language, more repeated words, and had more false starts in their speech to the male interviewer. The effects of discrimination can be cumulative, but the studies by Word and colleagues, and by Woodzicka and LaFrance, indicate that the effects of bias can be more immediate. Another study found subtle differences in the way interviewers behaved with job applicants presumed to be lesbian/ gay or heterosexual.[36] In terms of measures of overt discrimination, there were no significant differences in employers stating that jobs were available, no differences in frequency of being given permission to complete an application, and no differences in receiving a call back after the completion of an application.[37] However, in the examination of more subtle forms of discrimination, there were differences between how gay or straight applicants were treated. Consistent with the principles of subtle prejudice, employers were more verbally negative, spent less time, and used fewer words, when interacting with the lesbian and gay applicants. The authors conclude that employers were able to control their more overt discriminatory behaviors, but some of their negative feelings may have been expressed through subtle channels.

These three studies have important implications for the success of minorities in the early part of the employment process. First, African Americans as well as those presumed to be gay or lesbian were not overtly discriminated against, but were discriminated against in subtle ways. Second, mistreatment, even in subtle forms, has a negative impact on the recipient of such mistreatment including initiating the self-fulfilling prophecy of performing ineffectively or nervously during the interview. While these forms of discrimination are subtle and apparently benign, they affect the success of those who are subjected to them.

Finally, even if discrimination does not occur during the interview, stereotyping can occur during *recall* of the interview. People's stereotypes about certain groups can negatively affect their memories of how well an interview went. Ricardo Frazer and Uco Wiersma[38] had white US undergraduates conduct employment interviews with either a white or black applicant who was actually a trained interviewee working for the experimenter. Based on information provided to them prior to interviews, the interviewers believed that their applicants were either highly qualified for the position or not well qualified. Participants read each applicant's file and then used an interview guide provided by the researchers to interview an applicant. Frazer and Wiersma found that interviewers were equally likely to want to hire the black and white candidate immediately after the interview. However, when participants/interviewers returned a week later and were given the interview questions and asked to recall the performance of the applicants during questioning, disturbing differences emerged depending on whether or not the applicant had been white or black. African American applicants were *remembered* as having given less intelligent answers, when in fact, their actual responses to the items were identical to those of the white applicants. The time delay built into the study enabled the participants' racism to be revealed. Participants/interviewers correctly recalled performance differences between the low and high quality applicants – indicating that their memories were not generally inaccurate. These findings suggest that to some extent, people may be able to control their *behavior* and to choose not to discriminate. However, when recall is involved and the schema *black person* is called up African Americans are thought of as being less capable than the whites. These findings might speak to why members of minority groups might be hired at the same rate as whites, but may not be promoted as often as whites due to people's inaccurate memories of ethnic minority acheivement.

Internalized bias: wage entitlement

A study conducted with college educated full-time workers by the American Association of University Women[39] in 2007, found that men have higher salaries than do women – even after important variables such as college major, type of profession, experience, and training have been controlled for. This difference is seen one year after graduation from college, with women earning only 80% as much as men and only 69% of what men make ten years after college. Similar patterns are found in the UK.[40] By now, reading this book, it should be clear that benign bigotry likely accounts for some of the differences in pay between women and men. Contributing to the existence and internalization of benign bigotry is the phenomenon of *entitlement*. This internalization can manifest in the expectations of men and women in regard to gender differences. But an important area of research, the work on entitlement, begins to explain how bigotry can come to be internalized to manifest in gender differences in what women and men feel they have coming to them. Entitlement is a sense, belief, or assumption about what one deserves. It is the conviction that you have something coming to you. Women and men have a different sense of entitlement when it comes to what they think their work is worth. Brenda Major and her colleagues[41] conducted one of the classic experiments on women's and men's assumptions of monetary entitlement. US college students individually completed tasks and were given a few dollars to distribute amongst themselves based on how much they thought they deserved for completing the task. They were instructed to leave any remaining money. Each participant had access to a list of the amounts of money that participants who came before them gave themselves. In one condition of the study, the women participants saw a list showing that other women paid themselves *more* money than they left behind. In a second condition, women saw a list indicating that other women paid themselves *less* money than they left behind. Similar conditions were set up for men. The third condition did not reveal any information about what previous participants had paid themselves and therefore the participants in this condition had to decide for themselves (without external information) how much money they deserved. Participants only experienced one of the three conditions. Would you expect gender differences in how participants paid themselves in these three conditions? When both women and men participants saw what others paid themselves (i.e. when external standards were available), there were no gender differences in how much participants paid themselves. In other words, women and men alike used the information they saw about how much previous participants had paid themselves as a reference point for how much they should take for themselves. However, when participants had no information about what others had paid themselves for the same task, there were gender differences. Women paid themselves significantly less than men paid themselves. Men actually paid themselves more in the absence-of-information condition than when social comparison information was available, whereas women's self-pay did not differ significantly between the condition that provided information about what others gave themselves and the condition that did not provide such information. What these findings suggest about women's and men's entitlement is that men and women decide what to expect based on what others are getting. When there is social comparison information, men will match what they pay themselves with what others have paid themselves (as will women), but without social comparison information, men behave with less restraint, apparently feeling they have more coming to them than do women. Men's sense of entitlement, then, is not unbridled; they are guided by what others feel entitled to as much as women are. But without such comparison information, men feel they deserve more than do women.

Imagine you have been offered a job. If you know what others employed in the same position are being paid, you probably feel comfortable expecting a similar salary. But what if you do not know the going rate for your position? What if your soon-to-be employer asks you if you have a "salary requirement," (commonly used jargon)? What salary do you expect? Major and colleagues' study suggests that men will expect a higher salary than will women. Think about how differences in starting pay will impact the amount of money available for a raise, if raises are based on percentages of one's present salary. Therefore, one's starting salary can determine thousands of dollars in salary differences between women and men over several years of work.[42]

In a second experiment, Brenda Major and her colleagues[43] paid students a fixed amount of money to perform a task in which the students could work for as long as they thought was fair. The task entailed counting the number of dots on a page, and the counting was done either in private or in front of the experimenter. When women and men cannot choose how much they deserve because the salary is fixed, does their sense of entitlement affect how long they will work? Major and her colleagues found that women will go to great lengths to not give themselves what they have coming. Their study found that women: (1) worked longer than men did (they worked especially longer in the public condition, whereas the time men worked was unaffected by the public–private condition); (2) they completed more dot sets than men; and (3) did so more accurately; and (4) worked more efficiently than men. After the main part of the study, participants were asked to provide evaluations of their own performances. Despite the fact that women worked longer than men, completed more work, and worked more accurately, women and men did not differ in their self-rated performance evaluations. Taken together, these two experiments from Major and her colleagues suggest important differences between women's and men's sense of entitlement.

Many have interpreted Major's findings as evidence that women's lower sense of entitlement, compared to men's, signifies that women do not feel entitled enough – that women have "depressed" entitlement while men have a normal, healthy sense of entitlement. It is true that in these kinds of studies, women tend to pay themselves less than men for the same or better quality work, and believe the allocation to be fair.[44] However, a recent experiment finds that the issue does not seem to be that women's entitlement is *deflated*, but rather that men's is *inflated*. Brett Pelham and John Hetts[45] asked American college students to solve easy, moderate, or difficult anagrams of scrambled words. Participants were asked to evaluate their own performance and then paid themselves for their work. You might guess that those who felt they performed poorly would pay themselves less than those who believed they performed well. That was the case for women, but not for men. Specifically, women only underpaid themselves for their work when they worked on a difficult task and felt that they had performed poorly. Men paid themselves well even when they believed they had performed poorly. In other words, women based their own pay on their perceived performance, but men's pay was not connected to their perceived performance – men thought they should get paid well, even when they did not do a good job. Pelham and Hetts speculate that the men in their study based their level of self-pay on their self-esteem rather than on their performance, whereas women do not consider self-esteem as a legitimate source of entitlement. That is, men seem to feel that their personal feelings of worth entitle them to a certain level of payment, regardless of the quality of their performance. The women in these studies based their level of self-pay on their evaluations of their *work* rather than their evaluations of their *worth*.

Perceptions of competence

The research on entitlement examines what we think we have coming to us which, no doubt, is at least partly a result of how women and men are socialized to value their own work differently.[46] How do others perceive women's and men's performance? And do people use the same criteria to judge the competence of people of color and of whites? One study found that standards of competence shift depending on race and gender. Monica Biernat and Diane Kobrynowicz[47] asked American undergraduates to evaluate job applicants in terms of: (1) the minimum criteria that would be used to determine that a candidate was qualified and would therefore pass an initial screening for a position; and (2) the standards they would use to document an applicant's actual ability to do the job (e.g. percentage of work responsibilities for which the applicant would be competent). They found that the minimum standards for passing an applicant on to a second interview were lower for African Americans than for whites and for women than for men. However, when making ability inferences, judges set higher requirements for African Americans than whites and for women than men. Biernat and Kobrynowicz interpret their data to mean that low-status individuals are held to lower minimum standards because they are compared to members of their own group for which there is a lower standard (e.g. "He's fine, compared with other blacks" or "She's pretty competent, for a woman"). When considering higher ability standards, however, African Americans and women have to work even harder to enable documentation of their abilities. In this study, women and African Americans had to show more examples of skills than did men and whites, to prove their worth. This study lends supports to an oft-cited complaint by women and people of color who express their feelings that they have to jump through more hoops than white men to prove that they are competent. For low status groups, minimum standards are lower but ability standards are higher, while for high status groups, these two sets of standards do not differ. Biernat and Kobrynowicz's results are analogous to being short-listed versus being hired. More women and people of color might be put on a short list from which the person hired will be drawn, but white men may be more likely to be hired. The illusion of fairness can be maintained because an organization can show that many minorities are seriously considered. White men, however, still tend to be the ones who are actually hired. The work on minimum standards represents one of many double standards that make up the benign bigotry faced by subordinate groups in the workplace.

Demonstrating competence is especially difficult for women trying to achieve in male-stereotyped jobs. Recall the study conducted by Madeline Heilman and her colleagues[48] described in Chapter 3, "Feminists are man-haters." American college students were asked to evaluate either clearly successful or ambiguously successful candidates for a position as assistant vice president in an aircraft company. When students rated the obviously successful candidate, women and men were rated equally – they were both given credit for their successes. However, when information about the candidate's performance was ambiguous, the woman target was rated as less competent than the man. When the candidate was rated for likeability, the successful woman was liked significantly less than the successful man. The woman was rated as less hostile than the man in the ambiguous performance outcome condition but was rated as *more* hostile than the man in the clearly successful condition. Women, although rated as less competent and less achievement-oriented than men when information about them was ambiguous, were also rated as less hostile interpersonally. When evaluating successful candidates, however, the difference is dramatic – women who are acknowledged as successful are viewed not merely as indifferent to others but as hostile. And these patterns hold for both women and men raters, so these gender stereotypic norms, and the tendency to penalize those who violate them, are enforced for both women and men. Heilman conducted a third study and found that dislike of an employee was associated with not being recommended for promotions or for salary increases. Heilman concludes that while there are many things that lead an individual to be disliked in the job setting, it is only women for whom a unique propensity toward dislike is caused by success in a non-traditional work setting. People, both women and men, seem to be more comfortable with a less-qualified, woman and threatened by a successful woman.

Attributions of success and failure

Another way benign bigotry can manifest is in the attributions people make about behavior. As we saw in Chapters 1 and 2, attributions are explanations for the causes of behavior. Most relevant to the topic of affirmative action are the attributions people make about academic and workplace success and failure. The attributions made about women and people of color affect perceptions of their belongingness in an organization or university. The four most common attributions about success and failure are: *ability*, *effort*, *luck*, and the *nature of the task* (whether it is easy or difficult).[49] Let's look at attributions of success – explanations for why an individual succeeds. At first glance, one might think, *as long as I am successful, who cares about how people* explain *it?* But attributions are important because they tap into the dimension of intrinsic intelligence. For instance, if a student earns an A on one of her exams, if we attribute the high grade to her *ability*, we can expect her to do well on future exams. Attributions of ability are stable and static – if you are able today, we can expect that you will be able tomorrow. What if the student earned an A because the test was extremely easy, or because she just got lucky and all the information on the exam happened to be the information she studied carefully?

We cannot make predictions about her future successes because we cannot assume that she has the ability to achieve future success. There is a temporariness of attributions based on the nature of the task or on luck – in these cases we assume that the person is not internally successful, but instead, she might just get lucky sometimes. Earlier I discussed a study[50] on letters of recommendation for medical faculty. The attributions of success were different depending on whether the letter writer was describing a woman or a man. Letter writers were more likely to attribute men's success to their ability, using such terms as "accomplishment" and "achievement." On the other hand, women's success was more likely to be attributed to hard work, rather than native intelligence.

Social psychology experiments find similar patterns. A sample of high school students, college students, working people, and retired people from southern Spain evaluated candidates for a leadership position in an industry that was either congruent (traditional) or incongruent (non-traditional) with gender roles. Participants generally made internal attributions, such as ability, about men's successes, whether the job was congruent or incongruent with their gender. However, when women were being considered for a position that was incongruent with beliefs about tasks at which women are considered good, people were more likely to attribute success to something external such as luck.[51]

Like luck, or like an easy task, success due to hard work has an unstable quality to it. Even though hard work is valued and seems less capricious than luck or the ease of a task, success does not reside in the person who succeeds because she has worked hard. People are more comfortable with those who succeed due to their ability, not due to their hard work. If you had to choose a doctor to perform open-heart surgery on a close relative, would you rather have a doctor who is a great surgeon due to working hard (because the talent doesn't come naturally) or a doctor who is a great surgeon because of inherent gifts as a surgeon? Most people would probably prefer the stability of inherent gifts to the somewhat transitory nature of hard work.

What attribution patterns are associated with ethnicity and gender? Jeffrey Greenhaus and Saroj Parasuraman[52] examined attributions made about managers by their supervisors in three types of US companies: communications, banking, and electronics. This large field study comprised 1,628 managers, half of whom were African American and half of whom were white, and their supervisors. When the role of employee gender and race in supervisors' attributions about their employee's success was examined, specific patterns emerged. First, attributions of ability were more often made about men than women, but only in regard to the most highly successful managers. There were no gender differences in attributions of moderately successful managers. Why were there differences only among the most successful managers? Other research[53] has found that different attributions about women and men are likely to be evoked when woman's success violates gender-based expectations. Perhaps moderately successful women are not sufficiently successful to really violate their supervisors' expectations. People expect women to be moderately successful in the workplace, but not highly successful. The same study found that attributions of ability were also more likely for white than African American managers, particularly if the employee had limited experience (one year or less). There were no gender differences in attributions of effort and in whether the employee got help from others, but there were racial differences in these attributions. Attributions of effort were more likely for white managers than black managers. Attributions of effort can be a double-edged sword – on the one hand, the person is admired for working hard, but on the other, the person may be viewed as needing to work hard to compensate for a lack of ability. However, regarding white managers, supervisors attributed their work to both ability and effort, a combination that, when taken together, serve as a complement. Whites work hard *and* are smart. In sharp contrast, attributions of help from others were stronger for black managers than for white managers, particularly for managers with extensive experience. These attributions suggest that African American managers with a lot of experience are believed to have succeeded because they were helped by others, not because of their own efforts or abilities. Attributions about black men specifically were particularly damning. Their success was more often attributed to luck (than it was for white men and black women) and easiness of the job (than it was for black women and white women). These attributional patterns imply that white men solidly belong in the workplace and are legitimately managers, while the legitimacy of African American women, white women, and, especially, African American men is more tenuous.

Of course it's possible that in Greenhaus and Parasuraman's study, the success of white men as managers really was due to their ability and hard work, and for others, success was due to luck, help from others, and the easiness of the task. But given the large number of participants in the study, the number of work domains covered (communications, banking, and electronics), and the findings of experimental evidence revealing similar patterns for gender, it seems likely that the attributions made about the managers in the study were based less on actual behavior and more on stereotypes.

Successful minorities: How are they perceived?

Women and people of color are often not accorded the praise or recognition for their successes that is routinely accorded whites and men. How is the responsibility of success distributed in successful work groups? Madeline Heilman and Michelle Haynes[54] asked American undergraduates to evaluate women who work in successful woman–man work teams whose job is to create an investment portfolio. Creating an investment portfolio is a male-stereotyped task so Heilman and Haynes were interested in people's assumptions about who would be responsible if a woman and man together produced a joint product of very high quality. They found that when the successful performance information was about joint work on a male task, women team members were regarded more negatively – as being less competent and as having been less influential and having taken less of a leadership role – than their men counterparts, even though there was no actual information suggesting such a difference in contributions. When feedback was based on individual performance, women were not evaluated lower than men. So, unless there was clarity about individual contributions to the successful group outcome, women were seen as contributing less. Short of ensuring that the woman played a key role in the success of the team, the default assumption seemed to be that she did not. By the way, there were no differences in women and men raters' assessment – women raters were just as likely as men to make sexist attributions. What if there is information about past performance such that there is no way of assuming negative performance on the part of women? If there is explicit information confirming a woman's past on-the-job performance excellence, her contribution is recognized. So stereotypes can be averted when negative stereotype-based performance-expectations about women are undercut by a clear indication of past performance excellence.

These results suggest that without a compelling reason for the rater to believe otherwise, negative expectations of women who perform male-stereotyped tasks persist even in the face of clearly successful joint outcomes, resulting in the devaluation of women's competence and their contribution to the work product. Heilman and Haynes conclude that for women, working together with men in traditionally male domains can be detrimental – even when the work outcome is highly favorable. Unless (1) there was specific information about the woman's individual performance excellence; (2) the woman's contribution to the successful joint outcome was irrefutable; or (3) there was definitive information about the excellence of the woman team member's past performance effectiveness, women were thought to be generally less competent, less influential in arriving at the successful outcome, and less apt to have taken on a leadership role in the task than were men. Of course, it would be highly beneficial for a man to work in a successful mixed-gender work group because the credit would go to him. And from what we learned of the research on gender and entitlement discussed earlier in this chapter, the woman might work longer hours and possibly do more accurate work, yet expect less credit than the man.

Finally, what happens when those from the dominant group are confronted with a minority group member who may be *more* competent than them? In one study, when white men students were introduced to either high or low ability African American or white supervisors, the students judged the competence of able whites as higher than their own, but able African Americans were judged as less intelligent than themselves.[55] Of course, the level of competence of the white or African American comparison person was the same. Thus, when the competence of African American supervisors surpasses that of whites, whites appear to perceive the situation as though African Americans of lower competence are being given preferential treatment. This same pattern has been found when men are confronted with highly competent women.[56] People's schemas make them see false preference of minorities rather than the actual competence of minorities.

What are the implications of these studies for affirmative action? The research I have described suggests that when things *are* equal, they often are not *perceived* as equal. From the very first stages of the application process, women and people of color are disadvantaged. The playing field is not level at any stage of the application process, in salary expectations, in perceptions of experience and competence, and in explanations of success and failure. When women and people of color perform at the same rate as or better[57] than white men, they are *perceived* to be less competent. The fact that whites and men tend to misperceive the competence of people of color and women helps to justify their resistance to affirmative action.[58] Insufficient competence, not race or gender, becomes the apparent rationale justifying resistance. Similarly, deficiencies in qualifications, not bigotry, become the dominant articulated theme for protesting affirmative action policies. Many people may support the principle of affirmative action in the abstract but may oppose the actual implementation of affirmative action on the basis of an apparently non-race-related rationale.[59]

Benign bigotry and reactive anti-discrimination laws

In the beginning of this chapter, I differentiated the *proactive* monitoring system of affirmative action from the *reactive* equal opportunity practice. The studies I have reviewed should make clear that passive assurances of equal treatment, such as anti-discrimination laws, are not enough. Benign bigotry occurs at so many places that even when people think they are behaving fairly, they may not be.

Many activists and scholars see the need for affirmative action through a backward-looking framework of corrective justice, similar to, say, slavery reparations. That is, many people believe that affirmative action programs are designed to redress past discrimination. This inspires some from the dominant group to say, "*Why should I be punished for things my ancestors did?*" Since legalized slavery has been gone for 150 years, Jim Crow segregation in the US has been illegal for fifty years, and women have been able to vote for nearly 100 years, isn't the playing field level? In an article on the myth of "reverse racism" Stanley Fish[60] describes the absurdity of mistreating groups of people throughout history, then deciding to allow them equal opportunity.

But blacks have not simply been treated unfairly; they have been subjected first to decades of slavery, and then to decades of second-class citizenship, widespread legalized discrimination, economic deprivation, and cultural stigmatization. They have been bought, sold, killed, beaten, raped, excluded, exploited, shamed, and scorned for a very long time. The word "unfair" is hardly an adequate description of their experience, and the belated gift of "fairness" in the form of a resolution no longer to discriminate against them legally is hardly an adequate remedy for the deep disadvantages that the prior discrimination has produced. When the deck is stacked against you in more ways than you can even count, it is small consolation to hear that you are now free to enter the game and take your chances.[61]

I agree with Fish that legacies of past discrimination necessitate redress in the present. However, it is also my contention that discrimination in the *present* is sufficient reason to support affirmative action. A backward-looking framework helps people understand how racism and sexism are systems of inequality – they have been codified in our laws and are an integral part of our institutions. The studies I have reviewed in this chapter, however, suggest that there is prejudice *today* that can be ameliorated by affirmative action. A *presentist* framing[62] of the argument in favor of affirmative action that exposes and responds to pervasive subtle bias provides an independent and compelling case for affirmative action, regardless of what happened in the past.

As I said in the Introduction to this book, biases are produced by the current, ordinary workings of human brains – the schemas they create, and the behaviors they produce. While this is true, the targets of bias, the content of stereotypes of targets, and the effect of prejudice directed at targets, are the result of tens or even hundreds of years of systematic marginalization of some groups and the unjustified privileging of others. The experiments I have reviewed here allow us to see discrimination in the present. That bias is often automatic, inconspicuous, and unconscious, presents a challenge for the use of old-fashioned approaches designed to combat discrimination. Anti-discrimination legislation requires a showing of explicit discrimination. A model that supposes that discrimination takes place explicitly espouses views that have become woefully out of date.[63]

Systematic prejudice and the diversity-as-compelling-interest argument

In addition to the argument for affirmative action as a remedy for past discrimination, many scholars and activists argue in favor of affirmative action on the basis of the benefits of increased diversity. The argument is that diverse classrooms and work settings are beneficial to all; that we can all learn from people who are different from us. Affirmative action would allow more diversity in the workplace and at colleges and universities. After all, with the Internet and other technology, global commerce, and global imperialism, individuals need to learn how to understand and interact with people from diverse ethnic backgrounds, nationalities, religions, sexual orientations, and social classes. Affirmative action would allow entry into institutions previously closed to a variety of people, thus making those institutions more diverse, benefiting the dominant group.

The diversity argument is compelling, but, as Tim Wise[64] details, it is a dangerous argument to make for affirmative action. Arguing in favor of affirmative action to increase diversity contains several problematic assumptions. For instance, the diversity argument suggests that an institution's lack of diversity "just happened," as if by coincidence, rather than because of systematic institutional discrimination and individual bias. The diversity argument also implies that discrimination is a thing of the past and that diversity is the only reason affirmative action is necessary. Also, making the diversity argument a primary defense of affirmative action implies that women and people of color *are* less qualified, but that colleges and workplaces are nonetheless better off with them. And finally, the diversity argument supports the white male status quo. It exoticizes those who are different from the norm. In effect, it allows the dominant majority to say, *"Let's let a few of them play in our game."* White, middle-class men will still remain the norm which, with diversity arguments, lets minorities in for "local color."[65] While adding diversity to the workplace or the university certainly has benefits, the advantages of diverse settings should not cloud the real reason affirmative action is necessary: discrimination.

Deconstructing "reverse racism": Looking at privilege

Finally, an examination of the affirmative action debate cannot be complete without an examination of the role of privilege. In Chapter 3 I talked about *center-stealing*, male privilege, and the perceived threat of losing the center of societal attention.[66] When members of a privileged group imagine a threat, and when attention, even if temporary, turns away from them and towards members of a marginalized group, the dominant group members attempt to take back the spotlight to which they feel entitled. On an institutional level, there have been many cynical attempts and successes by affirmative action foes to undo the relatively brief (in historical terms) and modest gestures that make up affirmative action. California's Proposition 209, a ballot initiative passed by the voters in 1996, legally banned affirmative action. The proposition, cynically called the "California Civil Rights Initiative," dismantled whole categories of anti-bias initiative in California.

As scholars and activists such as Christina Accomando[67] point out, attacks on affirmative action "are cloaked in the language of neutrality and *anti*-discrimination."[68] Accomando continues, "opponents of affirmative action do not say they oppose equality; instead they deploy the language of equality that masks the social inequalities that necessitate affirmative action policies."[69] Former California governor and one-time presidential candidate

Pete Wilson, who helped lead the charge against affirmative action in the state, describes affirmative action as "preferential treatment" and those who benefit from it as members of "protected" and "preferred groups" who are only "so-called underrepresented" minorities.[70] Wilson's strategy, then, is to redefine affirmative action as a violation of (white men's) civil rights and the elimination of affirmative action as supporting equality and fairness. Like many who are opposed to affirmative action, to make his topsy-turvy point Wilson evokes the words of Abraham Lincoln, Thomas Jefferson, and, of course, Martin Luther King, Jr. (who supported affirmative action). Specifically, Wilson refers to King's "I Have a dream" speech, in which King dreams of an America where his children will be judged by the content of their character and not by the color of their skin. Cynical supporters of the status quo appropriate civil rights rhetoric, recode affirmative action as discrimination, misrepresent the status quo as bias-free, and paint proactive measures such as affirmative action as a violation of civil rights and equality.[71] Affirmative action can only be seen as reverse discrimination if the status quo is truly bias-free and women and people of color have chances of gaining admission into the university and the work place equal to those of white men.

Another strategy used by opponents of affirmative action is the rhetoric of false parallelism. In Chapter 3, I described the process whereby sexism can be downplayed by recoding sexism into a "battle-of-the-sexes" competition. Re-framing sexism into a battle between women and men undermines the fact that men are the privileged beneficiaries of sexism and women are the victims of it. Battle-of-the-sexes rhetoric reduces patriarchy and sexism to a *parallel* misunderstanding between women and men, not the systematic oppression of women. Here, in the affirmative action debate, a similar process creates a false parallelism through the notion that, historically, whites had it better than blacks, which was called *racism*, but now, with affirmative action, blacks have it better than whites, which is supposedly *reverse* racism. "Reverse racism" can only exist if what happens to whites under affirmative action is comparable to what happened to people of color historically and presently in the US. Obviously, the hundreds of years of white oppression against people of color, which included exclusion from academic institutions, involuntary servitude, denial of citizenship rights, forced sterilization, internment, forced removal from land, and genocide, are not comparable to any affirmative action program.

In terms of individual feelings about affirmative action, many whites and men come to perceive the prospect of actual equality as a disadvantage because they are so accustomed to having privilege that their privileged position feels normal. Because advantaged group members fail to acknowledge the privileges they receive based on their group membership, those who are experiencing a loss of or *perceived* loss of privilege may view their changing fortunes as discrimination. Men and whites, then, might employ discrimination explanations strategically as a means of improving how they feel about the negative outcomes they do experience, or expect that they might experience in the future. Attributing perceived or infrequently encountered negative events to discrimination may reflect attempts to protect self-esteem and to eliminate self-blame. This may be more likely for men than for women because of men's greater sense of entitlement and their lower likelihood of encountering consistent and severe group-based discrimination. These beliefs could be an anticipatory excuse for not doing well or may be a self-protective way of explaining poor performance when placed in competitive situations with women.[72]

There are reasons to suspect that some employers may be misusing affirmative action in a way that perpetuates the fear that some whites and men have about the extent to which affirmative action affects them. I have a colleague who is a professor and scholar of Latin American studies. She is a white woman. When she searched the job market for academic positions in ethnic studies and Latin American studies departments, she was a very attractive candidate because of her strong record of teaching, and research in her area of specialization, Latin American studies. She had many interviews across the country. During one such interview, she met with the chair of the department. The chair told her that she was an exceptional candidate, but that the department needed to hire a Latina/o for the position. She soon found out that, indeed, she did not get the job. While my colleague was disappointed she understood the desire to have a Latina/o scholar hold the position. She eventually landed a position elsewhere. About a year after she interviewed for the Latin American studies position, she attended an academic conference in her area of specialization and had the opportunity to meet the person who was hired for that position. Who was hired for the position in Latin American studies? A white man. Although there is no way of knowing why my colleague didn't get the position and why a white man, instead of a Latina/o, did, I wonder whether the chair told my colleague that she was highly qualified but they needed to hire a Latina/o simply to ease the rejection of not getting the job. Affirmative action can be used as an excuse for the numerous qualified applicants that do not get hired.

Putting it all together

Reactive equal opportunity laws may be adequate in conditions in which discrimination is overt and unabashed. However, because most discrimination is underground and subtle, we need the proactive measures of affirmative action programs. In this chapter, we saw that discrimination occurs at every level of the hiring process. It also occurs in college admissions.[73] In addition to the history of elite colleges and universities barring women and people of color from even applying, present practices such as legacy admissions, "development cases," and athletic scholarships for upper-class sports, serve to support the privileged.

In terms of employment, at every level of the application process including the content of letters of recommendation, interviews, the interpretation of applications, perceptions of competence, and explanations of success and failure, subtle bias exists, preventing a true measure of merit or quality from occurring. As I have outlined here, from the very first stages of the application process, women and people of color are disadvantaged.

Affirmative action is needed because of present discrimination. While more diversity in communities and organizations is beneficial, particularly to the dominant group who likely have less experience interacting with people different from themselves than do people of color, we should be cautious about a diversity-only argument in favor of affirmative action. As Tim Wise[74] points out, a diversity-only argument for affirmative action implies that discrimination is a thing of the past and that people of color and women are less qualified, but that an organization is benefited by including them to add "local color."

Strategies for change

Because affirmative action is a set of actual plans to reduce discrimination, there are many strategies for change relevant to this issue. The following strategies are more relevant to affirmative action plans in the workplace than plans for college and university admissions, although many of the suggestions can be applied to university admissions as well. Certainly, one critical change in university admissions is the ending of legacy admissions. Legacy admissions are blatant violations of fairness and merit. They specifically reproduce white privilege, by securing the admissions of children from privileged families. Oxford and Cambridge universities have both ended this practice.[75] Also, abolishing preference for donors is crucial to reducing preference for the privileged. Daniel Golden argues for a firewall between the admissions office and the development office to reduce potential conflicts of interest between admissions and fund-raising offices.[76]

Affirmative action plans

In her book, *"Why are all the Black Kids Sitting Together in the Cafeteria?"* Beverly Daniel Tatum[77] distinguishes between *goal-oriented* and *process-oriented* affirmative action plans. Process-oriented programs focus on creating a fair application process, assuming that fair process will produce a fair outcome. If a job opening is advertised widely, and anyone who is interested has a chance to apply, and if all applicants receive similar treatment during the evaluation of resumes and interviews, then the process is presumed to be fair. The search committee can truly choose the best candidate believing that no discrimination has taken place. In this regard, sometimes the best person will be a woman or a person of color, sometimes it will be a white man. In theory, process-oriented plans seem fair. They are certainly an improvement over word-of-mouth recruiting. But while the process-oriented approach may protect against blatant forms of discrimination, it will not protect against the various manifestations of benign bigotry presented in this chapter. Process-oriented programs time and again seem to find that the "best" candidate is from the dominant group. A "fair" process and even a diverse candidate pool do not necessarily produce a fair result because benign bigotry will still make an appearance at the end of the process. Recall Biernat and Kobrynowicz's study finding that women and people of color might be more likely to make an applicant pool short-list but are less likely than white men to be hired.[78]

Therefore, Tatum suggests using a *goal-oriented* approach. Goal-oriented affirmative action plans have the same open process as process-oriented programs and entail identifying a *pool of qualified candidates.* Hiring an unqualified person is never the goal of any affirmative action program, even if the hiring meets a "diversity requirement." Hiring unqualified minorities does neither the candidate nor the organization any good and defeats the aim of affirmative action by perpetuating the stereotype that affirmative action hires are less qualified than "real" hires. Once a qualified pool of candidates is established, the committee chooses those who move the organization closer to its diversity goals. According to Tatum,[79] in a well-conceived and implemented affirmative action plan, the first thing that should be done is to establish clear and meaningful selection criteria. What skills does the person need to function effectively in this environment? How will we assess whether the candidates have these required skills? Will this be on the basis of demonstrated past performance, scores on an appropriate test, the demonstrated completion of certain educational requirements? Once the criteria have been established, anyone who meets the criteria is considered qualified. If one candidate meets the criteria but also has some additional education or experience, it may be tempting to say this candidate is the "best" and should be hired. But if the candidates' extra talents are not part of the qualification criteria, those extra talents should not be considered. It's just too easy for search committee members to push ahead a white or male candidate using the rationale that he has extra special qualifications. In reality, sometimes there is an implicit assumption that those extra qualifications are whiteness or maleness. A tendency I have witnessed while serving on search committees is for an applicant from the dominant group being favored more than an equally qualified person of color when search committee members express vague concerns regarding the minority canditate such as *"I just don't think she's a good match for us,"* or *"He probably won't be happy here."* I suspect these comments reveal more about the committee member's discomfort with the applicant than they do the applicant. One myth about affirmative action is that unqualified people are hired. A sound goal-oriented affirmative action program will not do this.

Support at the top is crucial

Support for affirmative action by top management and university administration is key for successful implementation. Management and administrative personnel have a naturally disproportionate impact on organizations because of their status as authorities. When people are asked to adopt new attitudes, they first assess the credibility of the person who is promoting the adoption. Administrators and top management of organizations should clearly articulate that affirmative action is a fair policy that is rooted in egalitarian principles. Avoiding discussion of affirmative action in the hope that ignoring it will minimize resistance to it may backfire.[80] Justifying the use of an affirmative action plan can lead to more positive evaluations but can backfire if the justification focuses solely on under-representation of the target group. Affirmative action plans tend to be more readily accepted when the argument of organizational diversity or employment discrimination is utilized, rather than that of under-representation.[81] Given the limitations of defending affirmative action as it relates to increasing diversity, as I described above, I suggest focusing on discrimination and making diversity needs secondary. Also, affirmative action plans that are clearly defined and articulated find more support than those that are ill-defined or vague.[82] When affirmative action plans are nebulous, people assume that they involve quotas and preferences and are therefore unfair. It is also worth noting that companies perceived as progressive and fair have more productive, satisfied, and loyal workers than do other companies.[83] As we have seen in other chapters such as Chapter 3, the degree of commitment to anti-bias norms and the inevitability of the commitment and the changes that go with the commitment are critical in prejudice reduction. Support for affirmative action in an organization should be unequivocal and non-negotiable.

The way affirmative action is embraced by an organization can be critical to the job satisfaction of people of color as well. In organizations in which affirmative action is willingly and positively pursued, people of color have more commitment to the organization, more job satisfaction, and more confidence in their performance, compared to organizations with members who feel that affirmative action was imposed on them.[84]

Institutions and supervisors should help everyone understand that people hired under affirmative action are as qualified as others in the organization.[85] This task will probably involve convincing people that prejudice, and subtle prejudice in particular, still exists. Also, new employees, as well as the organization, should be made aware of what employers see as their specific strengths. Were it not for affirmative action, those abilities might well have gone unnoticed. General comments about a person are less useful than specific information about her abilities.[86]

Blind reviews

Some search committees use blind review of applications. While this would not be relevant in a goal-oriented affirmative action plan like the one described by Tatum, there might be circumstances in which blind reviews would be useful. This strategy has worked successfully with orchestra auditions, during which musicians sit behind a curtain, and play without the judges knowing whether or not they are women or men. Women who were previously shut out of prestigious orchestras because of gender bias have been just as likely to be chosen as men are. In their review of affirmative action strategies, Jerry Kang and Mahzarin Banaji[87] suggest the use of a two-step process of blind reviews. In the first step, a candidate's identity is cloaked during the evaluation of "merit." Once a

326 • Benign Bigotry

qualified pool of candidates is established, the veil can be lifted for further evaluation of the applicant.

Increasing the number of women and people of color
in a candidate pool

This next suggestion cannot be carried out if blind reviews are conducted. But there are many circumstances under which conducting truly blind reviews would not be possible or practical. For instance, membership in some organizations noted on a resume may reveal a candidate's ethnicity or gender. Studies have shown that when women candidates make up only a small portion of an applicant pool, their gender is salient – which makes them distinctive and different from the male norm of "appropriate" applicant. But when women constitute a substantial number of applicants, their gender becomes less salient and they are more likely to be seen as "applicant" and not "woman applicant."[88] The same process may also occur regarding people of color. If women and people of color make up a critical mass of the applicant pool, they will be less likely to be seen as exceptions, or as distinct or deviant because of their race and gender. *Imagining* a woman or person of color in the position will then become easier for those making the hiring decision.

Interviews

One review of the literature found that interviews produce more biased outcomes than decisions made via the use of paper records.[89] Awkwardness leads to worse interviews. For instance, while many whites may feel that they can interview a person of color professionally, and be free of bias, they may not realize the extent to which their discomfort, anxiety or bias manifests in awkward interactions.[90] If interviews are conducted, they should be standardized to make sure every applicant is asked the same questions.[91]

Interviewers should be educated about equal opportunity employment laws so they know what questions should and should not be asked.

Standardize and clarify performance criteria

When criteria used for hiring and performance evaluations are unclear, informal (not written), or not directly related to specific job performance, bias will creep into the evaluation process. Organizations should have a clear and articulable set of performance criteria that every employee or potential employee understands. At the same time, people's ideas of how to do a job are usually influenced by earlier jobholders' performance. Thus, it is tempting to see the characteristics of a previous jobholder as *the* necessary characteristics for good job performance, rather than seeing them as *one* set of traits that help a person do the job well.[92] Recognizing that there is more than one way to do a job well will allow for potential employees that may have not previously been on an employers' radar to get on it. Also, beware of stealth or bonus qualifications that hide privilege. For instance, one candidate might appear particularly appealing because she has traveled extensively. If being well traveled is not part of the standardized performance criteria, it should not be considered. The creation of explicit, valid criteria can only help an organization and its applicants.

Role models and mentors

Some people think that having role models in the workplace is important for women and people of color because it gives them successful people to emulate, a goal to strive for. Others caution against the use of role models because their presence can make women and people of color feel inferior if they do not succeed to the extent that the role model has. Thus, the challenge of role models is that they tend to be *exceptional* individuals, who not only work hard and are competent, but have also had unusual advantages that most competent and hardworking people have not. If there is only one person of color or one woman in a position of authority and you are dissimilar to her, you have no reason to think that there is room for you.[93] Role models tend to require women and minorities to be assimilationist, to suffer burdens not placed on whites and men, and perpetuates a system-reinforcing meritocratic myth that if you work hard, you can succeed, "just like me."[94]

Virginia Valian argues that, instead of role models, people need concrete suggestions about how to do their best work and how to maximize the chances that their work will be recognized and rewarded.[95] Mentors can educate employees about the unwritten norms and expectations of the department and organization, facilitate networking, nominate mentees for awards, and create collaborations on assignments such as grants.[96]

Diversity training

In order to comply with anti-discrimination law and to avoid costly lawsuits, many organizations conduct some kind of "diversity training" with their employees. Employees might be required to attend a day-long or hour-long workshop at required intervals, that reviews proper hiring procedures, the organization's affirmative action program, definitions of workplace harassment, Americans with Disabilities Act requirements, etc. While diversity training is probably helpful in explaining laws and company policies, as well as in educating the ignorant about blatant forms of discrimination, it is not likely to be very useful in detecting and preventing the subtle forms of discrimination described in this chapter. Most people are not aware of the extent to which their behavior and ideas are guided by their schemas. Making the unconscious conscious is an important step in ending discrimination, but it may not be accomplished through traditional kinds of diversity training.[97] Because benign bigotry is subtle and hard to detect, typical one-time diversity training courses and non-discrimination policies may do little to alleviate the existence of everyday discrimination in the workplace.[98]

NOTES

1. p. 170, Wilson, P. (1996). The minority–majority society. In G.E. Curry (Ed.), *The affirmative action debate* (pp. 167–174). New York: Addison-Wesley.

2. Crosby, F.J., Iyer, A., Clayton, S., & Downing, R.A. (2003). Affirmative action: Psychological data and the policy debates. *American psychologist, 58,* 93–115.

3. Harrison, D.A., Kravitz, D.A., Mayer, D.M., Leslie, L.M., & Lev-Arey, D. (2006). Understanding attitudes toward affirmative action programs in employment: Summary and meta-analysis of 35 years of research. *Journal of applied psychology, 91,* 1013–1036.

4. Wilson, P. (1996). The minority–majority society. In G.E. Curry (Ed.), *The affirmative action debate* (pp. 167–174). Reading, MA: Addison-Wesley.

5. Lerner, M.J. (1980). *The belief in a just world: A fundamental delusion.* New York: Springer.

6. Valian, V. (1999). *Why so slow? The advancement of women.* Cambridge, MA: The MIT Press.

7. Johnson, S.D. (1980). Reverse discrimination and aggressive behavior. *The journal of psychology, 104,* 11–19.

8. Crosby *et al.* Affirmative action.

9. Crosby, F.J. (2004). *Affirmative action is dead; long live affirmative action.* New Haven, CT: Yale University Press.

10. Kang, J., & Banaji, M.R. (2006). Fair measures: A behavioral realist revision of "affirmative action." *California law review, 94,* 1063–1118.

11. For one review, see: Fiske, S.T. (2004). *Social beings: A core motives approach to social psychology.* Hoboken, NJ: John Wiley & Sons.

12. Katz and Hass refer to these attitudes by whites as *ambivalent racism:* Katz, I., & Hass, R.G. (1988). Racial ambivalence and American value conflict: Correlational and priming studies of dual cognitive structures. *Journal of personality and social psychology, 55,* 893–905; Katz, I., Wackenhut, J., & Glass, D.C. (1986). An ambivalence-amplification theory of behavior toward the stigmatized. In S. Worchel & W.G. Austin (Eds.), *Psychology of intergroup relations* (pp. 103–117). Chicago: Nelson-Hall, Inc.

13. This description fits what Gaertner and Dovidio call *aversive racism:* Gaertner, S.L., & Dovidio, J.F. (1986). The aversive form of racism. In J.F. Dovidio & S.L. Gaertner (Eds.), *Prejudice, discrimination, and racism* (pp. 61–89). Orlando, FL: Academic Press, Inc.

14. Dovidio, J.F., Mann, J., & Gaertner, S.L. (1989). Resistance to affirmative action: The implications of aversive racism. In F.A. Blanchard &

F.J. Crosby, (Eds.), *Affirmative action in perspective* (pp. 83–102). New York: Springer-Verlag.

15. Tougas, F., Brown, R., Beaton, A.M., & Joly, S. (1995). Neosexism: Plus ça change, plus c'est pareil. *Personality and social psychology bulletin, 21*, 842–849. See also: Swim, J.K., Aikin, K.J., Hall, W.S., & Hunter, B.A. (1995). Sexism and racism: Old-fashioned and modern prejudices. *Journal of personality and social psychology, 68*, 199–214. See also: Glick, P., & Fiske, S.T. (1996). The Ambivalent Sexism Inventory: Differentiating hostile and benevolent sexism. *Journal of personality and social psychology, 70*, 491–512.

16. Dovidio, J.F., & Gaertner, S.L. (2000). Aversive racism and selection decisions: 1989 and 1999. *Psychological science, 11*, 315–319.

17. Rock, C. (Writer), & Gallen, J. (Director). (2004). *Never scared (Black ambition tour)* [DVD]. Washington, DC: Home Box Office, Inc.

18. Frey, D.L., & Gaertner, S.L. (1986). Helping and the avoidance of inappropriate interracial behavior: A strategy that perpetuates a nonprejudiced self-image. *Journal of personality and social psychology, 50*, 1083–1090.

19. Bergmann, B.A. (1996). *In defense of affirmative action.* New York: Basic-Books; Crosby, *Affirmative action is dead*; Golden, D. (2006). *The price of admission: How America's ruling class buys its way into elite colleges – and who gets left outside the gates.* New York: Crown Publishers; Wise, T.J. (2005). *Affirmative action: Racial preference in black and white.* New York: Routledge.

20. Golden, *The price of admission.*

21. Karabel, J. (2005). *The chosen: The hidden history of admission and exclusion at Harvard, Yale, and Princeton.* New York: Houghton Mifflin Company.

22. Golden, *The price of admission.*

23. *Ibid.*

24. See page 506 in Karabel, *The chosen.*

25. Karabel, *The chosen.*

26. *Ibid.*

27. Golden, *The price of admission.*

28. Bertrand, M., & Mullainathan, S. (2004). Are Emily and Greg more employable than Lakisha and Jamal? A field experiment on labor market discrimination. *The American economic review, 94*, 991–1013.

29. Dovidio *et al.* Resistance to affirmative action.

30. For a review, see: Kraiger, K., & Ford, J.K. (1985). A meta-analysis of ratee effects in performance ratings. *Journal of applied psychology, 70*, 56–65.

31. Fidell, L.S. (1975). Empirical verification of sex discrimination in hiring practices in psychology. In R.K. Unger (Ed.), *Woman: Dependent or independent variable* (pp. 774–785). New York: Psychological Dimensions, Inc.

32. See Tables 4 and 5 in: American Association of University Professors (2007, March/April). Financial inequality in higher education: The annual report of the economic status of the profession. Retrieved May 23, 2007, from www.aaup.org/NR/rdonlyres/B25BFE69-BCE7-4AC9-A644-7E84FF14B883/0/zreport.pdf

33. Trix, F., & Psenka, C. (2003). Exploring the color of glass: Letters of recommendation for female and male medical faculty. *Discourse and society, 14*, 191–220.

34. Word, C.O., Zanna, M.P., & Cooper, J. (1974). The nonverbal mediation of self-fulfilling prophecies in interracial interaction. *Journal of experimental social psychology, 10*, 109–120.

35. Woodzicka, J.A., & LaFrance, M. (2005). The effects of subtle sexual harassment on women's performance in a job interview. *Sex roles, 53*, 67–77.

36. Hebl, M.R., Foster, J.B., Mannix, L.M., & Dovidio, J.F. (2002). Formal and interpersonal discrimination: A field study of bias toward homosexual applicants. *Personality and social psychology bulletin, 28*, 815–825.

37. However, in all three measures, the "gay" applicant was told about job availability, permitted to complete an application, and called back less frequently than the "straight" applicant, on average, but the differences were not statistically significant.

38. Frazer, R.A., & Wiersma, U.J. (2001). Prejudice versus discrimination in the employment interview: We may hire equally, but our memories harbour prejudice. *Human relations, 54*, 173–191.

39. Dey, J.G., & Hill, C. (2007). Behind the pay gap. AAUW Educational Foundation.

40. Martin, L. (2006, June 4). Top women cheated by pay gap. *The Observer*, p. 18. Gender pay gap wider than thought. (2004, October 20). *BBC news*. Retrieved March 24, 2008, from http://news.bbc.co.uk/1/hi/business/3765535.stm

41. Experiment 1: Major, B., McFarlin, D.B., & Gagnon, D. (1984). Overworked and underpaid: On the nature of gender differences in personal entitlement. *Journal of personality and social psychology, 47*, 1399–1412.

42. For a hypothetical calculation of salary differences over several years, see: Valian, *Why so slow?*

43. Experiment 2: Major et al. Overworked and underpaid.

44. Hogue, M., & Yoder, J.D. (2003). The role of status in producing depressed entitlement in women's and men's pay allocations. *Psychology of women quarterly, 27*, 330–337.

45. Pelham, B.W. & Hetts, J.J. (2001). Underworked and overpaid: Elevated entitlement in men's self-pay. *Journal of experimental social psychology, 37*, 93–103.

46. For a review of gender socialization as it relates to entitlement, see: Valian, *Why so slow?*
47. Biernat, M., & Kobrynowicz, D. (1997). Gender- and race-based standards of competence: Lower minimum standards but higher ability standards for devalued groups. *Journal of personality and social psychology, 72,* 544–557.
48. Heilman, M.E., Wallen, A.S., Fuchs, D., & Tamkins, M.M. (2004). Penalties for success: Reactions to women who succeed at male gender-typed tasks. *Journal of applied psychology, 89,* 416–427.
49. For a review of the research on how attributions affect women and men in the workplace, see: Valian, *Why so slow?*
50. Trix & Psenka, Exploring the color of glass.
51. Garcia-Retamero, R., & López-Zafra, E. (2006). Congruencia de rol de género y liderazgo: El papel de las atribuciones causales sobre el éxito y el fracaso. *Revista Latinoamericana de psicología, 38,* 245–257.
52. Greenhaus, J.H., & Parasuraman, S. (1993). Job performance attributions and career advancement prospects: An examination of gender and race effects. *Organizational behavior and human decision processes, 55,* 273–297.
53. Heilman, M.E. (1983). Sex bias in work settings: The lack of fit model. *Research in organizational behavior, 5,* 269–298.
54. Heilman, M.E., & Haynes, M.C. (2005). No credit where credit is due: Attributional rationalization of women's success in male–female teams. *Journal of applied psychology, 90,* 905–916.
55. Dovidio *et al.* Resistance to affirmative action.
56. Dovidio, J.F., & Gaertner, S.L. (1983). The effects of sex, status, and ability on helping behavior. *Journal of applied social psychology, 13,* 191–205.
57. Heilman & Haynes, No credit where credit is due.
58. Dovidio *et al.* Resistance to affirmative action.
59. *Ibid.*
60. Fish, S. (2000, January/February). Reverse racism, or how the pot got to call the kettle black. *Crisis, 14–21.*
61. *Ibid.*, page 17.
62. Kang & Banaji, Fair measures.
63. *Ibid.*
64. Wise, *Affirmative action.*
65. *Ibid.*, for an extensive argument against the diversity defense regarding affirmative action.
66. Grillo, T., & Wildman, S.M. (1997). Obscuring the importance of race: The implication of making comparisons between racism and sexism (or other isms). In A.K. Wing (Ed.), *Critical race feminism: A reader* (pp. 44–50). New York: NYU Press.

67. Accomando, C. (2004). Exposing the lie of neutrality: June Jordan's *Affirmative Acts*. In M. Grebowicz & V. Kinloch (Eds.), *Still seeking an attitude: Critical reflections on the work of June Jordan* (pp. 33–47). Lanham, MD: Lexington Books.
68. *Ibid.*, page 33.
69. Ibid., page 35.
70. Wilson, The minority–majority society.
71. Accomando, Exposing the lie of neutrality.
72. Kobrynowicz, D., & Branscombe, N.R. (1997). Who considers themselves victims of discrimination? Individual difference predictors of perceived gender discrimination in women and men. *Psychology of women quarterly, 21*, 347–363.
73. Golden, *The price of admission*; Karabel, *The chosen.*
74. Wise, *Affirmative action.*
75. Golden, *The price of admission.*
76. *Ibid.*
77. Tatum, B.D. (1997). *"Why are all the black kids sitting together in the cafeteria?" and other conversations about race.* New York: Basic Books.
78. Biernat & Kobrynowicz, Gender- and race-based standards of competence.
79. Tatum, *"Why are all the black kids sitting together in the cafeteria?"*
80. Harrison *et al.* Understanding attitudes toward affirmative action programs in employment.
81. *Ibid.*
82. *Ibid.*
83. Arthur, J.B. (1994). Effects of human resource systems on manufacturing performance and turnover. *Academy of management journal, 37*, 670–687; Grover, S.L., & Crooker, K.J. (1995). Who appreciates family responsive human resource policies: The impact of family friendly policies on the organizational attachment of parents and non-parents. *Personnel psychology, 48*, 271–288; Hall, D.T., & Parker, V.A. (1993). The role of workplace flexibility in managing diversity. *Organizational dynamics, 22*, 5–18; Kinicki, A.J., Carson, K.P., & Bohlander, G.W. (1992). Relationship between an organization's actual human resource efforts and employee attitudes. *Group and organization management, 17*, 135–152; Koys, D.J. (1991). Fairness, legal compliance, and organizational commitment. *Employee responsibilities and rights journal, 4*, 283–291.
84. Niemann, Y.F., & Dovidio, J.F. (2005). Affirmative action and job satisfaction: Understanding underlying processes. *Journal of social issues, 61*, 507–523.
85. Valian, *Why so slow?*

86. Pettigrew, T.F., & Martin, J. (1987). Shaping the organizational context for Black American inclusion. *Journal of social issues, 43,* 41–78.
87. Kang & Banaji, Fair measures.
88. For a review of research in this area, see: Valian, *Why so slow?*
89. Kang & Banaji, Fair measures.
90. Reported in: Dovidio, J.F., Gaertner, S.L., Kawakami, K., & Hodson, G. (2002). Why can't we just get along? Interpersonal biases and interracial distrust. *Cultural diversity and ethnic minority psychology, 8,* 88–102.
91. Saks, A.M., & McCarthy, J.M. (2006). Effects of discriminatory interview questions and gender on applicant reactions. *Journal of business and psychology, 21,* 175–191.
92. Valian, *Why so slow?*
93. *Ibid.*
94. Kang & Banaji, Fair measures.
95. Valian, *Why so slow?*
96. Niemann & Dovidio, Affirmative action and job satisfaction.
97. Valian, *Why so slow?*
98. Deitch, E.A., Barsky, A., Butz, R.M., Chan, S., Brief, A.P., & Bradley, J.C. (2003). Subtle yet significant: The existence and impact of everyday racial discrimination in the workplace. *Human relations, 56,* 1299–1324.

Conclusion

We have come to the end of a journey – a journey that has allowed us to explore the world beneath the surfaces we see in our everyday interactions. The analysis in this book has framed some ordinary, often unconscious, "common-sense" assumptions as myths rather than as pieces of wisdom whose correctness is self-evident. Although it appears that we can make sense of the world around us by applying common sense, what travels socially as "common sense" is, in many instances, nothing more than misguided assumptions – a combination of underlying misinformation, repetitions of traditional biases, and prejudices. These shared, unexplored assumptions about the world come from the status quo (and its attendant distribution of power). These assumptions have the effect of explaining our world and justifying its organization in terms of race, ethnicity, gender, and sexuality systems of social inequality. These assumptions produce the very myths we have explored in this book. These myths feel harmless to many people if they believe they are based on truths, rather than reflecting biases and bigotry.

The apparent fact that members of "minorities" seem to share some of these beliefs does not constitute assent or agreement, nor does it make these myths any more true. As Beverly Daniel Tatum says, we all breathe the smog of racism.[1] On the contrary, what appears to be consent is an illustration of the pervasiveness and effectiveness of mystification and myth-making in the service of systems of power.

We explored six pervasive and pernicious myths, but this list is not in any way an exhaustive accounting of the living myths that organize and guide the culture wars waged against marginalized and misrepresented people. We have directly challenged these claims with empirical evidence derived from experimental research and real-life social evidence. These sources of data allow us to turn these "common-sense" assertions (the myths) into questions, and then to go about answering them in systematic ways.

The first belief, that "those people all look alike" is based on routine categorization, but status, power, and privilege determine who is harmed by it. For while everyone is capable of seeing people outside their own group as looking and acting alike, dominant groups, such as whites, are more likely to think members of subordinate groups look and act alike, than vice versa.[2] The stereotypes of the dominant group are more consequential than the stereotypes of the subordinate group. As I stated in the Introduction to this book, stereotypes control people[3] but the consequences to those with less power, such as people of color, can be disastrous. The outgroup homogeneity effect affects how whites read anger into the neutral faces of African American men, and surely plays a role in the belief that black men are linked with criminality, discussed at length in Chapter 2.

You can see how thinking categorically, in conjunction with specific cultural stereotypes, can lead to the "they must be guilty of something" assumption. The belief that those who have been accused of a crime are probably guilty is a taken-for-granted assumption rooted, in part, in people's belief that the world is a just place. The world feels like a more understandable and predictable place if we believe that bad people get locked up and good people remain free. In addition to one's belief in a just world, the idea that some people (e.g. the poor and people of color) seem to matter less than others, as we found in Chapter 1, contributes to the guilty-of-something belief.

The United States is one of the few countries that practice state-sponsored executions, sharing this distinction with China, Iran, Pakistan, and Saudi Arabia. The procedure for drawing a "death-qualified" jury adds yet another layer of bias stacked against the defendant. Death-qualified jurors (those who are not opposed to the death penalty and who agree to be willing to vote to execute the defendant who has not even been proven guilty yet) tend to be pro-prosecution, more punitive, and simply more likely to find a defendant guilty than are jurors who have not been death quali-fied.[4] Death-qualified juries are even less likely to take the delibe-ration process seriously, and are less accurate at remembering evidence than are juries that are not death qualified.[5] Given the proof of bias in every stage of the criminal justice process, capital punishment requires a confidence in one's justice system that is simply unwarranted in the United States. Regardless of one's poli-tical orientation, one's opinion of the death penalty, and one's view of whether or not the world is a just place, no one wants an innocent person to go to prison or the death chamber. In addition, every time an innocent person is convicted, a guilty person is free to commit more crimes. If we are truly concerned with public safety, minimizing bias and respecting due process should be everyone's goal.

Our discussion of feminism underpinned some major consider-ations, including preconceptions (held by both women and men), the operation of social schemas, and the failure to adequately inspect some of the operating instructions, that inform our ordinary day-to-day conduct. These particular myths actually stem from misogyny and, as they remain active and unchallenged, contribute to the subordination and marginalization of women across all segments of society. In so doing, artificial barriers are created under which the interests of men and the interests of women are positioned as incompatible and irreconcilable. We are led to believe that feminism, insofar as it is a way of looking at the world that advocates for social, economic, political, and legal equality for women, actually somehow diminishes the quality of life and the adequacy of regard and resources therefore available to men. We have seen that nothing could be further from the truth.

Feminists are described by many in the mass media as angry[6] and anti-male.[7] Yet there is no empirical evidence to suggest that feminists' attitudes toward men are more negative than those of non-feminists. In fact one study finds that feminists reported *lower* levels of hostility toward men than non-feminists.[8] The work in the area of ambivalent sexism and ambivalence toward men suggests that women who adhere to traditional gender roles, those who are unlikely to be feminists, may resent men's power, while endorsing the paternalistic chivalry of benevolent sexism.[9]

Feminists, like other non-traditional women, such as lesbians, women athletes, and women leaders, are viewed negatively because they transgress traditional expectations of women staying quiet and "behaving themselves." Feminists upset the status quo, and, as we saw in Chapter 1, those who are against the status quo are viewed as extremists, even when they are not.[10] Part of the threat of feminism is that feminists are more likely to see gender inequality as systemic, not as a problem between individual women and men. So while anti-feminist women might resent men, as we see with women's ambivalence toward men, feminists resent the unfairness of the system of gender inequality. Some people mistake feminists' fight against patriarchy as a fight against individual men.

Finally, the whole enterprise of feminists-as-man-haters needs to be deconstructed and dismantled. Women are not bashers, they are more often bashees, the targets of men's violence, or in the case of lesbians, lesbian-baiting. Calling feminists "male-bashers" shifts the focus from the systemic problem of men's violence against women to a focus on men who have gotten their feelings hurt by feminists and feminism. The feminist critique may be disconcerting to men and some women. It might hurt their feelings, it might seem unfair, and it might seem to disregard men's good intentions. This may make men feel uncomfortable but it's not male-bashing. Feminists are not critical of men simply for being men. The target of feminist critique is sexism in a male-dominated society.

Beliefs about feminism and feminists are not the only supposed threat to traditional heterosexuality. Lesbians and gay men are thought to disrupt the heterosexual norm by being hypersexual. In Chapter 4, the belief that homosexuals are conspicuous and provocative about sex and sexuality in ways that heterosexuals are not was explored. The research on illusory correlation finds that those negative and stereotypical portrayals of lesbians and gay men will be more memorable and meaningful to the viewer than negative portrayals of the heterosexual majority. People are also more likely to remember schema-consistent information than schema-inconsistent information. In other words, we are more likely to remember things in line with our stereotypes and disregard what we consider exceptions to our schematic rules. Furthermore, heterosexuals tend to believe that they can identify lesbians and gay men by the way they look. Without realizing that lesbians and gay men who do not conform to stereotypes are missed from the perceiver's radar. The (inaccurate) belief that lesbians and gay men can be spotted by how they look has important implications for homosexuals and heterosexuals. This belief produces a tyranny of gender role rigidity whereby anyone who does not conform to gender roles – a man who acts or looks a bit too feminine, a woman who acts or looks a bit too masculine – regardless of their actual sexual orientation, can be a target of gay-baiting or gay-bashing. Therefore, there is pressure for women and men to conform to gender stereotypes both in the way they look and in the way they act. Homophobia attempts to keep everyone, regardless of sexuality, in their place.

Declaring that homosexuals flaunt their sexuality is a declaration of heterosexual privilege. The implication is that heterosexuals are normal, that their romantic and sexual behavior is normal and natural. As Allan Johnson notes,[11] heterosexual privilege means that heterosexual people do not get reduced to a single aspect of their lives: who they are intimate with. In contrast, lesbians', gay men's, and bisexuals' openness about their sexuality is akin to flaunting it. From a heterosexual perspective, as evidenced by judges who view acknowledging one's sexuality as a gay person as dangerous to children, or the firefighters[12] who are accepting of gay firefighters as long as the topic never comes up in a conversation, openness equals *flaunting*. Imagine what it would be like to ask heterosexuals in the work place, whether it be an office, or fire station, to never mention any aspect of their sexuality – no discussion of dating, weddings, bachelor parties, vacations, sexual intercourse, what they did over the weekend, nothing.

As we have seen throughout this book, race and ethnicity play a significant role in how people interact with others. In an era when prejudice is frowned upon but still exists, there is pressure to appear unprejudiced. Many whites want to not notice race, or at least, not to appear to notice race.[13] Colorblindness, the subject of Chapter 5, is an attractive ideal: if a person does not see race, how can she be a racist? White people who think that they do not see color may believe their interactions with people of color are seamless, when, in fact, they may be awkward.[14] Thus, one problem with colorblindness at the individual level is that people are in fact *not* colorblind, they *do* notice race and they treat people differently depending on race. A self-perception of colorblindness is linked to a variety of attitudes centered on a lack of empathy. Posed as a goal for racial equality, the idea of colorblindness reflects and creates a complex and problematic view of racial equality. Belief in colorblindness protects whites from realizing that they benefit from racism. Many writers and politicians who endorse colorblindness are political conservatives[15] who argue in favor of racial color-blindness as part of an anti-affirmative action position. By 1980, the colorblind position had become part of the US Republican party platform.[16]

A major problem with the colorblind position, particularly in politics and mass media, is that as long as race is hidden from consciousness, the dominant racial and ethnic group can maintain the illusion that they are not responsible for the state of race relations because they do not knowingly engage in racist behavior, and even consider talking about race off limits. Colorblindness is problematic on a social level in terms of ethnic relations. When the colorblind approach has been compared to a multicultural approach to improving ethnic relations, the multicultural approach proves to be more effective.[17] Because of power differences between groups, colorblindness in society uses "whiteness" as the imagined norm by "whiting" out differences and perpetuating the belief of sameness. The denial of power imbalance, unearned privilege and racist domination are couched in the rhetoric of equal treatment and equal opportunity.[18] White individuals may have no awareness of their privileged status even as they protect their interests. While whites will acknowledge that disparities in education or other realms exist, they are more likely to attribute these to a lack of ambition and effort on the part of minorities than to structural favoritism toward whites that has been built into US institutions for generations.[19] Colorblind racism forms an invisible yet impregnable ideological wall that shields whites from America's racial reality.[20]

More cynical uses of colorblindness have included shutting down any discussion that race and ethnicity matter. In the current color-blind political era, those in the public arena who write about the realities of race and racism are the ones accused of fostering racial divisions.[21] By regarding race-related matters as *non*-racial, natural, or being rooted in personal choices, whites deem proposals to remedy racial inequality as illogical, undemocratic, and "racist," in reverse.[22]

Affirmative action is one of the most controversial political issues in the United States. To some extent the argument against affirmative action rests on a colorblind premise: we must be color-blind, and if we can be truly colorblind, affirmative action programs are unnecessary. After a review of people's attempts to be colorblind, as well as colorblind approaches to prejudice reduction, it seems clear that racial colorblindness cannot bolster the anti-affirmative action argument. Reactive equal opportunity laws may be adequate in conditions in which discrimination is overt and unabashed. However, because most discrimination is underground and subtle, we need the proactive measures of affirmative action programs. In Chapter 6, we saw that discrimination occurs at every level of the hiring process.

Anti-affirmative action activists re-frame affirmative action as discrimination as if the status quo is bias free and the playing field is level. Subsequently, the narrative of affirmative action is that it is reverse discrimination.

Each chapter ended with strategies for change specific to the issues described in the chapter. Most of the strategies described have been empirically investigated for their efficacy. One of the most thoroughly researched strategies is the *contact hypothesis* described in Chapters 1, 4, and 5. The *jigsaw technique* (discussed in Chapters 1 and 3) for fostering cooperation and interdependence in classrooms is one type of contact between groups that has shown promise. The jigsaw technique has also been shown to increase empathy between groups. *Inducing empathy* through other techniques is discussed in Chapters 1 and 5. The development of complex identities was discussed in Chapter 1. Studies have shown that a person with a *complex social identity* – an identity based on more than one role – tends to feel more commonalities with more people than a person who focuses on only one identity. Viewing outgroup members with more complexity is related to prejudice reduction as well. The role of *decategorization* and *salient categorization* is discussed in Chapter 5. Attempts at controlling one's stereotyped cognitions, stereotype suppression, have produced mixed results, as discussed in Chapters 1, 4, and 5. *Values confrontation*, when people are confronted with behaving in ways inconsistent with the way they view themselves, has shown some promise for those who are low in prejudice. Values confrontation is discussed in Chapter 5. *Cognitive dissonance* is discussed in Chapter 4. Cognitive dissonance plays a role in prejudice reduction and relates to the contact hypothesis and values confrontation. For instance, working closely with someone for whom you have prejudiced attitudes can produce dissonance: *if this person is so repugnant, why do I have contact with him?* Dissonance reduction entails adjusting one's attitudes to be consistent with one's behavior. And, in some cases, teaching young people about discrimination shows promise in bolstering their resistance to it (Chapters 3 and 5).

Beyond the exposure and analysis of each of the myths I have outlined specific strategies narrowly tailored to the topic. For instance, Chapter 2, describes approaches for reducing bias during police investigations, the importance of video recording interrogations, the risk of presenting false evidence or offers of leniency to false confessions, and the biases inherent in the death qualification process. In Chapter 3, the influence of women's studies and gender studies courses on people's attitudes about women and men shows promise. Suggestions and individual strategies to reduce bias in employment are offered in Chapter 6, including blind reviews, standardizing interviews, and clarifying performance criteria.

We have examined in this book relationships that are fundamentally political. In this sense, "political" refers not to contests or parties or elections. Rather, in our exposition, the idea of the political relies on a willingness to see, expose, and challenge the unequal distribution of power in our social lives. As we have seen, this power is expressed in benign bigotry: the small, daily, and personal ways and in large, society-level ways. In order to understand the operation of power, it is necessary to take a hard, cold, and clear-eyed look at the automatic assumptions that inform our thoughts, actions, and reactions to the behavior of those around us. One crucial discovery we have made together is that our lives are informed and scripted by cultural myths. Many myths masquerade as truth in our world, and many myths travel in the guise of principle, ideology, or folk wisdom. Most of these myths are fairly easily debunked with a cursory review of the historical record and a willingness to challenge cherished fairy tales. Some myths are more intractable and resist argument, evidence, and even apparently good intentions. We can now understand, as a result of our work with this book that conventional wisdom and common sense are frequently agents of social subordination, instruments of maintaining a power distribution we would not endorse if asked to. We now have a clearer understanding of the existence of everyday, *benign*, bigotry.

In these final pages, I address the reader directly. As I said at the beginning of this final chapter, this book has taken us on a journey of exploration of the world beneath the surfaces we see everyday. This journey might have involved introspection, during which you have made some excursions into your own unexplored thoughts, motives, and rationales for your own conduct and the behavior of others around you. This journey may have produced a range of feelings in you, including defensiveness, frustration, anger, embarrassment, guilt, and shame. This book is designed finally to combat such feelings and replace them instead with energy and equipment necessary to fight prejudice and promote social justice from the most ordinary and mundane kinds of social interactions to the largest levels of social policy and legislation.

With the insights gained from this book, we can no longer simply be observers watching (or failing to notice) injustices from the sidelines. You can never again say that you have not been told. Recognizing our shared responsibilities and our shared roles in seeing and undoing bigotry – at every level – sometimes feels overwhelming. But we will not end oppression by pretending it isn't there. And we, collectively, will never end oppression by abdicating our individual responsibility to take action and to voice objections to these ordinary forms of bigotry. Dominant groups tend to not see the trouble of bigotry as *their* trouble, which means they do not feel obliged to do something about it. Whether you are a member of a dominant group or subordinate group, this *is* your trouble. Although it is true that disadvantaged groups take the brunt of the problem of bigotry, privileged groups are also affected by it, partly because misery visited on others comes back to haunt those who benefit from it, especially in the form of defensiveness and fear.[23] Derald Sue[24] describes bigotry as a clamp on one's mind, distorting one's perception of reality. In maintaining one's schemas, one's perceptual accuracy is diminished. The harm to subordinate groups actually diminishes dominant group members' humanity because they lose sensitivity to hurting others. Stereotyping nearly always involves the loss of the ability to empathize. Bigotry is bad for those who engage in it because they misperceive themselves as superior thereby engaging in elaborate self-deception.

We might think that we do not individually have the power to make change. But it might be more about our reluctance to use our power.[25] This reluctance to acknowledge and use power comes up in the simplest everyday situations, as when co-workers laugh at a homophobic joke and you have to decide whether or not to laugh as well, say nothing, or publically object. We know how uncomfortable this can make the group feel and how they may fight off their discomfort by dismissing, excluding, or even attacking us as bearers of this kind of social bad news of taking exception to such humor. Sometimes we think that it doesn't matter that we are silent in situations like this. If you think what you do doesn't matter, watch how people react to the slight departures from established paths and how much effort they expend trying to ignore or explain away or challenge those who choose alternative paths. Breaking silence is important for dominant groups because it undermines the assumption of solidarity that privilege depends on.[26]

Fear and guilt often accompany changing our behavior. While fear and guilt are legitimate emotions, they do nothing for subordinate groups. Some people fear the discomfort and disruption that sometimes results from raising difficult issues. Loss of privilege remains a deeply held fear. Once we recognize the unearned and extremely beneficial privileges that accrue to us as a result of our sexuality, our gender, our race, our religion, our class, it becomes momentarily frightening to face relinquishing some of that privilege. If we fight against privilege and oppression, we may be afraid of being seen as divisive. Frightening, at least, until we remember the world of inequality, deprivation, hate crimes, and mutual alienation we nourish through our silence and inaction.

Prejudice and bigotry produce some of the most vicious individual and collective behaviors that human beings can enact. But, at the base of it all, they are really just habits of thought and habits of association. They are habits that are so often repeated and reinforced and seemingly shared that they begin to appear to be natural and correct. But as habits, they can be identified, they can be undone, and they can be replaced by other habits that we mean to have, that are the result of deliberate thought and intention.

We all share a social responsibility, a moral obligation to seek out evidence, to challenge our own assumptions, to attempt to understand the social world as it is and not as a projection of what we wish or fear it were. Only through this fierce, courageous and informed process can we then begin to imagine the world as we want it to be, and only then can we be part of making it so.

NOTES

1. Tatum, B.D. (1997). *"Why are all the black kids sitting together in the cafeteria?" and other conversations about race.* New York: Basic Books.
2. Meissner, C.A., & Brigham, J.C. (2001). Thirty years of investigating the own-race bias in memory for faces: A meta-analytic review. *Psychology, public policy, and law, 7,* 3–35.
3. Fiske, S.T. (1993). Controlling other people: The impact of power on stereotyping. *American psychologist, 48,* 621–628.
4. Fitzgerald, R., & Ellsworth, P.C. (1984). Due process vs. crime control: Death qualification and jury attitudes. *Law and human behavior, 8,* 31–51; Cowan, C.L., Thompson, W.C., & Ellsworth, P.C. (1984). The effects of death qualification on jurors' predisposition to convict and on the quality of deliberation. *Law and human behavior, 8,* 53–79. See also: Thompson, W.C., Cowan, C.L., Ellsworth, P.C., & Harrington, J.C. (1984). Death penalty attitudes and conviction proneness: The translation of attitudes into verdicts. *Law and human behavior, 8,* 95–113.
5. Cowan *et al.* The effects of death qualification.
6. O'Beirne, K. (2006). *Women who make the world worse: And how their radical feminist assault is ruining our schools, families, military, and sports.* New York: Sentinel.
7. Mansfield, H.C. (2006). *Manliness.* New Haven, CT: Yale University Press.
8. Anderson, K.J., Kanner, M., & Elsayegh, N. (2009). Are feminists man-haters? Feminists' and nonfeminists' attitudes toward men. *Psychology of women quarterly, 33,* 216–224.
9. Glick, P., & Fiske, S.T. (2001). An ambivalent alliance: Hostile and benevolent sexism as complementary justifications for gender inequality. *American psychologist, 56,* 109–118; Glick, P., & Fiske, S.T. (1999). The Ambivalence toward Men Inventory: Differentiating hostile and benevolent beliefs about men. *Psychology of women quarterly, 23,* 519–536.
10. Ebenbach, D.H., & Keltner, D. (1998). Power, emotion, and judgmental accuracy in social conflict: Motivating the cognitive miser. *Basic and applied social psychology, 20,* 7–21.
11. Johnson, A.G. (2006). *Privilege, power, and difference* (2nd edition). New York: McGraw-Hill.
12. Ward, J., & Winstanley, D. (2006). Watching the watch: The UK Fire Service and its impact on sexual minorities in the workplace. *Gender, work and organization, 13,* 193–219.
13. Norton, M.I., Sommers, S.R., Apfelbaum, E.P., Pura, N., & Ariely, D. (2006). Color blindness and interracial interaction: Playing the political correctness game. *Psychological science, 17,* 949–953.

14. Ibid.

15. Including former California governor Pete Wilson in: Wilson, P. (1996). The minority–majority society. In G.E. Curry (Ed.), The affirmative action debate (pp. 167–174). Reading, MA: Addison-Wesley. See also ,Terry Eastland in: Eastland, T. (1996). Ending affirmative action: The case for colorblind justice. New York: BasicBooks. See also William Bradford Reynolds in: Reynolds, W.B. (1996). An experiment gone awry. In G.E. Curry (Ed.), The affirmative action debate (pp. 130–136). Reading, MA: Addison-Wesley.

16. Carr, L.G. (1997). "Color-blind" racism. Thousand Oaks, CA: Sage Publications, Inc.

17. Richeson, J.A., & Nussbaum, R.J. (2003). The impact of multicultural-ism versus color-blindness on racial bias. Journal of experimental social psychology, 40, 417–423. See also: Wolsko, C., Park, B., Judd, C.M., & Wittenbrink, B. (2000). Framing interethnic ideology: Effects of multi-cultural and color-blind perspectives on judgments of groups and indi-viduals. Journal of personality and social psychology, 78, 635–654.

18. Sue, D.W. (2003). Dismantling the myth of a color-blind society. Black issues in higher education, 20, 106.

19. For example, Brodkin's study of the impact and legacies of the 1944 GI Bill shows that white American men disproportionately received its housing, educational, and employment benefits, while people of color and women were systematically excluded. Brodkin describes the program as one of the biggest and best affirmative action programs in the history of our nation for white men. See: Brodkin, K. (2007). How Jews became white folks and what that says about race in America. In P.S. Rothenberg (Ed.), Race, class, and gender in the United States (7th edition, pp. 38–53). New York: Worth.

20. Bonilla-Silva, E. (2003). Racism without racists: Color-blind racism and the persistence of racial inequality in the United States. Lanham, MD: Rowman & Littlefield Publishers, Inc.

21. Ibid.

22. Ibid.

23. Johnson, Privilege, power, and difference.

24. Sue, D.W. (2003). Overcoming our racism: The journey to liberation. San Francisco: Jossey-Bass.

25. Johnson, Privilege, power, and difference.

26. Ibid.

Index